WHY WE HATE

MORE PRAISE FOR *WHY WE HATE*

"Timely, valuable, and accessible, Levin and Rabrenovic amass an impressive range of examples to explore the prevalence and insidious nature of a phenomenon that faces us all—hate. By going behind the headlines they offer us important insights into the power of hatred and offer suggestions on how it might be managed."

ROGER MAC GINTY, Department of Politics, University of York

"Written in a compelling narrative style . . . [t]he book not only provides a cogent analysis of the problem: it also offers valuable understanding of the conditions under which hate and bigotry have been resisted and challenged, taking scholarship in the field in a much-needed direction with lessons about how hate can be overcome."

PAUL IGANSKI, Department of Sociology, Essex University, England, and editor of *The Hate Debate: Should Hate Be Punished as a Crime?* and *A New Antisemitism? Debating Judeophobia in 21st Century Britain*

"Provides a comprehensive, chilling, and utterly compelling analysis of the insidious mystery of hatred. . . . With stunning clarity, they explore the dark causes and consequences of hatred, while offering pragmatic solutions that lift the spirit of the reader. This is a book to be studied by everyone interested in the future of our civilization."

DR. LAWRENCE LOWENTHAL
New England Director American Jewish Committee

"September 11 polarized people around the globe, deepening old wounds and creating new ones. The communication of opposites is one of the many ways in which intellectual discourse can pacify expressions of prejudice. That promise is brightly articulated in *Why We Hate*."

MARK S. HAMM
author of *In Bad Company: America's Terrorist Underground*

WHY WE HATE

JACK LEVIN &
GORDANA RABRENOVIC

 Prometheus Books

59 John Glenn Drive
Amherst, New York 14228-2197

Inquiries should be addressed to
Prometheus Books
59 John Glenn Drive
Amherst, New York 14228–2197
VOICE: 716–691–0133, ext. 207
FAX: 716–564–2711
WWW.PROMETHEUSBOOKS.COM

08 07 06 05 04   5 4 3 2 1

Library of Congress Cataloging-in-Publication Data

Levin, Jack, 1941–
    Why we hate / Jack Levin and Gordana Rabrenovic.
        p. cm.
    Includes bibliographical references and index.
    ISBN 1–59102–191–X (hardcover : alk. paper)
    1. Hate crimes. 2. Hate. 3. Violence. I. Rabrenovic, Gordana, 1957– II. Title.

HV6773.5.L484 2004
302.5'4—dc22

                                                                        2004004496

Printed in the United States of America on acid-free paper

CONTENTS

CONTENTS

PREFACE

If it had a silver lining, the cloud of the September 11 terrorist attack informed Americans they could no longer assume that the United States was universally respected and admired or that developed nations were immune from terrorism. Thanks to 9/11, it became all but impossible to ignore the scourge of hate and violence around the world.

Then, on March 11, 2004, exactly 911 days after the attack on America, extremists set off a series of bombs on trains in Madrid, Spain, killing more than two hundred rush-hour commuters and injuring another fifteen hundred. Al Qaeda claimed responsibility. Three days later, Spain's Popular Party headed by Prime Minister Jose Mario Azar, who had supported the Bush administration's invasion of Iraq despite popular opposition, was soundly defeated at the polls by the antiwar Socialist Party.

Was the outcome of the Spanish election a result of democracy, terrorism, or both? Did it indicate that public opinion counts or that an entire nation can be manipulated by fear and violence? In the aftermath, European leaders, including the newly elected Spanish prime minister, pledged to intensify their efforts in the fight against terrorism. Would their strategy of greater cooperation among nations and coordination of intelligence efforts be more successful than the military toughness that has been advocated by the United States?

Of course, hate violence was a major force in political life long before Osama became a household name. Throughout history, hostility between groups has dominated the social, economic, and political landscape, finding expression in civil war, international conflict, and the persecution of vulnerable minorities.

In this book, we ask the most significant question: Why do we hate? Why the continuing bloodshed? Why the inhumane treatment of one group by another?

We examine the reality of hate as expressed in widespread violence, fear, and revenge, and explore the roots of hate in human nature, the mass media, culture, politics, and the economy. Perhaps, most importantly, we suggest strategies and tactics for reducing intergroup violence around the world. Along the way, we find lessons for coming to grips with hate violence in the experiences between Catholics and Protestants in Northern Ireland, between Christians and Jews in Bulgaria during World War II, between India's Hindus and Muslims, between Israelis and Palestinians, and between blacks and whites in the United States. And, in the hope of ending hate and violence, we focus on the contemporary conflict involving Muslims, Christians, and Jews in a post-9/11 world.

Many of our generous and insightful colleagues—researchers, teachers, and practitioners—contributed to this book. We were inspired by the good works of Paula Aymer, Eric Berman, Paul Bookbinder, Kevin Borgeson, Margaret Brearley, Greg Bura, Jeanine Chau, Richard Cole, Ed Dunbar, Raphael Ezekiel, T. C. Franklin, Mindy Fried, Kay Gillespie, Ryken Grattet, Mark Hamm, Ray Hammond, Ron Holmes, Paul Iganski, Val Jenness, Carol Kaufman, Nancy Kaufman, Phil Lamy, Fred Lawrence, Yueh-Ting Lee, Rob Leikand, Toni Lester, Bill Levin, Brian Levin, Larry

Lowenthal, Ron McAllister, Roger Mac Ginty, Petar Emil Mitev, Susan Ostrander, Barbara Perry, Carolyn Petrosino, Mark Potok, Michel Prum, Lorna Rivera, Laura Roskos, Angela Raven-Roberts, Michael Sutton, Cindy Tolin, Meredith Watts, Steve Wessler, and Scott Wolfman.

We are indebted to our colleagues at Northeastern University: Robin Chandler, Jeff Doggett, Michael Dukakis, Luis Falcon, Amy Farrell, Jamie Fox, Steve Harkins, Tony Jones, Maureen Kelleher, Debby Kaufman, Bill Kirtz, Tom Koenig, Bill Lancaster, Jack McDevitt, Tim Meisel, Bill Miles, Steve Nathanson, Donnie Perkins, Glenn Pierce, Debby Ramirez, Jim Ross, David Schmitt, Tom Shapiro, Jim Stellar, Naomi Thompson, and Kathrin Zippel.

The following students at Northeastern University deserve recognition for their assistance in helping us to crystallize our thinking about intergroup hostility: Christina Braidotti, Phyllis Brashler, Katie Conner, Vin Ferraro, Janese Free, Katrinka Heyman, Colleen Keaney-Mischel, Henrik Lenard, Eric Madfis, Jason Mazaik, Melissa Mazdel, Jeff O'Brien, Nelly Oliver, Elizabeth Ridge, and Stas Vysotsky.

Betty and Irving Brudnick, whose generous support and encouragement made possible the research for this book, have been true partners in the search for strategies to reduce hate and bring people together. As good Samaritans of the first order, the Brudnicks inspire hope and optimism in those who seek goodness and altruism in human nature.

The following people also deserve special recognition: Linda Regan, our editor at Prometheus Books who skillfully moved the book from idea to reality; Flea Levin for her competent editorial assistance; Mary A. Read, also at Prometheus Books, who expertly oversaw the production process; and Craig Bailey, Mike Lench, and Will Holton for their willingness to share their interesting photographs.

Last but by no means least, we thank the members of our respective families: Flea Levin; Bonnie and Brian Bryson; Michael Levin; and Andrea and Michael Segal; and Ljiljana Rabrenovic; Glenn Pierce; Olivera, Boris, and Aleksandra Vragovic; and Boyan and Sonya Kovacic—who have been more than generous with their patience, their encouragement, and their companionship. This book is dedicated to our children. May they live in a future world of security, peace, and respect for differences.

Jack Levin
Gordana Rabrenovic

CHAPTER 1
IN THE AFTERMATH OF 9/11

The horrific September 11, 2001, terrorist attack on the Twin Towers and the Pentagon knocked Americans out of their complacency and into the recognition, perhaps for the first time, that a cold-blooded and widespread form of anti-Americanism was being actively practiced around the world. Network newscasts played and replayed videotaped scenes purportedly showing a group of jubilant Arabs dancing and singing in the streets as they gleefully savored media accounts of the "Attack on America" in which some three thousand innocent civilians lost their lives. Many Middle Easterners adamantly denied that Arabs or Muslims were in any way responsible, instead blaming outsiders for the wanton destruction. Others in the Middle East praised Osama bin Laden as well as Middle Eastern suicide bombers whom they characterized as heroic figures.[1]

Americans who traveled abroad used to be called "ugly." They might have been ridiculed or scorned for their conspicuous consumption, but they were hardly treated as *the enemy*. By contrast, the reactions of some Middle Easterners to the September 11 attack suggest that Americans are now being regarded as morally bankrupt infidels who deserve nothing less than to be eliminated from the face of the earth.

The recent upsurge of negativity toward Americans is palpable. According to George Gallup,[2] more than 60 percent of the citizens of Pakistan, Iran, Saudi Arabia, and Jordan express unfavorable views of the United States. Even our "allies" in Saudi Arabia are overwhelmingly negative in their appraisal of America. About two-thirds of all Saudis are convinced, for example, that America "adopts biased policies in world affairs," has a "high rate of crime," and is "aggressive" and "conceited." More than half characterize Americans as "ruthless" and "arrogant."

This is not to say that most of the Islamic world condoned 9/11. Indeed, in almost every Muslim nation, strong majorities condemned the Attack on America, arguing consistently that such acts of terrorism were morally unjustifiable. Even in Pakistan and Iran, where negative views of America have long prevailed, approximately two-thirds of all citizens expressed their unqualified condemnation of the September 11 attack.[3]

At the same time, residents of Muslim countries were not willing to accept the idea, widely held as an obvious truth in the Western world, that Arabs were responsible for 9/11. Remarkably, the overwhelming majority of residents in Pakistan, Kuwait, Iran, Indonesia, and Lebanon rejected this notion. Instead, many Muslims blamed Israel, non-Muslim terrorists, or the United States itself.[4]

Why did so many people around the world still doubt if and how the September 11 attack occurred? Even though they saw on television the jets crashing into the twin towers, they simply couldn't believe their eyes. Television has unreal qualities; its images can be fabricated or exaggerated the way that motion picture fantasies are constructed to appear as real life. In the United States, Americans not only saw the events on TV; some also had friends, neighbors, family, and friends of friends who were killed or who witnessed the attacks. They also read newspaper stories about the victims and survivors and participated in collective events to memorialize the victims of the attack. All of this served as a reality check that was unavailable to citizens of other nations.

On the second anniversary of 9/11, some Iraqi citizens who were interviewed about the attack expressed disbelief that it had been accomplished without the help of American intelligence agencies. How could such a powerful country that so easily defeated them in two wars be so ill-informed as to the hijackers' plans? As Sheikh Hussein Al Fayez, an Iraqi tribal leader, said in an interview: "Such incidents surely could not be missed easily by the FBI and the CIA. I just don't see how they didn't know about it before. At first, I believed bin Laden did this alone. But now I'm not so sure."[5] For many people the denial of the incident was easier to swallow than the thought that the most powerful country in the world could be terrorized by a "megalomaniac billionaire hidden in a cave who sends planes against American cities."[6]

Just as anti-Americanism soared among the citizens of Muslim nations, anti-Jewish sentiment in the aftermath of 9/11 increased dramatically. Most of the new anti-Semitism is primarily oriented toward Israel but the rhetoric echoes the old anti-Semitism. In Egypt, recent newspaper articles described Jews as the sons of monkeys and pigs or as vampires who baked cookies with the blood of non-Jews. In Pakistan, *Wall Street Journal* reporter Daniel Pearl was brutally executed on videotape by terrorists while being forced to proclaim his Jewishness. In Germany, after Arabs attacked two Jewish American tourists, police barricaded a synagogue, a religiously integrated school, and a Jewish restaurant. In France, anti-Jewish *and* anti-immigrant (anti-Muslim) right-wing extremist Jean-Marie Le Pen received 18 percent of the vote in the country's recent presidential election. In London, suburban Paris, Marseilles, Strasbourg, Istanbul, and Berlin, fire bombs have been exploded in synagogues. In Canada, synagogues have been burnt, and bomb threats and physical assaults have been lodged against Jews. Many of these recent attacks on Jews and synagogues in countries around the world have been perpetrated by identifiably Arab or Muslim youths.[7]

Yet not all recent destructive anti-Semitic or anti-Israeli activities have occurred outside our own borders. The deadly "fireworks" that erupted at the Los Angeles International Airport on the morning of July 4, 2002, were particularly telling. Hesham Mohamed Ali Hadayet waited patiently in line at the El Al airlines second-floor ticket counter, and then, without uttering a word, opened fire with his .45 Glock semiautomatic handgun. Before security guards could wrestle him to the ground, the Egyptian immigrant had managed to spray a dozen bullets into a crowd of people, fatally gunning down two innocent victims, both Israeli citizens.[8]

The forty-one-year-old assailant was a Cairo-born accountant who had migrated to the United States some ten years earlier. Unfortunately, his personal life had recently fallen apart, when the small limousine service he had been running out of his apartment in Irvine became mired in debt. And a few days before his deadly rampage at LAX, Hadayet's wife and two sons left him to return to Egypt.

Still, Hadayet's grievances were political as well as personal. He was outraged by the policies of the United States toward Palestinians. He had long argued that the government of his Egyptian homeland be overthrown. He had told an ex-employee that he despised all Israelis. And he had vented his anger at a neighbor for flying an American flag after September 11, 2001. Somehow, Hadayet's political views and personal problems intersected in his mind, as he searched in vain for some reasonable resolution to the circumstances that had left his life in shambles. In the end, however, he reacted to his problems by committing an act of terrorism.

It should be noted that some of the violence following the attack on the Twin Towers was directed by vengeful Americans *against* Arabs and Muslims. In the aftermath of September 11, some irate citizens were eager to victimize almost anyone who had a "Middle Eastern look," even if they traced their ancestry to India, Pakistan, Italy, Greece, or Latin America—whether they were Muslim or Christian, or whether they embraced the United States and its values. In Mesa, Arizona, a forty-nine-year-old Sikh Indian wearing a turban was shot down in front of his gas station. In Dallas, a Pakistani Muslim was found shot to death in his convenience store. In Huntington, New York, a Pakistani pedestrian was nearly run down by a motorist who had threatened to kill her. In San Gabriel, California, an Egyptian Christian was killed in his grocery store. In Somerset, Massachusetts, a group of teenaged boys lobbed a Molotov cocktail onto the roof of the Olde Village convenience store owned by a family from India. And in Boston, a Saudi Arabian man was stabbed as he left a Back Bay nightclub. These were all unprovoked heinous acts of hate.[9]

Even prior to September 11, 2001, Americans held Arabs in low esteem, depending on their role in current events. During the Persian Gulf War in 1991, Gallup[10] found that 41 percent of Americans said they had a "low opinion" of Arabs. For the duration of the first armed conflict in Iraq, the majority of Americans told survey researchers that Arabs were "terrorists," "violent," and "religious fanatics." Shortly after the World Trade Center was bombed in 1993, Americans' attitudes toward Arabs turned more negative: 32 percent expressed an unfavorable opinion regarding Arabs.

By the mid-1990s, Americans were becoming suspicious that almost any act of terrorism must implicate an Arab or Muslim perpetrator. In April 1995, for example, shortly after the bombing of the federal building in Oklahoma City, two bearded Middle Eastern men were reportedly observed leaving the scene of the crime. Until the arrest of Timothy McVeigh, many innocent Muslims and Arabs were targeted and assaulted by angry citizens who blamed them for the death of 168 innocent Americans.

Notwithstanding the negative public image of Arabs during periods of crisis prior to 9/11, however, the willingness of Americans to tolerate Arabs and Muslims again plummeted in the months following the Attack on America. According to Gallup, with the exception of North Korea which was identified by Pres. George W. Bush as part of the Axis of Evil, almost all of the nations despised by Americans were primarily Islamic: Iraq, Iran, the Palestinian Authority, Libya, Pakistan, and Afghanistan.[11]

Even Muslim nations that had been regarded before 9/11 in a favorable light—Egypt and Saudi Arabia—afterward received unfavorable ratings from a majority of Americans. At the bottom of the list, in advance of the "liberation" of Iraq, 85 percent of all Americans viewed Iranians unfavorably and 88 percent rated Iraqis unfavorably. To provide perspective on these results, we should consider that merely 5 percent of Americans rated Canadians in a negative light; only 27 percent evaluated Russians (citizens of the former Evil Empire) unfavorably.

The worsening of American attitudes toward Arabs and Muslims after 9/11 was fanned by fears of another terrorist attack in addition to anger over 9/11. Since the attack, Americans have felt a dramatically heightened sense of their vulnerability wherever they might be—whether in shopping malls, airplanes, cinemas, concert halls, sports' stadiums, government buildings, power plants, and even at home. Because of the modus operandi employed in the attack, however, numerous false reports emerged, especially at airports and on airliners, that were filed by frightened passengers searching for Middle Eastern would-be terrorists. The indicators were as obvious as they were unreliable—tan skin, a foreign accent, the wearing of a turban or a veil. In its first racial discrimination complaint against an airline, for example, the US government accused American Airlines of removing passengers from their flights—even American citizens who had tickets and had passed security checks—simply because they were perceived to be Middle Eastern, Asian, or Muslim.[12]

Almost three out of four Americans still support tightening immigration restrictions against Arabs and Muslims. And a national poll taken in August 2002 discovered that a large number of Americans have become phobic about terrorism. They avoid large crowds and national landmarks; they are suspicious of people of Arab descent. Some twenty million Americans now refuse to fly, but millions more are anxious when they do. And because of 9/11, many Americans have bought guns or avoid vacations in places they deem vulnerable to attack.

It didn't take much time for Americans' fear of terrorism to spread to numerous innocent people. A couple of days following the first anniversary of the 9/11 terrorist attack, three Muslim medical students were detained when a woman in a restaurant from Cartersville, Georgia, reportedly overheard them talk about blowing up buildings and joke about the attack on the Twin Towers. The police searched their car but failed to uncover any explosives. And after seventeen hours, the three men were released without being charged with any crimes. Unfortunately, the hospital in Miami where they were to begin their medical internships, having received threatening phone calls, sadly decided to rescind its offer.[13]

Whatever one's opinion of the woman is, she certainly did follow the recommendation of the Bush administration for all citizens to be on guard in our war against terror. The incident in a small-town Georgia restaurant happened in the midst of a heightened state of national alert surrounding the first anniversary of the 2001 terrorist attack. Americans were told to be alert to the possibility of terrorism, but were given almost no guidelines on what to look for or where. When official sources of news are not forthcoming, individuals will create their own news, drawing on questionable sources and skimpy threads.

Moreover, Americans are generally convinced that the threat of terrorism soared after 9/11. They are unaware that almost five hundred terrorist acts had occurred in the United States between 1980 and 2001; or that the vast majority of such acts were homegrown. Thirty-six percent were international in origin, whereas 64 percent were perpetrated by our fellow citizens.

And under such conditions, based only on the "bits and pieces" of the conversation the woman in Georgia overheard, it was just a matter of time before Americans generalized their fear from airports and planes to a wide range of venues and situations.

As for the Georgian woman, eyewitness testimony, even under the best of circumstances and a sincere wish to help, is notoriously unreliable. And, during times of crisis, individuals can easily succumb to hysteria. In the case of the three Muslim medical students detained by Florida police, it was widely reported that they had failed to pay a toll on Florida's Alligator Alley and were driving with inaccurate license plates. Later, a videotape showed the car's driver paying the toll. Moreover, a search of registry records indicated that their license plates were absolutely correct and in order.

For someone who is prone to violence, the distinction between anxiety and hatred has broken down. During a period of two months, thirty-year-old Larme Price of Brooklyn, New York, targeted immigrants whom he believed to be of Middle Eastern descent. Early on the morning of February 8, 2003, Price—wearing a dark jacket, a black-and-red Boston Red Sox baseball cap, and hooded sweatshirt—walked into a convenience store in the Ozone Park section of Queens, where he immediately confronted John Freddy. The native of Guyana was seated in a chair, nonchalantly scratching lottery tickets and having a cup of coffee before beginning his job at the supermarket across the street. Price, holding his .40 caliber revolver by his side, walked over to where Freddy was seated and shot the immigrant in the head. A few hours after killing his first victim and still sporting his hooded sweatshirt, Price entered another convenience store, where—again without provocation—he fatally shot Indian immigrant Sukhjit Khajala and then took $169 from the cash register.[14]

A few weeks passed before Price struck another time. He found his third and fourth murder victims: first, thirty-two-year-old Albert Kotlyar, the Russian-born manager of an all-night laundry in Bedford-Stuyvesant, New York, and then, ten days later, Abdul Nassir Ali, a fifty-four-year-old Yemini immigrant who was seated by the front door of the Stop II Food Market in Crown Heights. Both were shot at point-blank range.

Two more days passed before Price walked into a Brooklyn police station, claiming to know the identity of the immigrant killer and offering to help track him down. But then, it took only a few hours of being interrogated before Price gave his confession. Over his cell phone, the father of two children told police that his motive for fatally shooting four people was to exact a measure of revenge by eliminating "Arabs," the people he blamed for the 9/11 Attack on America. The reason for contacting the police was that he began to have second thoughts about the legitimacy of his killing spree. After reading the Bible and reflecting on his violation of the Sixth Commandment, Thou shall not kill, Price decided to turn himself in to the police. That's when he learned what newspaper headlines had shouted all along; namely, that only one of his murdered victims was an Arab.

Though aimed primarily at Muslim and Arab immigrants, the venom of homegrown hate and violence has quickly spread beyond Middle Easterners and Asians. Anti-Semites located in extremist groups around the country seized on the opportunity provided by

September 11 to place the blame on Jews and/or Israelis. Thus, the Web sites of white supremacists such as David Duke contained lengthy stories suggesting that thousands of Jews allegedly employed at the World Trade Center in New York City had been warned early on the morning of September 11 not to show up for work. When many Jewish names turned up on the list of those killed in the World Trade Center attack, the extremists decided instead that it was Israelis, not Jews, who had received September 11 wake-up calls. Only a few Israelis, they claimed, had lost their lives.

The small number of Israelis murdered comes as no surprise to those who recognize that the Twin Towers were located in New York City, not Tel Aviv. Yet for white supremacists who hate Jews, the absence of large numbers of Israeli victims only served to confirm in their minds that the attack on America resulted from a worldwide conspiracy among Jews, the Israeli government, and pro-Jewish forces working within the federal government of the United States. Imitating their Islamic militant counterparts around the world, American anti-Jewish extremists minimized the role of Muslim fundamentalists in favor of placing the blame for 9/11 on their historical and political enemies—the Jews. "The Jews did it; the Jews did it," they claimed, but only with the assistance of what anti-Semites call "America's Zionist Occupied Government" aka ZOG.

Not all of the fallout from 9/11 drove the flames of hate to new heights. For a period of several months following the attack on America, racial tensions, especially between blacks and whites, subsided. It appeared that terrorism and the threat of terrorism—a threat from without—had united American citizens of varying colors, races, and creeds. In almost every sector of American society, public opinion surveys reported that the credibility of the police, the president, and Congress had skyrocketed. The same polls also discovered that black and white Americans had a more favorable attitude toward one another.

One year later, however, a reversal of good feeling between racial groups already occurred, suggesting strongly that the unifying impact of September 11 had been merely a temporary one. In July 2002, an event took place that was reminiscent of the beating of Rodney King. A black suspect in Inglewood, California—while handcuffed and apparently compliant—was shown on videotape being brutalized by a white police officer.[15] Moreover, in Boston, two white supremacists were tried and convicted for plotting to blow up African American and Jewish landmarks. In a separate case, a thirty-four-year-old black man in New York City shot three people: two whites and one Asian. He then attempted to set fire to customers at a trendy Manhattan wine bar.[16]

The intense anger we refer to as hate is often expressed through violence and fear; it has also, at times, taken the form of revenge. Until recently, the term *hate* was used generically to refer to any intense dislike or hostility, whatever its object. In everyday conversation, for example, an individual might be said to "hate" his father, the taste of spinach, his job, or even himself. Thus, hate could, in this use of the term, be directed at a person, a group, an idea, some other abstraction, or an inanimate object.[17]

Beginning in the mid-1980s, however, *hate* became increasingly applied, in a much more restricted sense, to characterize an individual's negative feelings toward the members of some other group of people, because of their race, religious identity, ethnic origin, gender, sexual orientation, age, or disability status.[18] As incorporated into the concepts of "hate crime" and "hate violence," this more recent usage overlaps terms such as *prejudice* and *bias* (as in such more specific forms as racism, sexism, ageism, homophobia, and xenophobia).

Among the concepts in the lexicon of bigotry, *hate* is not alone in having undergone a significant shift of meaning. A parallel transition occurred from the original definition of the kindred term *prej-*

udice from "any prejudgment" to "a hostile attitude directed specifically toward the members of any group regarded as inferior by virtue of its presumed defects of environment or heredity."[19]

Though overlapping, *hate* and *prejudice* also have subtle differences that are important to emphasize. *Hate* tends to focus less on cognition (i.e., stereotyping) and more on the emotional or affective component of bigotry. Indeed, until hate became recently associated with intergroup hostility, researchers focused almost exclusively on the cognitive dimension of prejudice. In other words, sociologists and psychologists have offered many more insights into the nature of stereotypes and other cognitive processes related to prejudice than they have into its emotional basis.[20] Many have therefore ignored hate.

In the chapters that follow we use the terms *hate* and *prejudice* to examine the experiences of groups in conflict. As two sociologists who have studied hate and violence for more than twenty years, we will explore the reasons why hostility develops in the relationship between groups and why violence so often flares up when social conflict arises between them. We will examine how grievances and frustration can escalate into violence with disastrous consequences. We will also seek to explain why hate exists—why we hate "outsiders," but also why "outsiders" hate us. We ask: Are human beings born with a propensity for hate and violence? Or, do they learn to hate? Do you have to hate in order to commit a hate crime? Or, can there be more rational reasons for attacking "outsiders"? And, do we necessarily reduce hate when society makes efforts to reduce ignorance?

We take the position that it is important to be looking beyond the prejudice and hate in order to determine those factors responsible for the hostility. Specifically, we recognize that hate is frequently employed as a justification for acting in a despicable manner. Moreover, violence has its seeming advantages—psychological, social, and economic—for those who choose to be hostile and vicious toward those who are different.

More important, perhaps, we will make recommendations on how to discourage hostility from arising, in the first place, and how to combat hate and violence once they emerge. We suggest that ordinary people working collectively in a nonviolent effort have made a big difference in the past and can make a big difference in the future. The risk factors for hate violence vary by society and culture. It is always possible to locate good Samaritans who are willing to risk their prestige, their friends, and even their lives for the sake of a vulnerable group of people. Yet many societies do not provide the ingredients for molding a large number of such courageous human beings. Consequently, groups that are out of favor are often left without allies. They become convenient scapegoats for the expression of hate and violence.

CHAPTER 2
HATE AS VIOLENCE

Frustration increases the likelihood that an individual will turn violent. People who cannot fulfill their goals and are dissatisfied with their lives may decide to strike back against those they regard as responsible for their plight. Yet violence is often aimed not at the true source of the frustration, but at an innocent target. Retaliation may be out of the question when the perpetrator turns out to be a harsh and threatening parent, a belittling and unappreciative boss, or a physically powerful peer. Moreover, there are circumstances in which the true source of the frustration is difficult if not impossible to identify. Exactly where do we place the responsibility for the September 11 attack on America? The culprit seems to be a shadowy figure named Osama bin Laden, the leader of a previously obscure terrorist group located thousands of miles from the United States. For nearly all Americans, the extent of their contact with bin Laden is having seen him a few times on low-quality videotapes or in some newspaper photographs.[1]

When the source of our difficulties is very powerful or difficult to identify or both, we tend to redirect or displace our anger to some innocent target, especially a target that is both visible and vulnerable. In other words, we tend to attack someone who is easily identifiable and likely incapable of striking back. Psychologists refer to this phenomenon as *scapegoating* or *displaced aggression*. Thus, if you can't locate Osama bin Laden, you can at least attack and victimize Arab-Americans, Muslim-Americans, and all immigrants for that matter.

In the history of the United States, black Americans have made convenient scapegoats when times were tough. Their skin color easily marked them for violence; their lack of power to retaliate made them a safe target for the wrath of the majority. In the closing decades of the nineteenth century, when former slaves began to compete effectively against their white counterparts in the job market, the number of assaults and murders committed against blacks soared.[2]

High levels of residential segregation by race are a relatively new phenomenon in American cities. Research by historians shows that prior to the twentieth century, African Americans lived in all sections of major cities.[3] The sharp increase in residential separation is attributable to the Great Migration, when during the period from 1916 to 1930, over a million African Americans moved from the South to Northern cities. The white population responded to this influx by institutionalizing social and legal policies to keep the races apart. Many city governments created special residential zones for black residents; but when in 1917 this type of policy was ruled unconstitutional, racially restrictive covenants were instead written into the buyer's real estate deed.[4] Also, white residents created property owners' associations in order to keep their neighborhoods white by pressing realtors and merchants to boycott black residents. Some used arson and mob raids on the homes of African Americans who moved into white neighborhoods.

The persistence of residential segregation is partly explained by those historical trends and by the desire of groups to live in neighborhoods with individuals who share their ethnic, religious, and socioeconomic background. Even in cities we still have a dual housing market where housing is differentially available to white and African American households. Again, many studies conducted by sociologists have shown how real estate agents act as gatekeepers for segregation; the real estate agents show black house seekers property in black neighborhoods and white house seekers property in white neighborhoods. One study showed that African Americans have a one-in-five chance of being discriminated against in the sale of a home, and a one-in-two chance of being discriminated against in a rental.[5]

Even when real estate agents do abide by the law and use "race neutral" practices, homeowners themselves still have discriminated against black applicants. This is what happened in a suburb of Boston in 2000. Michael Demon, a visiting professor at MIT, was looking for a house in Belmont. He liked the community for its easy commute to Boston and its excellent schools. He was shown a house that was perfect for his family. Filling out all the paper work, Demon wrote a check for the deposit. But the deal fell apart when he submitted a letter from MIT as proof of his source of income. The letter said that he would be the Martin Luther King Jr. visiting associate professor. At that point, the owner of the house discovered that Michael Demon[6] and his family were black. She had never met the Demons nor had any desire to meet them. Just the fact that they were black was enough for her to reject the deal. According to the *Boston Globe* account, her rationale for discriminating against the Demon family was that her neighbors would be unhappy.[7]

During the 1930s, Hitler targeted Jews whom he blamed for the serious and worsening economic plight experienced by the German people. Like blacks in the United States, Jews made a perfect scapegoat. Since they comprised only one-half of 1 percent of the German population, their small numbers made them very vulnerable. And their position in the German economy—occupying middle-class and upper-middle-class jobs—gave them visibility on an everyday basis. To an impoverished German Christian, the relative wealth of his Jewish neighbor—the butcher, the owner of a small grocery store, the reporter, the doctor, the artist, the professor, or the lawyer—must have seemed vastly more threatening than the more concealed wealth of the non-Jewish major industrialists. Moreover, German Jews represented a broad range of religious orientations. Some were totally assimilated and never attended religious services; others were conservative and observant; still others were ultra-Orthodox and dressed in a way that made them easily identifiable. Finally, Jewish immigrants from countries in eastern Europe were highly visible by virtue of differences in their language and clothing.

The vulnerability and visibility (and even invisibility) of women and girls have certainly contributed to making them the recipients of brutal violence around the world. In Turkey and in Jordan, under the assumption that a female family member has dishonored the family by committing immoral behavior, hundreds of girls and women have been murdered. In Zimbabwe, many women on farms and in rural areas have been raped with impunity by militants who seek to intimidate the farmers into giving up their land. In Uzbekistan, local officials have limited the number of divorces available within a certain period of time, forcing women who seek a legal separation into remaining with their abusive partners. In the Ukraine, one in every three women suffers domestic violence. In the former Yugoslavia, the Democratic Republic of the Congo, Indonesia, Guinea, and Tanzania, young women have suffered numerous rapes and other forms of physical violence during periods of armed conflict in which one side has the upper hand over the other and targets the civilian population. Husbands or boyfriends throwing sulfuric acid into the face of an "uppity woman" have been reported in Bangladesh, Egypt, England, India, Italy, Jamaica, Malaysia, Nigeria, Vietnam, and the United States.[8]

Some of the most commonplace acts of hate violence have been committed not by Nazis, white supremacists, or Klansmen, but by alienated young people who spray paint anti-Semitic graffiti on a building or a car, burn a cross on the front lawn of a black family, shout racial epithets, or physically attack total strangers because they are different. Thus, some groups of teenagers (and they represent only a small percentage of all teenagers) have been known to go out on a Saturday night, looking for someone to bash either verbally or physically in order to impress their friends or gain a sense of their own importance. Bored and idle, they typically travel by car or on foot to an area of town where they are likely to locate an appropriate member of an "inferior" group. Or, they might come across an outsider at a party or celebration at which a number of their hate-filled friends have come together for a good time, but it ends up at someone else's expense.

Targets regarded as inferior or undesirable make especially good victims for groups of thrill-seeking youngsters. The "thrill seekers" feelings of guilt are easily assuaged or nonexistent, since they have been taught through immersion in their culture or in their homes that certain individuals in their midst are inferior beings, deserving of only the most brutal forms of punishment and abuse. It isn't necessary, however, for all these youthful perpetrators to be exceptionally hateful. Instead, they have a burning desire to feel important or to gain bragging rights with their friends. Such motivations may seem trivial, but not to a teenaged boy who is at odds with his parents, rejected by the popular youngsters at school, or trapped in a dead-end job. Even those few who join organized hate groups may not be entirely motivated by intense bigotry. In a study of women who join white supremacist groups, sociologist Kathleen Blee discovered that many of her respondents became

more hateful only *after* joining the movement. They were originally motivated less by hate and more by a desire to remain in
good standing with their comrades.[9]

Gays and lesbians are frequently the victims of brutal thrill
attacks perpetrated by teenaged hatemongers and their buddies. A
recent example occurred in 2003 at a July 4 fireworks celebration in
Boston, Massachusetts. Two (assumed to be) lesbian partners, Lisa
Craig, age thirty-five, and Debbie Riley, thirty-seven, were walking
to buy ice cream for their two young daughters when a group of
teenagers, shouting antigay epithets, confronted them on the street.
Three of the girls and a boy punched Craig to the ground and kicked
her in the head. She required surgery to stop the bleeding in her
brain and two hundred stitches to close her wounds.[10]

White straight teenagers have not cornered the market on hate,
however. Thrill-motivated hate crimes have also been committed
by minority youngsters who feel marginalized and alienated from
mainstream society and have become convinced that white people
are the enemy. At some level, they are able to justify their bigotry
by referring to the history of oppression, beginning with slavery,
suffered by people of color in the United States. For these very
angry youths, bashing a white person may give them a feeling of
power that they feel has been missing from their lives.

On May 1, 2003, a group of eighteen middle-school students in
Cleveland, Ohio, which included eleven black girls, five black
boys, one Latino girl, and one white girl, was charged with beating
and kicking a thirteen-year-old white girl as she walked home from
school. The youthful defendants told police that May 1 was "beat
up a white kid day." One attacker said, "I hit her and got my stomp
in." Another referred to the victim as "white trash."[11]

Hate violence may have a more practical purpose than just
giving some teenagers a thrill. In many cases, the violence is
designed to send a message from the residents of segregated neigh-

borhoods, schools, and college dormitories to the "outsider" who had dared to move in. Study after study suggests that hate crimes escalate when black or Latino families move into previously all-white neighborhoods.

Susan and David Weston[12] were a white couple living in Anoka, Minnesota. They had a fifteen-year-old biracial son, whose biological father was black. On a Thursday morning in July 2003, Susan woke up to find racial slurs and obscenities spray-painted on the garage of their family home. Among the epithets, they found the words "Go Away" and the letters "AAB," a reference to a group of white supremacist high-school students known as the All-American Boys who had been previously involved in a number of racial incidents. In 1998, three members of the All-American Boys had pleaded guilty to disorderly conduct in a race-based assault.

The Westons learned that the police had arrested a sixteen-year-old boy and a fourteen-year-old girl, both white. Captain Tom Anderson suggested that the two teenagers might face hate-crime charges. The officer added that the graffiti on the Westons' garage appeared to be partly motivated by racial bias, but also "just stupid kid stuff."[13]

Hate speech and graffiti are too often regarded as a childish prank, as just "stupid kid stuff" not to be taken too seriously. Though, as noted, some teenagers "just" looking for a thrill will pick on an outsider to harass, it's a mistake to downplay the seriousness of these acts. By trivializing "even" verbal assaults, members of the community and the police may give hate an opportunity to escalate into more serious forms of aggression. Most hate attacks designed to send a message to a neighbor, coworker, or classmate are not the least bit trivial from the victim's standpoint, but they do not always begin as a physical assault. When the victim refuses to leave the block, however, perpetrators may decide to take their persuasive methods to the next level, becoming increasingly more violent in the process.

Victims often report receiving harassing phone messages, notes in their mailbox, and attacks on their personal property. Many decide not to contact the police about these incidents because they fear escalating the problem unnecessarily and hope that the offenders will simply lose interest. Unfortunately, hate crime perpetrators, unless stopped, more typically continue to intensify the violence until the victims "get the message."

David Palmer[14] knows all too well how hate violence can escalate when it isn't taken seriously. The twenty-nine-year-old black resident of Pemberton Township, Pennsylvania, was recently targeted by two white supremacists after he moved onto a predominantly white block of single-family houses. Shouting racial slurs at Palmer and his wife as they stood on their own front lawn, the two bigots tried to get them to leave the neighborhood. Sadly, none of Palmer's other white neighbors was reportedly willing to give him support or encouragement. Nobody urged him to stay in the area; not a single white person on the block assured him that they were respectful of differences.

If they saw the verbal attack on Palmer as an isolated and trivial event, then his white neighbors were totally wrong. Three weeks later, the same two hatemongers (who have since been arrested) invaded Palmer's home in the dead of night, this time brutally beating him and his wife with baseball bats. Fortunately, the Palmers were able to escape with stitches and broken bones, but they also felt alone and unwanted, as if nobody in the neighborhood really cared. They have since relocated to another community, where they might feel more secure. And the bigots' escalation of violence against them accomplished exactly what they had intended: It drove a black family out of a white neighborhood.

Black Americans are not alone in being singled out as victims of hate offenses. Since the 9/11 attack on America, immigrants have increasingly come under attack from ordinary Americans who are concerned about terrorism as well as a rising unemployment rate. Four white teenagers were charged with a hate crime committed in the early morning of July 4, 2003: the firebombing of a small two-story house in the town of Farmingdale on Long Island, New York. Inside and asleep were the members of an immigrant family—a Mexican couple and their two young children—who escaped burning to death when neighbors roused them by shouting and banging on the doors. This is how these teenagers purportedly celebrated America's Independence Day. Referring to the young perpetrators of the crime, Patrick Young, chairman of the Long Island Immigrant Alliance, said, "These young men grew up in an atmosphere where adults claiming to be speaking for the community depicted Latinos as criminals and terrorists."[15]

A couple of years earlier, two Mexican immigrants living next door in the same neighborhood were taken to a warehouse under the ruse of offering them a job, but instead were beaten and stabbed and then left for dead. The perpetrators turned out to be two young white supremacists, tatooed from head to toe with neo-Nazi slogans, who decided to execute the immigrants they so despised.[16]

The same sort of hate violence has been noted not only in the United States but also in countries around the world, when newcomers cross that divide between two racial, ethnic, religious, or national groups. We have recently witnessed attacks on immigrants in England, France, Italy, Russia, and China. Even in Scandinavian countries, where tolerance for difference has long been espoused, immigrants from African nations have been assaulted and even murdered for their very presence in a section of a city that some white residents declare as "off limits" to newcomers. In one horrifying incident, on the night of January 26, 2001, fifteen-year-old Benjamin Hermansen—the dark-skinned son of a white Norwegian mother and a black Ghanaian father—was chased by three neo-Nazi skinheads through the streets of Oslo's multiracial Holmlia suburb. They knocked Hermansen to the ground and repeatedly stabbed him in the chest, back, and arms. He staggered along for a few yards, but was dead when he hit the ground.

Throughout the 1990s, there were thousands of attacks in German cities against Turks, Africans, Romanians, and Vietnamese. In 1991, for example, six hundred right-wing German youths attacked hundreds of Vietnamese and Mozambicans in the streets of Hoyerswerde. In 1992, hundreds of hate-filled youngsters in the city of Rostock assaulted the apartments housing Asian immigrants with gasoline bombs and rocks.

The new millennium brought little if any relief for threats to newcomers. In September 2001, a group of German teenagers firebombed a home for foreigners and a nearby Asian grocery store in Rostock. More than one hundred residents of the building—all immigrants from Asian nations—fled in panic to avoid being burned alive.[17] Then, in December 2001, thirty-five hundred members of the extremist National Democratic Party held the largest neo-Nazi rally in Berlin since the collapse of the Third Reich in 1945.

German citizens are certainly not alone in their disdain for newcomers. In France, widespread resentment against its six million Muslim immigrants has provoked the French government to tighten its policies restricting illegal immigrants. According to public opinion pollsters, 76 percent of all French citizens believe there are too many Arabs in their country.[18] In England, over the last two years alone, there were two thousand racial attacks on immigrants that ranged from spray painting graffiti to murder.[19] In Sweden, the racist youth movement has been more active recently, using white-power rock music to spread its xenophobic message to target its enemies who include blacks, Jews, and immigrants.[20]

In the United States, hate violence has been implicated in hundreds of acts of domestic terrorism and scores of assassinations perpetrated by angry and alienated individuals who act alone rather than as members of organized political groups. In the aftermath of the September 11, 2001, tragedy, it is easy to lose sight of the fact that the majority of terrorist acts on American soil have been perpetrated by American citizens who hate the federal government or despise certain kinds of Americans. Unlike international terrorism, the American version has been inspired not just by politics but also by psychopathology.

The assassination of John Lennon was perpetrated by a troubled young man, Mark Chapman, whose vicious act was more psychotic than political. John Hinckley, who attempted to kill then president Ronald Reagan, was inspired not by extremist religion or politics, but by a delusional belief that he needed to get some publicity in order to impress actress Jodie Foster.

In October 2001, near Manchester, Tennessee, a passenger slashed the throat of Greyhound bus driver Garfield Sands with a boxcutter. Sands recovered from his ordeal, but the bus crashed, killing six passengers. The assailant turned out to be not a Middle Easterner but a mentally deranged twenty-nine-year-old Croatian war veteran who had been in the United States since 1999. He had post-traumatic stress syndrome after fighting in Croatia's war for independence from Yugoslavia in 1991. In January 2002, fifteen-year-old Charles Bishop, who had no connections to Islam apart from being inspired by the attack on America, committed suicide by flying his plane into a building in downtown Tampa, Florida.

And in our nation, political motivation has also played a role in provoking some terrorist acts. Middle Easterners aren't the only ones who think that America is a bully. Politics certainly had something to do with Timothy McVeigh's 1995 bombing of the Oklahoma City federal building which killed 168 innocent people. McVeigh, a former US serviceman, apparently had been associated with a civilian militia in Kingman, Arizona. His "bible" was the infamous *Turner Diaries*, a fictionalized account written by a white supremacist of a coming civil war, in which revolutionaries bring down the federal government by bombing federal buildings and disrupting public utilities.

In 1996, Eric Rudolph allegedly caused the deadly explosion that ripped through Centennial Olympic Park in Atlanta, Georgia, which killed one patron and injured at least one hundred others. He is also accused of the 1998 fatal bombing of an abortion clinic in Birmingham, Alabama, which killed a police officer and injured seven. Hiding in the hills of North Carolina, Rudolph was able to stay on the loose for five years until he was apprehended in 2003. Many believe he was helped by sympathetic residents of the area.

In 1999, Indiana University college student Benjamin Smith went on a rampage, shooting to death a Korean graduate student and an African American basketball coach. He also injured six Orthodox Jews. It turned out that Smith was a member of the white supremacist group World Church of the Creator.

In the international arena, hate may not always inspire warfare, but it usually keeps the conflicting parties from finding a peaceful resolution of their differences, whether in conflict or in war. The enemy is typically dehumanized, in an effort to reduce the feelings of guilt and shame associated with murdering decent and honorable human beings. Often the "other" has been referred to as a "cancer" that needs to be removed from society. Serving as the equivalent of the N-word for blacks, the term *gook* has, for example, been employed in a long history of supporting wars waged against Asians by the United States. This term is meant to reduce a person to an insidious stereotype. During World War II, the Japanese enemy was referred to as gooks; during the Korean conflict, it was the North Koreans who were given the label. During the Vietnam War, the term gook was reserved for North Vietnamese and the Viet Cong enemy. And during the 1970s, as large numbers of "boat people" migrated from Southeast Asia for a new beginning in the United States, the newcomers to America were vilified with the same gook label.

If a war has lasted long enough, its adversaries have defined one another as subhuman animals or demons. And there have been more than enough opportunities over the past thirty-four hundred years of recorded history to practice the fine art of dehumanization. During this period of time, human beings have been totally at peace for merely 268 of those years. By this measure, hate has historically reigned supreme. In the twentieth century alone, more than 108 million people lost their lives in war. Over the course of human history, the number killed in wars probably exceeds 150 million and may have encompassed as many as one billion. In addition, there are countless civilians who have been shot, stabbed, bombed, raped, starved, and driven from their homes.

Into the new millennium, peace in the world seems no better off than it was during the last century. Some three thousand civilians lost their lives in the September 11, 2001, attack on America. Moreover, in 2003 alone, at least thirty wars or armed conflicts took place in Afghanistan, Algeria, Burundi, China, Colombia, the Congo, India, Indonesia, Israel, Iraq, Liberia, Nigeria, Pakistan, Peru, the Philippines, Russia, Somalia, Sudan, and Uganda.[21]

The most extreme measure of large-scale hate is evident in acts known as *genocide*: those acts committed with the intent of annihilating an entire group of people based on differences in their race, religion, ethnicity, or national origin. Perhaps because of the growing presence of efficient weapons of mass destruction, the frequency and size of carnage of genocidal campaigns have grown dramatically over the last one hundred years, though even primitive weapons can do horrific damage.

The first genocide of the last century was the Armenian massacre of 1915–1916, which accounted for the deaths of one and a half million Armenians at the hands of the Turkish army. In the

1930s, a staggering twenty million citizens of the Soviet Union were murdered by its Stalinist regime. From 1937 to 1945, six million Jews along with at least five million Gypsies (Roma), Jehovah's Witnesses, gays, and other "enemies of the Fatherland" were exterminated by the Nazis. In the 1970s, almost two million Cambodians—more than one-quarter of the country's seven million inhabitants—were murdered by the Khmer Rouge. In 1987, fifty thousand Iraqi Kurds were slaughtered by their Muslim neighbors. From 1992 to 1995, more than three hundred thousand Muslims were killed in Bosnia by Serbs and Croatians. And in 1994, more than one million Tutsis and moderate Hutus in Rwanda were massacred by Hutus over a ten-week period.

How is it that apparently ordinary people can turn into killing machines and commit atrocities against their neighbors? Some of those "ordinary" people are "natural-born killers" who, when given the permission, kill with moral impunity. But most of the others join in acts of collective violence out of profound fear: Some are forced by their leaders to participate in the attacks. In many cases, leaders instill the notion that if their followers do not kill their opponents first, they will become victims themselves.

CHAPTER 3
HATE AS FEAR

Many white Americans sincerely believe that racism is ancient history. They point to the fact that America long ago abolished slavery and removed its separate water fountains and restrooms. They suggest that affirmative action legislation has helped create a viable black middle class, and point to the fact that a growing number of major cities now have black mayors.

What they don't usually recognize, however, is that black Americans—and especially black men—now suffer new indignities. The old forms of racism have to some degree but not completely abated, but they have been replaced by a pervasive and profound sense of *Afrophobia*—an irrational fear among many whites of African Americans.

Since the early days of the civil rights movement more than forty years ago, the traditional stereotype of blacks as "ignorant buffoons" and "happy-go-lucky Sambos" has gradually given way to an even more dangerous image. Some people project on African Americans the stereotype of potential thieves, rapists, and murderers to be avoided at any cost. Thus, many cab drivers won't always stop for a black man, nor will some white women share an elevator ride with a black stranger. When black or Latino men go driving through a white neighborhood, they are often stopped by a suspicious police officer; when they go shopping downtown, they are followed through stores by security guards.

This is what happened to Dee Brown, the black NBA player who was mistaken for a bank robber in a wealthy suburb of Boston. On Friday afternoon, September 23, 1990, Brown and his fiancée were seated in their car in front of the Wellesley, Massachusetts, post office, when seven police officers with their guns drawn surrounded their car and ordered them to lie face down (Brown's version) or kneel down (the police's version) on the ground. After twenty tense minutes, the police officers realized that they had the wrong man and let the couple go. But the damage had been done.[1]

The police had been summoned by a call from the manager of the bank across the street. The bank secretary saw Mr. Brown going into the post office and believed he looked like a man who had robbed their bank a week earlier. Other bank employees had confirmed the secretary's suspicion. What infuriated Brown was that he did not look anything like the bank robber. At the time, the professional basketball player was twenty-one-years-old, six foot one, with very dark skin. The robber turned out to be a thirty-year-old, six foot one, light-skinned black man with hazel eyes.

Wellesley is a town with only 1.8 percent black residents, a reality that can help explain how the bank employees' eyewitness observations could have been so faulty. For some white Wellesley residents, one tall, young black man looks exactly like any other tall, relatively young, black man. What made this story important news was the fact that Dee Brown was the Boston Celtics' top 1990 draft pick. Had he not been a celebrity, the story would likely have gone unpublished and unacknowledged as yet another example of discrimination.

Another case of mistaken identity comes from New York City. In July 16, 1999, black Broadway actor Alton Fitzgerald White was picked up by the police in the lobby of his apartment building in

Harlem. As he was exiting the building on his way to the gym, he was intercepted by the police looking for four Hispanic men with weapons who allegedly were dealing drugs in the building.[2] White and five other men were arrested, handcuffed, and strip-searched because they fit the witness's description of drug dealers. It did not help that White's neighbors vouched for him and even informed the police that he was a Broadway actor. After five hours in the police station, White and three of the other men—Charles Mason, a student affairs coordinator at Columbia University; John Martin, a public relations director, and Dennis Marshall,[3] a graduate student at Columbia University—were released, while two of the other men were charged with the crime. White's humiliation at being arrested came on top of having to miss his evening performance. Ironically, in his Broadway show, the actor plays the role of a black man who is confronted by racist firemen as he drives through a town in New York State.

This is why so many black men cringed in horror when they saw O. J. Simpson's courtroom appearances being telecast daily to a national audience or when they learned that NBA superstar Kobe Bryant had been indicted for allegedly committing a sexual assault. It wasn't only that they mistrust the criminal justice system; blacks were also concerned that the publicity would reinforce the Afrophobic stereotype by which they were being personally judged, on an everyday basis, as thugs, thieves, and rapists.

These views show how racial discrimination persists. A sociologist conducted research in which she sent black and white college students in search of low-skilled jobs. In this study conducted by Northwestern University's Devah Pager, in Milwaukee, Wisconsin, the job seekers were divided so that half were given bogus criminal records whereas the other half were not. As expected, black applicants with criminal records had very little chance of being called back after their first encounter. Only 5 percent were called for a return interview. However, the more surprising finding was that the black applicants without criminal records were less likely to be called back than the white applicants *with* criminal records. Specifically, 14 percent of the black applicants without criminal records were called back compared with 17 percent of the white applicants with criminal records. Most likely to get a second interview were white applicants who did not have records; fully 34 percent were called back.[4]

Similar results were found in research conducted by economists Marianne Bertrand of the University of Chicago and Sendhi Mullainathan of the Massachusetts Institute of Technology. In their study, conducted in Boston and Chicago, applicants were given names that could be assumed by employers as either white or African American. Their findings once again showed discriminatory recruitment practices. Applicants with names that "sounded" white, such as Greg Kelly or Emily Walsh, were 50 percent more likely to be called for interviews than applicants with names such as Jamal Jackson or Lakisha Washington. Even more disturbing was their finding that, for purposes of getting a job interview, a white-sounding name was worth as much as an extra eight years of work experience![5]

One explanation that has been proposed by labor market researchers for the lower employment rates of black Americans is their assumed lack of so-called soft skills including abilities, talents, and traits that pertain to personality, attitude, and behavior rather than to formal or technical knowledge. Soft skills include interaction proficiency such as an ability to interact with customers, coworkers, and supervisors; friendliness; teamwork; ability to fit in; appropriate affect; grooming and attire; as well as expressions of motivation such as enthusiasm; positive work attitude; commitment to job; dependability; and willingness to learn.[6]

This stigmatizes an entire race based on assumptions, but there are young blacks and others of deprived backgrounds who, according to the labor market argument, may lack the necessary socialization experiences so useful in the workplace. Thus, they are advised to learn how to present themselves and communicate in ways acceptable to a majority white culture. But, as the Bertrand-Mullainathan and Pager studies show, this is not always enough. All the job applicants in this study were college students who already had soft skills, and still their race trumped their effectiveness in communicating in a middle-class manner. Thus, potential employers having typically a limited amount of time to screen job applicants, seem to depend a great deal on stereotyped preconceptions about race.

Some Afrophobics justify their concern by citing national statistics which show that black Americans commit a disproportionate number of homicides—more than 50 percent of all murders. Yet any white person who rationally approaches this statistic would recognize that it is totally invalid as a basis for protecting oneself from harm. First, while half of all murders are committed by African Americans, only less than one-half of 1 percent of all blacks commit murder. Indeed, the overwhelming majority of black Americans are decent, law-abiding citizens whose lives have been impacted by the criminals in their midst and are anxious to eliminate drugs, guns, and gangs. To put the problem of prediction in some perspective, consider the fact that men commit more than 90 percent of all murders in the United States. Just as in the case of African Americans, however, only less than one-half of 1 percent of all men are responsible for these homicides. On this basis, it would be ridiculous to advise women everywhere who are concerned for their personal safety to avoid, at all costs, interacting with men. Indeed, it might be more rational to advise instead that they avoid dealing with certain kinds of men (and women) who have the potential to become violent: those who are possessive, sociopathic, impulsive, and quick to anger. The same should be said for black Americans.

Moreover, just like their white counterparts, black killers target the members of their own group: their friends, neighbors, and family members. Thus, whites tend to kill whites; Asians tend to kill Asians; Latinos tend to kill Latinos; and blacks tend to kill blacks.

Finally, the most hideous and grotesque crimes in America are perpetrated by whites. In fact, 70 percent of all sadistic serial killers and mass murderers are white. Thus, almost everybody was shocked when in October 2002, the Beltway Sniper turned out to be two black men. This is because serial killers, torturers, and snipers are predominately white male perpetrators.

The real variable for predicting criminality is poverty, not race. During the nineteenth century, impoverished Irish Americans who had recently immigrated to the New World and had high rates of crime were scorned and stigmatized by groups of Americans who had settled there earlier. During the early years of the twentieth century, impoverished Italian Americans were widely regarded as the kingpins of organized crime. Some of the images linking these groups with crime were based on reality—a reality inspired by widespread poverty. To the extent that Irish and Italian Americans escaped their impoverished circumstances and moved into the middle class, their crime rates plummeted.

Phobics often avoid uncomfortable contact. Those who dread airplanes will take a bus or a train. In the same way, fearful white pedestrians have been known to cross to the other side of the street to avoid black passersby. Some white tourists who get lost in black neighborhoods are afraid to ask for directions. And, when a black family moves into a previously all-white neighborhood, its members run the risk of being shunned or worse.

Specific phobias frequently develop out of negative childhood experiences. Thus, Afrophobes grow up hearing racial jokes and slurs recited at the family dinner table and by their friends. They watch stereotyped versions of black Americans on TV. Some are warned, time and time again, to be wary of dark-skinned strangers.

Because whites and blacks often live in separate neighborhoods, there is little interaction between them that would allow for confronting those stereotypes. According to the US Department of Education, for example, in 86 percent of the public schools in the City of Chicago, more than 50 percent of the students are of color—black, Latino, or Asian; in 62 percent of the Chicago schools, more than 90 percent are students of color, and in 42 percent of these schools, the student population is made up entirely of children of color. In contrast, 65 percent of all public schools in suburban Chicago are more than 75 percent white and 40 percent are more than 90 percent white.[7]

No wonder that a black child who lived in the affluent suburb of Wellesley, Massachusetts, was mistakenly put on a bus to take him to an inner-city neighborhood. The five-year-old kindergartner was mistaken for a "Metco" student and put on a bus at the end of his afterschool program. Designed to aid in the process of school desegregation, Metco is a voluntary program that buses children from Boston neighborhoods to suburban schools in the city's metropolitan area. The error was made because the bus was late and the teachers still did not know all the children by name. In the confusion of the first day of school, the Wellesley child joined the Metco children waiting for the bus. It also happened that one of the children from the Metco program was picked up by his parent earlier in the day, so when afterschool teachers counted the children, the number was right. The mistake was discovered when another parent picked up her son in Boston and noticed the boy from Wellesley standing alone on the sidewalk.[8]

The stigma involved in being part of the Metco program became obvious recently when talk-show hosts John Dennis and Gerry Callahan, of local radio station WEEI-AM, joked about a gorilla that had escaped from the Franklin Park Zoo (located in Boston's inner city). After noting that the gorilla was seen at a bus stop, Dennis and Callahan speculated while laughing that the escaped animal must have been "a Metco gorilla . . . heading out to Lexington [a wealthy suburb west of Boston]." Metco students did not find their joke funny. Some were taunted by their white classmates who likened their black classmates to wild animals. After listeners and public leaders complained about Dennis and Callahan's remarks, the radio station suspended the pair for two weeks without pay.[9]

Many people hold the view that discrimination has all but disappeared. They say that it is class, rather than race, that holds blacks back. But research does not always support this conclusion. For example, studies conducted by the US Department of Education suggest that school suspensions are related to class. Poor children are indeed more likely to be suspended from school than their wealthier counterparts. However, this is not the same for black and white students. The percentage of white eighth graders who were suspended from school and who come from the lowest economic strata is only slightly higher than the percentage of suspended black eighth graders who come from the highest economic strata: 14.7 percent versus 13.6 percent.[10] Thus, the wealthiest black eighth graders and the poorest white eighth graders have similar suspension rates!

When hatred for a group is widely shared among members of society, it becomes part of the culture—the way of life of that society. America has been no exception. Children are indoctrinated from an early age to hate. As noted earlier, they hear their parents and later their friends tell and retell belittling ethnic jokes and make nasty ethnic slurs. They watch television programs dominated by young white males and an occasional Latino or Asian playing a stereotyped role. They are given textbooks that misrepresent or minimize the importance of minorities in the fabric of American life. They notice that disproportionate numbers of blacks and Latinos reside in the most impoverished, run-down, and crime-ridden neighborhoods, while there are few if any blacks and Latinos on their own block. Lacking historical and sociological insight, too many naively come to believe that minorities who live in squalor get what they deserve, due to lack of intellect or ambition. They become convinced that the "dangerous black man" lurks behind every act of violence perpetrated against "their kind of people."

The pervasive presence of antiblack stereotypes in our culture has been perpetuated by those who seek, sometimes for devious reasons, to deflect blame away from themselves. When Americans seek to create a scapegoat for a crime, they often resort to the stereotypic images that are so widely shared by the members of society, pinning the blame on someone who is black or Latino.

In their book about ethnic changes in the three Boston neighborhoods of Roxbury, Dorchester, and Mattapan, Hillel Levine and Lawrence Harmon wrote about the tactics used by Boston-area bankers and real-estate brokers to get white residents of Mattapan's Wellington Hill to sell their houses. This enabled the real-estate agents to make their salaries from more commissions. Here are some of the announcements that real-estate brokers made in 1968 in their unsolicited calls to residents: "The value of your house is dropping $1,000 every month. . . . You have a twelve-year-old daughter. What if she was raped. You'd have a mulatto grandchild. . . . If you still want to live here, fine. Just take a ride through the [predominantly black] Columbia Point housing project. Then come back and say you want to live here." [11]

One anonymous broker described real-estate brokers' tactics as follows:

We were told you get the listing any way you can. It's pretty easy to do: just scare the hell out of them. And that's what we did. We were not only making money, we were having fun doing what we were doing. We all liked selling real estate—if you want to call what we were doing back then selling real estate. And it got to a point that to have fun while we were working, we would try to outdo each other with the most outlandish threats that people would believe and chuckle about them at the end of the day. . . . I had fun at it. I'd go down the street with the [black] buyer and ask, Which house do you want? He'd pick one, and I'd ring the doorbell and say, these people want to buy your house. If the lady said no, I'd say the reason they're so interested is that their cousins, aunts, mother, whatever, it's a family of twelve, are moving in diagonally across the street. And they want to be near them. Most of the time, that worked. If that didn't work, you'd say their kid just got out of jail for housebreaking, or rape, or something that would work."[12]

The "dangerous black man" stereotype has time and again been resurrected to meet the needs of white America. Indeed, this image was frequently employed to justify keeping rebellious blacks enslaved and later lynching them. More recently, during the 1988 presidential campaign of the elder George Bush, commercials prominently featured rapist and murderer Willy Horton, a black inmate who had been furloughed in Massachusetts under the administration of Bush's Democratic rival, Michael Dukakis. While the political message may have been designed to discredit his Democratic opponent, Bush's references to Willy Horton also served to reinforce the image of the "black bogeyman" who threatens all of white America.

Charles Stuart may have gotten inspiration from the Bush commercials. On October 23, 1989, Charles Stuart claimed that a black stranger had shot to death his pregnant wife while the couple was driving through the Mission Hill area of Boston, on their way home from a birthing class in nearby Brigham and Women's Hospital. Boston police responded by rounding up and detaining dozens of African American men in the area of the killing, solely because of their race, eventually arresting a black resident of the Mission Hill neighborhood who turned out to be innocent. More than two months later, after admitting to his wife's murder, Stuart committed suicide by jumping from the Tobin Bridge.

On October 25, 1994, a young mother in Union, South Carolina, appeared teary-eyed and grief-stricken before the cameras at a televised press conference when she begged the kidnapper of her two sons, Michael, age three and Alex, age one, to release them unharmed. Susan Smith told the police that a black stranger, armed with a handgun, had stolen her car with her two boys seated in the back. Little more than a week later, Smith confessed that there had never been a black abductor and that she herself had knowingly drowned her two sons so she could be free to go off with her lover.

On November 28, 1994, Josephine Lupus, a junior at the State University of New York in Old Westbury, attempted to conceal her self-destructive behavior by claiming that while walking to her car on campus, she had been slashed in the face and stabbed in the stomach during a robbery. The assailant, according to Lupus's description to police, was a black male, approximately six foot tall, who wore a green army jacket, woolen cap, and a scarf wrapped around part of his face. He had allegedly fled on foot with the student's wallet. After the police noted inconsistencies in her account of the robbery, Lupus admitted fabricating the story and inflicting her own wounds. Even more suspicious to police investigators was the neatness of her injuries. An assailant lashing out with a knife would not have taken the time to slash his victim so symmetrically.

On July 23, 1995, fifteen-year-old Eddie O'Brien of Somerville, Massachusetts, ended the life of his best friend's mother, forty-two-year-old Janet Downing, by viciously stabbing her ninety-eight times in a fit of rage. In an effort to give himself an alibi and to explain away the cuts he had suffered while attacking his victim, O'Brien claimed to have been mugged and stabbed by a black man and a Hispanic man while shopping in nearby Union Square. O'Brien's alibi fell apart when the police discovered his fingerprints and blood inside Downing's Somerville home.[13] He was tried as an adult and convicted of first-degree murder.

In January 2003, two sixteen-year-old white boys, Derek Kraayenbrink and Nick Lokhorst, claimed to have been the victims of a vicious armed robbery that took place while they were working in a Hull, Iowa, convenience store. Both boys had been shot in the shoulder, according to their reports to the police, by a Hispanic man who walked into the store, shot them, took money from the cash register, and then fled the scene. A few weeks later, Kraayenbrink and Lokhorst finally confessed to quite a different sequence of events: In order to deflect blame for perpetrating the robbery, they had invented the story after shooting themselves, both in the left shoulder, and then taking $1,800 from the cash register. The two boys plead guilty to theft, conspiracy, carrying weapons, and making a false report to the police.[14]

Under the widespread belief that the criminal justice system can effectively combat crime by using tougher law-enforcement measures, the criminal justice system has expanded enormously over the last three decades. Between 1972 and 1988, spending on criminal justice grew by 150 percent. Between 1969 and 1989, per capita state expenditures on police and corrections increased tenfold. And between 1980 and 1990, the United States doubled the size of its national police force. By the year 1999, the United States had 420,544 law-enforcement officers: two and a half officers for every one thousand Americans.[15] We are currently spending $40 billion on housing, feeding, and caring for the prison population.[16]

The fear of crime and an expanded criminal justice system have led to a ballooning of our prison population. In 1972, the incarceration rate was approximately one hundred people per 100,000 population. By 2002, more than 470 people per 100,000 were incarcerated.[17] In 1990, 70 percent of the people arrested in the United States were between the ages of sixteen and thirty-four, and more than 80 percent were male.[18] There are presently some 6.7 million Americans who are under correctional supervision or about 3.1 percent of the United States adult population, out of which over two million Americans are serving time in a state or federal prison.[19]

This increase in the prison population was also due to the introduction of "get tough" measures such as mandatory minimum sentences, trying juveniles as adults, and restrictions on parole, especially for drug offenders. The new policies disproportionately affected African Americans. According to the Bureau of Justice Statistics, 10 percent of all black males age twenty-five to twenty-nine were in prison on December 2002, compared to 2.4 percent of Latino males and 1.2 percent of white males.[20]

Tougher sentencing also resulted in a substantial increase in the proportion of prisoners incarcerated for drug and property offenses, thus decreasing the proportion of prisoners locked up for violent acts. Some 85 percent of drug offenders have no history of prior incarceration for violent crimes and one-third of drug offenders are incarcerated for the possession or use of drugs. Moreover, 40 percent of federal drug offenders have no current or prior episode of violence in their records.[21] As a result, more than half of all incarcerations are a result of keeping nonviolent offenders in prison.

On occasion, the stereotyped images of a group have become so firmly entrenched in the culture that the victims of such false beliefs begin to accept them as accurate depictions of themselves. Black is bad; white is wonderful. Caucasian physiognomy is beautiful; thick lips and wider nostrils are not. Subcultural norms are worthless; the dominant culture is all-knowing, all-powerful. White culture rules!

A Latina college student whose skin color might be characterized as tan recently revealed she had been sent a strong message throughout her childhood: from her father she learned that dark skin color was ugly and that light skin color was attractive. What made it so difficult for Maria[22] was the fact that her own skin color was a few shades darker than that of her father or of her two older sisters. She was constantly being reminded of her "inferior" looks, her father complaining repeatedly that her skin color was too dark, forbidding her to go out in the sun even for a short period of time. Maria never learned to swim, out of fear that her skin would darken from an outing at the beach or a pool. In addition, her sisters referred to her jet-black hair as "frizzy" and "nappy," as "Nigger hair." By the time Maria had reached high school, she totally avoided white students because their presence only reminded her in a painful way of her own "inferiority." Now a college student, she continues to feel uncomfortable around whites.

Racial self-hate can have much more dangerous consequences than just causing a minority member to avoid those in the dominant group. Leo Felton was a white supremacist inmate, a member of a prison hate group known as the Aryan Brotherhood whose members despise blacks and Jews. Felton, whose body was literally covered with Nazi and racist tattoos, enjoyed listening to white power CDs that urged listeners to execute blacks and Jews. After serving his sentence for beating up a black cab driver, Felton then made plans to get even with his black and Jewish enemies. In order to inspire a race riot, he plotted to blow up monuments dedicated to civil rights leaders and to kill black leaders such as Jesse Jackson and Al Sharpton. Felton collected bomb-making materials, but was apprehended before he got a chance to use them. He is now serving a sentence of twenty-two years for conspiracy to commit murder. Ironically, Leo Felton's mother has been a white civil rights leader; Felton's father is black. If the Aryan Brotherhood had ever gotten wind of Felton's true racial ancestry, there is a good chance that they would have cut him into small pieces.

CHAPTER 4
HATE AS REVENGE

On occasion, violence has become a means of retribution and retaliation for an individual who—as the expression goes—seeks "an eye for an eye." On July 10, 2003, Doug Williams decided to exact a measure of sweet revenge. The forty-eight-year-old employee at a plant in Meridian, Mississippi, had long complained to his white coworkers that black Americans were nowadays being given preferential treatment.

And according to Williams, this was especially true where he worked. During his nineteen years with the company, he was repeatedly passed over for promotions. Instead, he was reminded of his bad temper and forced to attend anger-management classes. Then, he was carefully monitored by his bosses, as though he was some kind of a hothead.

Now, seated in a meeting with managers at his factory job, Williams once again felt angry. He felt he was being humiliated, told that he hadn't put racial issues aside; he wasn't trying to get along with his black coworkers. Having heard quite enough, Williams bolted from his chair and ran from the room. His parting words were: "Y'all can handle this."

Earlier in December 2001, Williams had verbally threatened a black coworker. Then in June 2003, he went to work wearing a white hood over his head that seemed reminiscent of that of the Ku Klux Klan. Then, he stayed home for several days rather than give in to the pressure to remove it. Now he was being reprimanded by the very managers who had refused to acknowledge his importance to the company, who had previously admonished him for his bad temper, and who had denied him the promotions he deserved.

On July 10, after leaving the meeting at which his insensitivity and anger were discussed, Williams returned with a rifle strapped to his back and a shotgun in his hands. He said, "I told you about fucking with me," and immediately sprayed the room with bullets, killing two of his coworkers. He then ran through the factory, firing at point-blank range at fellow employees. Three more were fatally shot before Williams took his own life. The final body count: Four blacks and one white. Williams had always claimed to be keeping score on those who offended him. From his viewpoint, he had just evened the score.

Williams was far from the first alienated American to settle a grudge with a gun. Numerous individuals feel bitter, deprived, and angry. Many do not know their neighbors; have few if any friends to count on for help; or may be divorced or separated and living alone. Importantly, they are also alone in a social psychological sense, having lost their connections with other people who might have supported and encouraged them. As a result, they have nobody to assist in getting them through hard times. Some of these alienated individuals settle their grudges through the barrel of a gun.

In March 2000, not far from the city of Pittsburgh, a thirty-nine-year-old black resident of Wilkinsburg, Pennsylvania, was at his wit's end. After a lifetime of racial insults and slights, Ronald Taylor felt that he could no longer tolerate what he believed to be the continuing racist neglect of his white maintenance man, John

DeWitt. The front door of Taylor's apartment unit had been broken for some period of time, so Taylor fixated on his white maintenance man.

On March 1, racial revenge was on Taylor's mind. Leaving his apartment, he remarked to a black neighbor living nearby that he wasn't going to hurt any black people—that he was just "out to kill white people." And Taylor was true to his word. Not finding John DeWitt, he instead fatally shot a carpenter who had been working in the building. Then, he walked to a fast-food restaurant in the Wilkinsburg business district, where he shouted, "White trash. Racist pig," and opened fire again, killing two and injuring two more. All of Taylor's victims were white.

But Taylor wasn't the only Pennsylvanian who had revenge on his mind. Just a couple of weeks later, Richard Baumhammers, an out-of-work white immigration lawyer in suburban Pittsburgh took a cue from Taylor regarding how to get even with his enemies. The thirty-four-year-old Baumhammers despised immigrants, blacks, and Jews. He feared that white Christian Americans were being pushed out by a growing presence of third-world upstarts. And he believed that American citizens would soon have to reside in isolated suburbs surrounded by immigrants from impoverished nations.

Baumhammers' first victim was his Jewish next-door neighbor, a woman whom he had known since childhood. After shooting her to death, Baumhammers then set her house ablaze and drove off toward two local synagogues, where he fired bullets into their windows. He then drove over a twenty-mile area, searching for anyone who might possibly be an immigrant or a person of color. An hour later, Baumhammers had killed four more people: a man of Indian descent who was exiting a local grocery store, a Vietnamese American worker, a Chinese American manager of a popular Chinese restaurant, and an African American man as he was leaving a karate school.

Many hate crimes have at least some element of revenge for a perceived wrong: The killers act as though they themselves are victims of injustice. They may take action against a family that moves into "their" neighborhood, a student who takes "their" seat in a classroom at a university, or a coworker who gets the promotion that "they" deserved to have. In such cases, a hatemonger might regard himself as avenging a specific intrusion, but his main objective is really not to get even. His goal is, in his eyes, much more practical and concrete: to move the outsider from the neighborhood, the job, or the classroom. In a retaliatory attack, by contrast, the primary goal is not to remove any particular victim from any particular location, but simply to hurt any member of a despised group, to inflict pain and suffering among the despised group, and to exact a measure of revenge for a perceived wrong. Rather than defend or protect his territory or turf from the intrusion of an "outsider," the individual seeks to even the score against outsiders generally. Retaliation is his objective and violence is usually the means that he chooses to employ.

According to sociologists Jack McDevitt, Jack Levin, and Susan Bennett, about 8 percent of all hate crimes are retaliatory in nature.[1] In these cases, the offenders may never have known the previous victim, but simply heard that a hate crime attack had occurred in the neighborhood, at work, or at school and decided "to get one of them for what they have done to one of us." The offenders seek out someone—perhaps anyone—in a group against whom to retaliate for a prior incident.

The desire to punish the perpetrators of a serious crime is often the first reaction of the victim or the victim's family and friends. This might be a natural reaction, a need to protect oneself in the future or to seek justice for the victim. Especially when the violence impacting a group is seen as unwarranted, cruel, or excessive, it arouses intense anger and a burning desire to act as soon as possible to avenge the harm. In seeking revenge, however, the victims can easily become the perpetrators.

Rather than seek justice through official channels, those identified with the injured side sometimes take the matter into their own hands. In their quest for revenge, they indiscriminately target any member of the perpetrator's group. The vicious cycle of aggression and retaliation between groups may not be broken until a formal authority has intervened in an effective manner or until all-out warfare has occurred. Moreover, a lack of any response by members of the victimized group can also send the wrong signal to aggressors. Hate-motivated crimes that go unchallenged implicitly send a message of support and encouragement to those who would perpetrate violence in the future. Those who are victimized should seek help from the proper authorities, and they should act accordingly.

As compared with victims of other crimes, victims of hate are especially likely to consider revenge. Research indicates that hate-crime victims are *significantly* more likely than the victims of other offenses to think about seeking revenge and getting even. This seems to suggest that the vicious cycle of aggression and retaliation is particularly likely in the event of an offense committed because someone happens to belong to a different race, religious group, ethnicity, sexual orientation, or disability status. Hate-crime victims have trouble letting go of the injury. Their central identity has been threatened or attacked, and they feel extremely vulnerable. For some, justice takes the form of getting even with people in the perpetrators' group, even if it means harming an individual or individuals who had nothing to do with committing the original offense.

The need to retaliate against *any* member of the perpetrator's group is a motivating characteristic found in many violence-prone individuals. John Geoghan, the former priest from Boston who was convicted of molesting children, was strangled to death in August 2003 by a fellow inmate at a maximum security prison, who had been sexually abused as a child, but not by Geoghan. The former priest's killer, Joseph Druce, was a thirty-seven-year-old neo-Nazi who was already serving a life sentence for strangling and mutilating a gay man from nearby Gloucester, Massachusetts. A year earlier, Druce had pled guilty to sending anthrax hoax letters and swastikas to a federal prosecutor and thirty-nine Massachusetts lawyers, because they had Jewish-sounding surnames. He apparently felt victimized by *his* attorney but decided to get even with Jewish lawyers in general.[2]

Revenge is frequently more than just an individual phenomenon. Entire communities and societies have become embroiled in violent forms of vengeance as a result of a single incident in which the members of one group harm a member of the other.

An important example of how the desire for general vengeance can lead to an escalation of conflict and violence between groups can be found in an incident that occurred in the Crown Heights section of New York City, which has long had a history of hostility between its black and Jewish neighbors. In August 1991, seven-year-old Gavin Cato, a black child who lived in the Crown Heights section, was accidentally killed when the car driven by an Orthodox Jewish motorist jumped the curb. In retaliation, a twenty-nine-year-old rabbinical student from Australia who was totally unconnected to the accident was stabbed to death.

In Crown Heights, mistrust and suspicion were palpable on both sides of the racial ledger. Many black residents were convinced that the motorist who hit the black child would get off scot-free due to the perception that Jewish residents enjoyed special treatment from city officials. At the same time, Jewish residents of Crown Heights were certain that the black mayor of New York City, David Dinkins, would do little if anything to bring the murderer of the Australian rabbinical student to justice.

For almost a week, blacks and Jews exchanged insulting

remarks, hurled rocks and bottles at one another, and broke windows in homes and cars. Dozens more were injured.[3]

The role of reprisal and revenge is even more central in the development of large-scale violence between national groups. Since the intifada against Israel began in September 2000, both sides—the Israelis and the Palestinians—have contributed to an escalating cycle of violence. On the Palestinian side, popular support has grown for suicide bombers who blow up Israeli civilians—men, women, and children—on buses, at outdoor cafes, and in discos. Indeed, suicide bombers are considered by many as martyrs to the cause of nationhood, with their images being displayed heroically as models for others to follow.

In response, Israel has gradually escalated its reprisals, temporarily reoccupying Palestinian land, using F-16 fighters in the Palestinian territories, and assassinating a number of leaders from radical political/military groups. After suicide bombings in December 2002 in Jerusalem and Haifa resulted in twenty-five lives lost, Israel retaliated again by destroying Arafat's heliport and confining him to what was left of his compound in the West Bank town of Ramallah. In June 2003, after Israeli missile attacks had killed twenty Palestinians, the militant group Hamas retaliated by sending a suicide bomber to kill seventeen Israelis aboard a Jerusalem bus.[4]

Two months later, twenty-nine-year-old cleric Raed Mesk, from the West Bank city of Hebron, dressed in the clothing of a Hasidic Jew, blew up a bus in Jerusalem, killing twenty-one and injuring another one hundred. A member of Hamas, the bomber had apparently decided to settle a personal score: His close friend Mohammed Sidr, an Islamic Jihad leader in Hebron, had been assassinated by Israeli troops a week earlier. Even in the international arena, it is still an eye for an eye, sadly and ironically in the biblical lands.[5]

The continuing Israeli-Palestinian fighting is only one situation among a number of ongoing violent conflicts between ethnic and religious groups that is fueled by retaliation and revenge, and has a long history. None has had more brutal assaults than the confrontations between India's Hindu majority and Muslim minority. Though dating back centuries, the Hindu-Muslim antagonism worsened dramatically after the separation of Pakistan from India in 1947 and continued to grow through the 1990s and into the new century. The ethnic riots that have periodically broken out in Indian communities have resulted in great losses to both life and property. Rioting and murders have spawned a rise of nationalistic political parties that further polarized and radicalized some among Hindu and Muslim local populations.

In February 2002, for example, nearly one thousand Muslims from the western state of Gujarat were killed, maimed, or gang-raped, and another ninety thousand Muslims were left homeless during a seventy-two-hour bloodbath perpetrated by an extremist Hindu mob. These terrible acts of violence were motivated by vengeance for another terrible incident, some sixty miles southwest of the city of Ahmedabad. A Muslim mob attacked a train carrying Hindus and burned alive more than fifty of them.[6]

Then, in June 2002, some fifteen hundred Hindus and Muslims rioted through the streets of Ahmedabad, burning each other's shops and stores. A week earlier, Muslims stabbed four Hindus and stoned to death a Hindu truck driver. Moreover, the police discovered stockpiles of homemade bombs in more than one hundred households of both religious groups, an indication of more intergroup violence to come.[7]

The process of collective retaliation continued in full force. In February 2002, in the city of Godhra—the birthplace of Mahatma Gandhi and a key industrial area of the country—a Muslim mob killed fifty-eight Hindu nationalists who were returning from the city of Ayodhya. Hindu nationalists had traveled to Ayodhya in order to campaign in support of building a Hindu temple on the site of the former Babri Masjid mosque, one of India's most venerated Muslim religious sites prior to its demolition by Hindus in 1992. The train carrying more than one hundred Hindu nationalists was firebombed as it entered the rail station in a Muslim-populated area. Many of the victims, who were burned alive in the conflagration, were women and children.[8]

The Muslims' brutal attack on Hindu civilians was an act of retaliation for the injustice committed against them by the demolition of their holy site and the apparent sacrilege of building a Hindu temple in its place. Thousands of Muslims and Hindus were killed in its aftermath. But the destruction of the mosque was, from the Hindu point of view, an act of revenge for numerous humiliating episodes suffered by Hindu nationalists at the hands of the Muslims over the past three hundred years. By some accounts, the Muslim firebombing of a train carrying Hindu nationalists was triggered by Hindus chanting religious slogans as they stopped at the railway station in a Muslim-dominated neighborhood.[9] In the aftermath of the train attack, clashes between Muslims and Hindus spread across the state, and hundreds of Muslims were attacked—with deadly consequences—in their shops, houses, and neighborhoods.

Revenge is, for many individuals, a personal form of justice. In their dealings with others, Hammurabi's code of "an eye for an eye" has provided the rule for responding to anyone at home, work, or school who is seen as responsible for their personal miseries. Someone who gets fired at a factory decides to sabotage the manufacturing process; a husband who suffers a nasty divorce harms his children to get even with his wife; a student who gets a failing grade gets even with his teacher by sending her threatening letters.

As harmful as the revenge motive can be for an individual who blames others for his personal problems, it becomes far more destructive when groups decide to retaliate for acts of injustice committed against them by other groups. The revenge motive often becomes the basis for a vicious cycle of violence and retaliation that seems all but impossible to break. Hate fuels violence which only escalates into ever more destructive levels of hate and violence. The results in places like India, Israel, the former Yugoslavia, and Northern Ireland have been disastrous.

CHAPTER 5
HATE AND HUMAN NATURE

uman beings come into this world possessing certain universally shared tendencies developed genetically over thousands of
years of evolution. Because of such inherited predispositions, individuals need not be taught to prefer the members of their own
group. This preference seems to have been hardwired into the
genetic structure of every human being and transmitted at birth
from generation to generation.[1]

For one thing, the survival of early humankind depended in part
on being wary of strangers. Members of a tribe cooperated together
for their mutual benefit to ensure shelter, food, and protection. Until
and unless they were proven otherwise, outsiders were considered
the enemy. Especially during periods of drought or famine, their
agenda could easily have included stealing food and possessions,
raping the women, or destroying the tribe. Those who lived to a ripe
old age were cautious and wary of outsiders and/or part of a group
that was successful in battle. This wariness of outsiders became, in
the Darwinian sense, a strength of those who were able to survive
and pass on their legacy to future generations. So what began likely
as genetic was soon learned behavior in each successive generation.

The naive and unsuspecting were likely to be enslaved or slain; the skeptical lived to fight another day.

Whether or not rational in the contemporary world, we continue to be wary of strangers. One of the favorite themes in motion pictures—for example, *Witness, The Fugitive, Phone Booth, A Fistful of Dollars, The Cable Guy,* and *To Sleep with Danger*—is the outsider who can't be trusted or, at least, that is a belief, right or wrong, to be explored.

Moreover, like attracts like. When it comes to their peers, human beings seem almost universally to be predisposed to prefer being among people like themselves—those who share their personal characteristics such as abilities, social class, drug use, and activities as well as their basic values concerning politics, family, and social issues. They may assume that those who differ in terms of appearance by race or culture also differ with respect to their attitudes and values. Thus, where they have choices, birds of a feather tend to congregate together in families, neighborhoods, classrooms, churches, voluntary organizations, and social clubs.

Humans seem to have a predisposition, even when entrenched in a homogeneous group, to find distinctions to sort out "us" and "them." If no ethnic or religious differences exist, humans will invent them to set up a hierarchy of those of us who are the richest, most intelligent, most morally superior, best hunters, and so on. We then often maintain our closest friendships with our peers and look down on the others.

The reason for the pervasive connection between similarity and attraction may be twofold. Similarity makes us feel that our own attitudes and values are correct; it is rewarding to hear our friends and acquaintances agree with our political and social views. We may also assume that others, simultaneously, will like us. Agreement may be taken as a sign of acceptance and friendship, whereas disagreement may indicate rejection.[2]

It is also true that how human beings feel about themselves seems to depend in part on how they feel about their group memberships. They may experience higher self-esteem if they believe that their group is superior; they may feel worse about themselves if they consider their group to be inferior to others. Social identity has a profound impact on personal identity.[3]

Indeed, it is merely the act of being assigned to a group, any group, that automatically triggers a preference for one's own group.[4] That is, all it takes is to be assigned arbitrarily, even by a flip of a coin, to a group named "A" rather than "B." This is enough to make an individual prefer the people in group A over B.

The two groups A and B can be identical in every respect; indeed, they don't even have to exist in reality. Still, those individuals who *believe* they have been assigned to A will come to be convinced that the members of A are better in almost every respect than the members of B.[5] Those who *believe* they belong to B will come to regard their fellow members as superior in almost every way to those who belong to A. Thus, strangers may be viewed as inferior, simply because they are outsiders who don't belong to the group.[6] Just being newcomers seems to set these thoughts in motion. Moreover, individuals will better recall the good deeds and positive characteristics of their own group—the "in-group"—and better recall the negative behavior of the other group—the "out-group."[7] If someone from the in-group steals or lies, his fellow members might have only a fuzzy memory of the details of the crime; if, on the other hand, a member of the out-group transgresses, all the minute details of his crime are likely to be remembered vividly.

Moreover, human beings have a predisposition to restrict their empathy and compassion only to those they know well—not to strangers, not to the members of other groups, and not to people who are physically distant. This limited breadth of empathy is in part functional for humans who might otherwise indiscriminately and pervasively feel, on an everyday basis, the weight of pain and suffering experienced by many millions of humans around the world. Instead, individuals are more likely to limit their compassion to situations close to home, both literally and figuratively, over which they might exercise some control.

For our forebears, extended empathy was probably much less problematic. In the absence of technological forms of either transportation or communication, the local community was, through much of human history, the extent of one's existence. Individuals interacted on a daily basis with extended kin and close neighbors. Their awareness of issues facing outsiders was at best minimal, dependent on the word-of-mouth descriptions brought to them by messengers and other travelers returning from faraway places. And those who came from faraway places were not to be trusted.

In sharp contrast, humans are now bombarded with media depictions of war, genocide, drought and starvation, terminal illness, violent crime, and natural catastrophes coming from countries around the world. Wire services, newspaper sections, network newscasts, and national cable telecasts all present us with images of human misery. What is more, millions of Americans have visited cities throughout the United States if not around the world. Among those who have traveled less are many who have read novels and short stories based in exotic settings far removed from their own everyday lives.

If empathy were boundless, individuals in the contemporary world would likely be overwhelmed psychologically by human misery. They might, at the same time, spread their emotional energy thinly on starving children in Africa, victims of suicide bombings in the Middle East, victims of bloody acts of terrorism in Northern Ireland, orphaned youngsters with disabilities in eastern Europe, homeless people sleeping on the streets of Bombay, and countless millions who suffer on a daily basis. This is not to say we humans should not help those less fortunate. Nevertheless, if individuals lacked priorities for focusing their compassion, they would be totally bogged down by the weight of empathetic anxiety. Their effectiveness in responding to any local examples of misery would be muted by their willingness to respond to *all* acts of misery, no matter where or when they occur. In fact, many individuals might feel so overwhelmed that they'd be paralyzed to act at all.

As a practical matter of survival, then, mechanisms for restricting breadth of empathy seem to be programmed into human beings. Even the most despicable serial killers have some empathy, though it is far more limited in scope than in most people. They typically have a small circle of family and friends for whom they care; these are the few who are off limits when it comes to killing. Thus, most serial killers target absolute strangers.

This same predisposition to restrict empathy to one's own group also permits normal, seemingly moral humans to kill one another in warfare, commit genocide, and commit unspeakable acts against prisoners of war as well as innocent civilians who happen to get in the way. It also makes it difficult to rally potential contributors of money, blood, or organs to those who live in far-off places or those who appear to be different in socially significant ways. To many white Americans, the problems suffered by black and Latino Americans in the United States seem as psychologically remote as those of blacks in Africa or Latinos in South America.

Of course, human beings vary in terms of where they draw the line that separates the in-group from the out-group. Religion has been known to dehumanize nonbelievers, making it possible for zealots to pillage, rape, and murder in the name of moral righteousness those of other religions. At the same time, religious doctrine may have the opposite effect by extending the range of our "kinship relations" to people we have never met or have little in common with, and to people who live thousands of miles away who are genetically independent of us. Just being identified with the same religious group may help make "brothers" and "sisters" of people on opposite sides of the globe. Of course, the remainder of humanity—those who are not of the same faith or are nonbelievers—are often seen as beyond the embrace of compassion, unless they're viewed as potential converts.[8]

We should examine the universal presence of innate predispositions that might reduce or enhance our ability to get along with the members of other groups. We should also, however, recognize the distinction between *preferring* in-group members and *despising* out-group members. An inborn preference for members of our own group is certainly not a sufficient condition for wanting to eliminate strangers from the face of the earth. Being wary of outsiders does not necessarily mean hating or attacking them. Hating "the other" is learned behavior, pure and simple. Hate originates in the environment, in the psychological desires of an individual, and in the socioeconomic characteristics of society.

White supremacists were *not* born loathing blacks and Latinos. Muslims were *not* born hating Jews and Christians. Americans were *not* born despising Arabs. Though humans have a predisposition to view outsiders with a degree of skepticism, hating outsiders, or those from specific groups, is taught. Haters learn such ideas either early in life from their parents or later in life from their friends, classmates, teachers, religious leaders, and the mass media.

The first few years of life have a disproportionate influence on the way that individuals will think about other people. Bigoted parents may praise their offspring for using racial epithets or repeating jokes that belittle others. As mentioned, they may ridicule or punish their children for expressing attitudes of tolerance and respect for differences.

After being encouraged to express their hate, children will frequently imitate the bigoted behavior of their parents and siblings.

By the age of three, most children are already aware of racial and ethnic differences. By the time they are five, they have learned the negative stereotypes about various groups in and out of their midst. By then, some already believe that Arabs are terrorists, Jews are money-grubbers, blacks are criminals, Latinos are lazy, and so on. In addition, children by their fifth or sixth year who have been taught to hate have already incorporated such negative feelings as fear, revulsion, contempt, and envy which are triggered by the mere presence of the despised group.

Thus, children are socialized to hate in exactly the same way they are socialized to accept other conceptions of what should be valued, such as motherhood, patriotism, and personal success. They are rewarded by their mentors for being hateful and ridiculed for being respectful of differences. Around the dinner table, children hear their parents discuss their fear of Middle Easterners, their disgust for immigrants living in inner-city squalor, their envy regarding Asian youngsters winning Merit Scholarships, their horror at the thought of belonging to a country club that allows in Jews and other "undesirables."

A 2002 study of three- to six-year-old Catholic and Protestant children growing up in a deeply divided society, Northern Ireland, suggests that as soon as children can talk, they are already able to express preferences for pictures and objects that depict their own communities. As the children grow they soon also learn to fear and loathe the members of the other group, be it Protestant or Catholic. This is not surprising in a deeply divided society where children live in ethnically segregated communities and where only 4 percent of children attend schools integrated by religion.[9] No wonder that a 2001 survey of the young people in Belfast, as noted earlier, found that the majority of the children and teenagers interviewed had never had a proper conversation with anyone outside of their own religious group.[10]

It is not only the content but also the form of child rearing that contributes to the acceptance of hate. Children who are raised under harsh and threatening child-rearing practices come to feel a profound sense of their own powerlessness. These children have been placed in a subservient role with the parents as all-powerful. To compensate, children raised in an authoritarian manner might later come to identify with powerful authority figures such as Hitler, Stalin, Milosevic, Ceausescu, or Charles Manson. They divide the world conveniently and absolutely between the weak and the strong, the good and the bad, and they avoid contact with outsiders whom they regard as inferior and possibly evil. They don't want to identify with the weak group and, by extension, feel their own sense of weakness again.[11]

According to psychoanalyst Carl Goldberg, many hate-filled individuals who start out as innocent victims later become bonded to hate and violence in response to their own pain and suffering. Authoritarian parents ignore their children's needs and demand absolute compliance, their only measure of parental adequacy being their child's "unprotesting obedience." Any attempt on the part of the growing child to express independent thought and behavior is met not with parental pride but with anger and/or worse.[12]

During premodern times, in a traditionalist conservative world, authoritarian parents might actually have prepared a child to deal with an authoritarian education, and life dominated by the church and government. But in periods of social change, authoritarian types have a particularly difficult time, since they are intolerant of ambiguities and have an excessive need for structure. Moreover, in the postmodern world, an authoritarian family background might prevent a child from realizing his potential or becoming a success. Instead, authoritarian adults find themselves marginalized and alienated from other members of society. And the child of an authoritarian parent may be doomed to failure, making him susceptible to the attractions of hate groups.

Violence may seem an acceptable alternative to peace when an individual's needs go unmet. The survival value of violent behavior has its basis in evolution. Aggression as a means to an end—the goal of staying alive and surviving another day—has been transmitted genetically over the course of thousands of years of development. Those who survived passed on their genes to the next generation. This is defensive violence meant only to protect, not to do injury gratuitously. Thus, an individual who is actually threatened may learn to shoot a firearm, but only to prevent his own death.[13]

According to psychoanalyst Eric Fromm, however, there is another type of violent behavior whose objective is the destruction of fellow human beings as an end in itself. This type of malignant aggression is, for Fromm, entirely learned and concentrated in individuals who feel a profound sense of their own powerlessness. They strike back in a violent fashion, and the more they can inflict pain and suffering on the "enemy," the better they feel about themselves.[14]

More contemporary experts might say that certain individuals are prone to anger and violence. Some have implicated hormones and chemicals in the brain; others have focused on the role of repeated head trauma or genetic factors. Those who study the effect of the environment have singled out abandonment and abuse during early childhood as an important ingredient in the etiology of violence. Still others have stressed the failure of an individual to bond with other human beings, particularly parents, as an important causal variable.[15]

However, according to Kevin Borgeson, a professor at St. Bonaventure University who studies hate groups, hate violence has a basis in economic deprivation. He suggests that members of the white supremacist organization known as Aryan Nations are drawn overwhelmingly from the ranks of the deprived, powerless, and downtrodden. In his study, Borgeson found that 78 percent of the members he interviewed were manual laborers or unemployed. They despised blacks, Latinos, and immigrants, but especially Jews, whom they considered to be children of Satan and behind the entire world's problems. According to Borgeson, what disturbs the members of Aryan Nations above everything else is that though many Jewish Americans came as immigrants in the past two or three generations, they have garnered relative success. However, this success coupled with age-old stereotypes fuel their hate. Jews as a group have climbed into the middle classes. If Jews have done it, why haven't they? In their minds, there must be some conspiracy to explain this.[16]

For a prejudiced person, stereotyping is an extremely useful activity. It reduces the uncertainties of everyday interaction, and makes life seem entirely predictable. If someone is Jewish, he is expected to be shrewd and mercenary, and perhaps part of a world-wide conspiracy, which explains his success. If an individual is black, she is seen as lazy and ignorant, and not to be befriended. If someone is Muslim, he is likely a terrorist, and not to be trusted. In short, the prejudiced person is *ethnocentric*, holding a generalized hostility toward a broad range of groups considered to be inferior. If he hates blacks, he probably also despises Latinos and gays and Jews and Muslims. This generalized hostility is a clue that prejudice serves an important psychological function. It permits someone who feels like a loser to cast off his self-negativism and translate it into contempt against outsiders. This is the essence of scapegoating. "No wonder I can't succeed," he tells himself, "since they control everything." "Compared to them, I am superior and morally correct."

The case of Slavica Nikolic[17] illustrates how people accept hateful ideology, when they are able to distance themselves from the suffering of others. Nikolic is a science professor at a major university who came to the United States from Serbia to obtain her PhD, married an American, and had among her friends people from Croatia, Slovenia, and Serbia. As a science professor, she was not interested in politics. Her interaction with her friends was mostly about children and family life. When war broke out in the former Yugoslavia, she was stunned. Slavica could not understand what was going on. The American newspapers were not very helpful in explaining the causes of the war. When she talked to members of her family in Serbia, they sounded frightened and angry. Her Croatian and Slovenian friends' accounts contradicted the stories that she heard from her Serbian relations.

After months of anguish, Slavica finally found solace in a newly formed Serbian local organization in the United States. There, she met others of Serbian descent who explained to her the events in Yugoslavia as attacks against her people. Serbs were the victims, they argued, caught in a propaganda war. All of a sudden, senseless events started to make sense to her. The ambiguity vanished. She found the community that embraced her and provided her with a route to meaningful actions. She became an active member of the organization, and then became its president.

Slavica was now a woman with a mission: to expose the injustices done to Serbs. Her anguish soon disappeared. You could not say that she was happy, but she found a way to channel her angst into an action that gave her life purpose and meaning. She did, however, lose her Slovenian and Croatian friends, but she also gained new friends. Slavica was looking for a "home" and she had found it. She felt comfortable talking to her fellow members. She now "understood" events that in the beginning of the war seemed incomprehensible to her.

What happened to Slavica is not a rare occurrence. Confronted with the complexities of life, many people look for simple explanations. Kathleen Blee writes about women who join hate groups. They are often attracted to these organizations because of a need for community.[18]

Hate can also increase or decrease in intensity for reasons unrelated to the feelings about a particular group of people. Groups of teenagers who get together on a slow night to bash minorities are usually led by a single hatemonger. Most go along to get along. They aren't particularly hate-filled, but they also do not want to be rejected by their friends. Only after they have assaulted someone from a different race, religion, or sexual orientation and they look to justify their criminal behavior, do many begin to despise their victims. After all, these "victims" got them into trouble. Rather than face their own abominable behavior, they see the outsiders whom they targeted all of a sudden as the children of Satan, animals, mud people, vermin, and enemies of all civilized human beings. If they were to recognize the humanity of their victims, they would also have to face the shameful effects of a guilty conscience. But bashing a child of the Devil needs no defense.

CHAPTER 6
THE POLITICAL USES OF HATE

In 1890, Chief David Hennessey of the New Orleans Police Department was brutally murdered on the streets of the city. He was cut down by five men who opened fire with shotguns and pistols. By the next morning, millions of people throughout the nation read in their newspapers that the prominent police chief had been murdered by the Mafia, based only on the word of a captain in the New Orleans Police Department who claimed that his dying friend had whispered that his assailants were "dagos."[1]

This charge fed directly into a widespread fear among local residents about the Mafia in New Orleans. Without a shred of evidence, the mayor made public a list of ninety-four Mafia murders in the city. He forgot to mention that these murders had taken place over a twenty-five-year period and that the list had included every homicide in the city where the victim had an Italian-sounding name. He also failed to indicate that ninety-one of the killings were still unsolved. Indeed, the mayor's assumption that the killers were Italian and Mafiosi was strictly speculation.[2]

The events which followed the murder of Chief Hennessey were carefully orchestrated by forces in local politics and business who resented and despised the Italians' growing economic and political power. Plantation owners were alarmed that these Italians, who had originally worked the sugar fields for slave wages, were suddenly buying up cheap land. Moreover, Sicilian fishermen and peddlers, shortly off the boat from the old country, were seen by the business leaders of New Orleans as monopolizing the fruit, oyster, and fish industries of the city.[3]

After the murder of Hennessey, nineteen Italians were arrested. The trial of the first nine defendants ended in a mistrial for three men and a verdict of not guilty for the other six. Even before the second round of trials could begin, an angry mob took matters into its own hands.[4]

The ensuing riot was anything but spontaneous. The morning after the jury's verdict was given to the court, local newspapers carried an advertisement inviting the citizens of New Orleans to attend a mass meeting "to remedy the failure of justice in the Hennessey case." Among the sponsors of the ad and leaders of the meeting were wealthy landowners, political leaders, and a political boss with a long history of violence.

These were the men who led some twelve thousand New Orleanians to storm Parish Prison, where the defendants were being held. After being stirred up to a frenzy by these community leaders, the angry mob slaughtered eleven Italians, three of whom had been previously acquitted, three whose court appearance had ended in a mistrial, and five more who had never even been tried. Another eight men escaped by hiding themselves in closets or under mattresses in their cells.

The cause of the largest mass lynching in American history cannot be attributed to sheer crowd madness. There was, instead, a deliberate plan on the part of those who stood to gain by eliminating the competition from Italians in local agriculture and industry. What began as well-planned local and political collusion became mass hysteria.[5]

Our examination of vengeance earlier suggests that in many instances, the desire for revenge does not always develop in a spontaneous fashion. Rather, it can be orchestrated and supported by political leaders who use revenge as a way to consolidate their power. The escalation of violence in the Indian state of Gujarat that we discussed in chapter 4 is another example. Even though the Indian national government called for calm and warned against revenge attacks, the killings of Muslims went unchecked. The violence, though, was not entirely one-sided. In response to Hindu attacks on Muslims, Islamic gunmen in September 2002 opened fire in the Hindu temple in Gandhinagar, Gujarat, shooting to death twenty-nine worshipers.[6]

One of the reasons why the violence between Hindus and Muslims continued unabated was that the state government did little to stop it, beyond espousing perfunctory warnings. And state officials may have had practical reasons for allowing, perhaps even encouraging, the killings to go on without restraint.[7] Following riots between Hindus and Muslims, Narendra Modi, the leader of Gujarat's branch of the Bharatiya Janata Party (BJP), the Hindu nationalist party, won the state election. In his campaign, Modi stressed the danger that Muslims presented to Hindus; and in his speeches he urged his voters never to forget the violence perpetrated by Muslims in Godhra. Modi's victory reversed eleven consecutive defeats for the BJP in other Indian states, showing how the politics of hate could be successfully exploited for electoral gain.[8]

The Bharatiya Janata Party came to power by mobilizing the nationalistic sentiment of Hindus, who represented about 80 percent of the Indian population. Once in power, however, the party toned down its nationalism in order to gain the support of more moderate Hindus. Although the BJP represented the upper castes, it depended as well on gaining the support of a coalition of other parties. The BJP even tried to accommodate Muslim voters by appointing two Muslims as ministers and by portraying itself as a party of law and order.

On the other hand, the Bharatiya Janata Party also sought to make India more Hindu-like and, in that way, continued to promote a nationalistic agenda that would infringe on the rights of Muslims. For example, the party advocated the adoption of a common civil code for all Indians, thereby eliminating the controls that the Muslim and Christian minorities had over their own personal laws. Without such controls, these minorities would have been forced to comply with a set of legal standards that seriously reduced their ability to practice the rituals and customs of their own religions. The party also sought to abolish the constitutional autonomy of India's only Muslim-majority state, Kashmir. The party's one-sided and biased position only fueled the fires of bigotry and violence among India's Hindu population.

By 2002, mounting economic and social problems in India undermined BJP's power, severely reducing the political clout of the BJP-led coalition government. The extremist Hindu-based party lost elections in one state after another.

Yet the Muslim riots in Gujarat presented Narendra Modi with an opportunity to reverse his party's downslide. Instead of addressing other pressing issues facing the state, such as economic development or public services, Modi campaigned to unite Hindus against the Muslim threat (Recall Willie Horton's role in the Bush versus Dukakis 1988 presidential race). He also got help from hundreds of out-of-state volunteers from the World Hindu Council, a Hindu nationalistic organization whose members came to assist him in his reelection efforts. Party slogans portrayed Muslims as loyal to Islam rather than India, and as engaging in acts that were harmful to Hindus, such as slaughtering cows, attacking temples, and kidnapping Hindu girls.[9]

Thus, the message that Modi sent to his voters was that only his government would be able to protect Hindu interests and provide them with safety. In the aftermath of the violence, fliers were circulated that called on Hindus to stop doing business with Muslims and to stop hiring them as workers. Not surprisingly, fliers also threatened Hindu employers with retaliation if they did not comply.

Such actions not only made Muslim residents less secure but apparently drove them into the arms of their own fundamentalists, a consequence that may further escalate the conflict in the future. Modi's propaganda attack also forced the more secular Muslims to choose sides. As Islamic Indians, they could not continue to coexist with the Hindus. And they would not be accepted by fellow Muslims if they did not conform to the more rigid set of expectations for their religious identity. As it happens in other ethnically divided societies, when the state fails to protect its citizens, they are forced to seek help from members of their own ethnic community. In Gujarat, many secular Muslims had to move to Muslim neighborhoods, thus further increasing the distance, both literally and figuratively, between India's Muslims and Hindus.

Other integrated social institutions were also affected by the intergroup violence. For example, Mallik Mohammed Ghazni had to move his three-year-old daughter from an integrated nursery school in a Hindu-dominated neighborhood to one run by an Islamic volunteer organization in a Muslim-dominated neighborhood. He recalled with horror an incident that occurred in his daughter's school during the riots when teachers were asked by Hindu protesters to give them a list of all Muslim students. Although the teachers refused, Ghazni worries that in the future they might be forced to comply with such demands. He continues to voice his concern.

"Things are better now, but I am happier that my daughter continues to learn among Muslims," Ghazni says. "There is safety in being with your own. Had a mob attacked her old school, [the school] wouldn't have been able to protect her."[10]

The danger of politicians exploiting ethnic violence to further their own personal objectives is as profoundly sad as it is pervasive. Instead of making victims more safe or providing them with justice, it turns them against the possibility of using a socially legitimate channel to resolve their grievances. Exploitive politicians also foster a desire for revenge that perpetuates the cycle of violence. In India, political manipulation has meant that Hinduism, a normally tolerant religion, is being turned into a vastly more contentious political force. That in turn threatens India as a secular, democratic, and pluralist nation.

Hindu nationalists were fighting to get permission to build a temple in Ayodhya. This was just the first of their demands. There are more than three thousand mosques in India that Hindu nationalists claim have been built on the former sites of Hindu temples and should be demolished. Even the famous Taj Mahal, constructed by Shah Jehan, a Mogul emperor in the seventeenth century, is a potential target for demolition.[11] And the list goes on, because the conflict is not just about the site of a temple, nor is it only about getting even for past wrongdoings, but it is also about who will wield power to define the future of India. This is why terrorist attacks increase when the peace process is discussed. Just as in Israel and Northern Ireland, certain radical elements within one or the other ethnic group believe that it will lose out by the imposition of a real peace. For selfish reasons, they fight to maintain, heighten, or even expand the conflict.

Rhetoric espoused by the Bharatiya Janata Party resembles that of numerous nationalistic parties whose members generally use cultural interpretations to justify their claims on territory and to deflect any outside influences on their own ethnic group. They accomplish this often by adopting a rigid understanding of truth that excludes any reasonable alternatives, competing interpretations, and claims of other ethnic groups. Under this arrangement, every group operates within its own set of "truths," and no effort is made to view the political situation from any other perspective or a broader, more encompassing viewpoint. The people in a region often live in peace for decades, until—as conflict reemerges—leaders try to justify the violence of their adherents by recounting previous conflicts and offering their one-sided interpretation of events. They often portray the members of their own group as being the true victims of injustice and suffering at the hands of members of the opposing group. Being a victim thus justifies their use of violence and their desire to get revenge for whatever misfortunes they had been made to suffer.

In the former Yugoslavia, for example, the Serbian nationalist parties defended the suspension of autonomy for the Kosovo region in 1989, even though more than 90 percent of the residents of that region were members of an Albanian ethnic group. Following the denial of their independence, more than twenty Albanians died in clashes with the police. Meanwhile, in Belgrade, tens of thousands of Serbian nationalists celebrated the Serbian takeover of the province. These Serb nationalists claimed that Kosovo was their sacred ancestral homeland, and that by giving it up they would be giving up their souls. At the same time, they demanded political autonomy for the Serbs living in Krajina, a region in Croatia. There was no recognition on the Serbian part that the Krajina region also had historical and symbolic value for Croatians. The fact that the two claims were contradictory did not undermine Serbian expansionist efforts or reduce the fervor among the nationalists. Not surprisingly, the conflict in Kosovo was but a prelude to a full-fledged war in Yugoslavia. In the three wars that followed, more than two hundred thousand people died and more than two million people were displaced.[12]

In time of economic instability, structural change, or political turmoil, the members of the majority group often react to a real or perceived threat to their position in society by turning against the members of the minority groups in their midst. Operating under a zero-sum definition of the situation (i.e., someone else's loss is viewed as a personal gain), they try to limit the minorities' civil rights and access to their country's economic resources. The inability of the formal governing structures to protect the human rights of all residents and to address growing social inequalities becomes the root cause of many ethnic conflicts. In their extreme forms, such conflicts can lead to expelling and executing minority group members for the purpose of creating ethnically homogeneous societies—"ethnic cleansing." This is what happened in Bosnia, Croatia, and Kosovo.

Ethnic cleansing and civil war in the former Yugoslavia provide an appropriate example of how an escalation of ethnic conflict can turn into ethnic cleansing and genocide. Post–Second World War Yugoslavia was built based on the ideal of an integrated and ethnically diverse society. However, economic and political crises of the late 1980s challenged this ideal to the extent that incidents of ethnic hatred that had been previously punishable by law were now officially ignored. An increasing number of such incidents reflected a weakening of the social order and of the ideology of ethnic coexistence. Furthermore, the inability of the existing party leaders and the federal government to come up with solutions for the troubled Yugoslavian economy created a power vacuum. By offering solutions to the country's problems, ethnic leaders emerged who promoted intergroup fear and hatred. Minorities were identified as a threat to the stability and safety of the majority group. Ethnic conflict and increased discrimination against minority residents thus developed as a part of the process of ethnic leaders seizing power in a power vacuum.

Why does a country move from peaceful coexistence to ethnic war? Certainly economic problems intensify the competition for scarce resources, and political leaders inflame the tension by

THE POLITICAL USES OF HATE

emphasizing ethnic differences so they can be used as a political weapon. Within the Yugoslavian context, the mass media played an important role in promoting ethnic hatred in general and trumpeting the ethnic rhetoric of nationalistic parties, in particular. Although opposition newspapers and radio stations existed, they were no match for the well-supported official media. National television stations, for example, broadcast images of suffering members of their own ethnic group without mentioning the suffering of others. Newspapers published the stories that documented abuses of "their" people at the hands of other groups without referring to the abuses to members of other groups tolerated or promoted in their own states. Also completely missing from the ethnic rhetoric were examples of cooperation and peaceful coexistence among different ethnic groups in the country.

Yugoslavia again is a telling example. In post-communist Yugoslavia, members of the Albanian minority group lost most of their ethnic rights when Slobodan Milosevic came into power. To consolidate his absolute control, Milosevic exploited Serbian fears and grievances against Albanians. By stripping Albanians of their self-rule privileges, Milosevic might have appeased Serbian nationalists, but he also led Yugoslavia to its destruction.

In their quest for realizing their nationalist aspirations, Serbs committed horrendous violence against other ethnic groups in Bosnia and Kosovo, and got expelled from the Krajina region of Croatia. (However, atrocities were committed on all sides.) After ten years of war, Serbia was left with a ruined economy, with thousands of refugees from Bosnia, Croatia, and Kosovo, and with a terrible reputation for the suffering that it inflicted on others. (This is particularly sad since the Serbs had so distinguished themselves for bravery in World War II.) Milosevic is currently on trial as a war criminal at The Hague tribunal.

From the time Milosevic came to power in 1987, he successfully worked on destroying his opponents and consequently any alternative to his rule, by controlling the sources of information and cultural expression.[13] By isolating Serbs and making them fearful of other ethnic groups, he could justify involving them in wars that brought them further misery and loss. Even under such conditions, however, many Serbs still held views that were favorable to working cooperatively with members of other ethnic groups.

In 1996, the Helsinki Committee for Human Rights in Serbia conducted a public opinion poll of five hundred Serbian respondents on their views of human rights for the ethnic minorities in their country. The question posed was: Should Serbs in Serbia have more rights than members of other ethnic groups? The majority of Serbs (54 percent) responded by rejecting the unequal treatment of others. What was troubling for achieving a resolution of ethnic conflict, however, was the finding that 40 percent of the respondents told pollsters that the members of the majority group should be granted more rights than their minority counterparts. Further results of the poll showed that Serbs were more willing to grant minorities some group rights, such as the right to practice their own religion, conduct cultural affairs, publish their own newspapers, and even have educational institutions in their own language. But the same set of respondents was also against giving minority residents the right to use their own language in formal institutions and local government, even in the regions where they comprised the majority. Serbians saw such rights as potentially destabilizing the nation as a whole.

On the one hand, some Serbians expressed a desire for equality; others favored their own group over others. A large number was willing to support policies that promoted accommodation rather than prolonged conflict. For example, most respondents (72.6 percent) thought that increasing the standard of living for the members of all ethnic groups would decrease the tensions between them.

Moreover, more than a third (37 percent) thought that the ethnic conflict might be solved by giving minority groups all of the rights enjoyed by other citizens. On the other hand, 29 percent of the respondents thought that the solution to ethnic conflict could be secured by encouraging members of the minority group, in a peaceful way, to leave the country, and 8 percent supported the forceful resettlement of minority residents. [14]

In order to maintain multiethnic societies, a government has to recognize and respect minority rights. In such circumstances, special policies for minorities are often enacted in order to remedy past injustices. Throughout history, some ethnic groups have received a "special" status.

For example, because of past grievances, Jews in the Middle Ages were exempted from paying certain taxes, Serbs in Krajina were granted autonomy by the Austrian Empire, and many African Americans in the United States have been beneficiaries of affirmative action as they enrolled in universities or sought employment. In times of crisis, those same special rights (for past wrongs) are used as a justification for attacking these so-called privileged groups.

In the early 1990s, as the United States went through an economic recession, the so called "angry" white men (a minority of white men actually) blamed African Americans and women for their loss of jobs and status. Similarly, Israeli secular Jews often made derogatory remarks against ultra-Orthodox Jews who were exempt from mandatory military service and received generous government benefits through student stipends and child support policies.[15]

Multiethnic societies are faced with the problem of how to balance human rights with ethnic rights. *Human rights* are often defined as individual citizenship rights that theoretically apply to each and every member of society, whereas *ethnic rights* refer to the special prerogatives granted to a minority group in order to address its particular needs. A growing number of governments are paying attention to handling intergroup relations by recognizing minority rights and by making special provisions for them. In India, the Muslim minority has the right to apply its own civil law in separate civil courts.

However, this right is one of the major issues that Hindu nationalists have used to argue that Muslims have privileged status in India, and thus have campaigned to abolish it. On a more promising note, organizations such as the Organization for Security and Cooperation in Europe (OSCE) and the Council of Europe are also actively promoting standards that enhance minority rights such as to "prohibit forced assimilation and population transfers, endorse autonomy for minorities within existing states, and acknowledge that minority claims are legitimate subjects of international discussion by both UN and European regional organizations."[16]

An analysis of the persecution of Gypsies, correctly referred to as the Roma, in Europe epitomizes how politics is used to flame hate. The worsening of economic conditions and political instability in the countries of central and eastern Europe where the Roma are a minority group have contributed to turning them into a scapegoat, blaming them for nearly all of society's ills. Moreover, renewed nationalistic ideologies have helped to channel the displaced hostility of a frustrated population toward this stigmatized ethnic group, stigmatizing it further.[17]

Consequently, Roma throughout Europe have faced increased discrimination by both national governments and local authorities in places where they reside. They are often victimized by a hostile media, widespread personal hatred, and violence perpetrated by lynch mobs, skinheads, and the police. In September 1994, two Roma refugees from the former Yugoslavia died in an arson attack in Germany, and in February 1995, four Roma were killed by a pipe bomb in Austria.[18] In Serbia, in October 1997, a pregnant Roma woman and a fourteen-year-old boy were beaten to death by the members of a Serbian neo-Nazi gang.[19] And shortly after the Yugoslavian forces withdrew from Kosovo in 1999, the expulsion and harassment of Roma by Albanians began. Their houses were burned, and they were beaten and murdered. In addition, when Roma have sought to flee from a menacing situation, they have frequently been denied safe havens as refugees.[20] Even international organizations often fail to step up and protect them, as the most recent outbreaks of continuous harassment and attacks against Roma in Kosovo illustrate.

We saw in previous examples how political leaders initiate or support hate-motivated acts of discrimination or violence. In order to drive their point home, they always bandy about images that are familiar to their subjects and claim that the action that they undertook, such as the torture, the starvation, and the murder of political opponents, will benefit their own victimized people. In the process of serving their people, however, these leaders often enrich themselves and bolster their positions by amassing tremendous power.[21] Thus, before India's independence, the British colonial officers glorified their role in spreading democracy to justify their presence. Meanwhile, they subjugated the people; and they themselves lived like royalty, appropriating India's resources.[22]

In many cases, political leaders put their own well-being above that of the people. This explains why the political manipulation of hatred tends to continue even after a peace agreement is signed. In Northern Ireland, for example, the firebombing of Catholic homes, the bombing of crowded shopping areas of Omagh, and the murder of a prominent Catholic attorney all followed the signing of the peace treaty known as "the Good Friday Agreement" in 1998.[23] An ordinary citizen, a Catholic resident of Ardoyne, was shot in the head and neck while walking near his home.[24]

In order to understand perpetuating violence when it seems to make no practical sense, we have to consider the role of political leaders, both major and minor, in the peacemaking process. Their self-interests are not always in tune with the interests of their nation or the groups that they lead. Although 86 percent of the people of Northern Ireland voted for the peace agreement, small minorities of both Catholic and Protestant extremists have not given up waging civil war. When Catholic organizations Sinn Féin and its military wing, the Irish Republican Army (IRA), signed the agreement, splinter groups emerged to advocate their own extremist agenda. On August 13, 1998, a breakaway group, the Real IRA, set off a bomb on a crowded shopping street in Omagh. Another splinter group, the Continuity IRA, also rejected the peace agreement and continued to use violence as its members pursued their goal of seceding from Great Britain. Fearing the consequences of peace, they acquired new weapons of destruction and planned to target the security forces operating in Northern Ireland.[25]

The Omagh bombing was particularly gruesome. Consisting of about 60 percent Catholics and 40 percent Protestant residents, the town had no history of sectarian violence. The bomb that exploded on a Saturday afternoon claimed the lives of twenty-eight—fourteen women, five men, and nine children. More than two hundred local residents were injured, many losing their limbs and being permanently disabled. Some were doing their back-to-school shopping; others were enjoying the end-of-summer heat; still others were working in local shops and stores.[26]

The terrorist incident in Omagh was one of the most devastating attacks on civilians during the last thirty years of the Northern Ireland conflict. The fact that so many of the victims had been mothers and their children, both Catholics and Protestants, guaranteed that the bomb blast would occupy a prominent position in the minds and memories of Northern Ireland's residents. Who could forget the untimely death of Avril Monaghan, pregnant with twins; her eighteen-month-old daughter, Maura; and Avril's mother, Mary Grimes: Three generations of one family wiped out in an instant.[27]

Prior to its tragic explosion in Omagh, members of the Real IRA had attempted a number of other bombings, destroying businesses in Belfast and Portadown without any human casualties. Many believed that the escalation into mass murder by these political extremists was an attempt to extend their operational base at a time when they may have seemed politically irrelevant.

Similarly, in an effort to sabotage the peace process, paramilitary units of the Irish Protestant side of the conflict continued to attack Catholics. Rosemary Nelson, a prominent lawyer and the mother of three young children, was killed by a bomb left in her car only a few hundred yards from her home. A group of Protestant loyalists claimed responsibility for the murder. The Red Hand Defenders group, another splinter Protestant organization whose members took responsibility for the murder of a Catholic citizen, is led by a man with a long history of using violence for political purposes.[28]

What looks for all the world to be senseless murder turns out, in Northern Ireland, to have a connection to the "troubles" and therefore has a political purpose. On July 12, 1998, the three brothers of the Quinn family—ten-year-old Richard, nine-year-old Mark, and seven-year-old Jason—were murdered in their sleep when their house in a predominantly Protestant neighborhood was firebombed in the middle of the night. Their parents, whose bedroom was on the ground floor, escaped with minor injuries, but they were unable to save their three boys who were trapped in an upstairs bedroom. Police believed that the Quinns' house was targeted by Protestant extremists because the mother was a Catholic. It did not seem to matter to the killers that the three boys themselves had been brought up as Protestants.[29]

For Protestants in Northern Ireland, July 12 is an almost sacred day. Every year Protestant Orangemen march in a traditional procession through their own and Catholic neighborhoods in order to celebrate the July 12, 1690, victory over Catholics at the River Boyne. The firebombing murder of the Quinn brothers coincided with a number of violent acts that broke out around the parade. More than 130 firebombings of Catholic-owned houses in the vicinity were perpetrated during the week of rioting and protests associated with the march. In retaliation, three Orange halls and a Protestant church were damaged by a petrol bomb, but luckily no lives were claimed.[30]

More than half the victims of the Northern Ireland conflict have been civilians, overwhelmingly male and overwhelmingly young Catholic men. Paramilitary groups were responsible for murdering 80 percent of the victims.[31] Although many Catholics were killed by security forces or by Protestant paramilitary groups, some lost their lives to Catholic paramilitary forces because of their real or perceived traitorous behavior.

At a superficial level, the "troubles" in Northern Ireland are simply a religious conflict. That is, the struggle is between those who wish Northern Ireland to remain part of the United Kingdom, the Protestants who are known as unionists, versus those who wish to see the unification of the island of Ireland, the Catholics who are known as nationalists. Yet a closer examination suggests that the conflict is more about economic and political inequality than about religion. There are many Protestants who are not unionists and many Catholics who are not nationalists. Traditionally, Protestants have controlled the reigns of power and have garnered a disproportionate amount of the wealth of the country. By contrast, Catholics have been more impoverished and have lacked political clout. The conflict is about one group seeking to enhance its standing in a society, but as seen as at the expense of another group. In Northern Ireland, the advantage of Protestants is regarded as the disadvantage of Catholics.

Although the violence in Northern Ireland is less pervasive than in Israel, low-level conflicts continue to simmer. "The Good Friday" peace agreement signed in 1998 failed to bring closure to the strife, because in part, political parties and paramilitary organizations in Northern Ireland were deeply invested in the conflict. What would they do if it stopped? They might have to address the more mundane but serious problems that residents of Northern Ireland face every day (such as unemployment, and lack of services and housing).

Although most political leaders agree that the situation in Northern Ireland is better today than in the past, both sides are still blaming each other for the slow progress of the peace plan. Though both sides have committed atrocities against the other, both expect the other side to accept full responsibility. The peace process brought some degree of normality to everyday life, allowing Northern Ireland's young people to enjoy a degree of freedom of movement not known by previous generations. Still, many young people are choosing to leave Northern Ireland for less sectarian places in the world as well as places that have jobs.

The story of the escalation of conflict between Protestant unionists and Catholic nationalists in the Northern Belfast neighborhood of Ardoyne suggests how easily the peace process can be tested, especially in the poorer neighborhoods. Beginning in September 2001, over a period of three months, parents and children from the Holy Cross Primary School, a Catholic elementary school for girls ages three to eleven that is located in a Protestant enclave of the mainly Catholic Ardoyne neighborhood, suffered daily harassment from their Protestant neighbors as they tried to bring their daughters to school. As they walked the three hundred yards that separate their Catholic housing project from the school's main entrance, the little girls in their crisp dresses had curses hurled at them as well as stones, balloons filled with urine, and gasoline bombs. The two sides were separated from each other by hundreds of police and military troops, who could do little more than keep the Protestant and Catholic residents physically apart.

Residents of the Ardoyne Protestant enclave demanded that the Catholic parents and their children stop using the front entrance to the school that passes through their neighborhood, and instead use the back door of the school that can be accessed from Crumlin Road within the Catholic neighborhood. School officials agreed, recommending that parents take an alternative rear entrance in order to protect their children.[32]

But many of the Catholic parents refused to use the alternative entrance to school, arguing that it was offensive to them and their daughters. "The only thing we'd miss," argued one irate father, recalling Nazi treatment of Jews, "would be the yellow stars."[33] For many parents, therefore, using the front entrance symbolized their right to equal treatment under the law. If the government could not defend their children's right to an education, then how realistic was it to expect equality and freedom from the state? In order to underscore the symbolism of their situation, parents compared their struggle to the civil rights battles of African Americans in the United States during the 1960s and recalled images of places such as Little Rock, Arkansas, and Selma, Alabama. "The very phrase—back door entrance—is an image that Catholics will not accept. They say Catholics will no longer go through back doors, up back streets, or second class anything. They are determined to go up the main road."[34]

As is usually the case in hate-motivated conflicts, there was no consensus about who started these confrontations. The reason for blocking the passage, some Protestant residents argued, was the constant harassment they had faced from their Catholic neighbors when they had tried to use neighborhood facilities such as playgrounds, the library, and the post office in the Catholic area. These

Protestants contended that the presence of nationalist flags and graffiti and vandalism to their houses and property were making their lives difficult.

The Catholic explanation was somewhat different. Some attributed their neighbors' anger to the changing neighborhood demographics that had made Protestants the minority in Northern Belfast, causing them to lose some of their power. Catholic girls, they argued, had walked the same route to school for the last thirty years, and even during the worst outburst of violence in Belfast had not suffered harassment by their Protestant neighbors.[35]

The Catholics also blamed new Protestant residents who had arrived during the previous year. The newcomers were the families of the members of the Ulster Defense Association, the largest loyalist terror group in the country, who had moved to this North Belfast neighborhood after being expelled from a large Protestant enclave in West Belfast due to their feud with another loyalist group. Many of the new residents were believed to be supporters of hardliner Johnny "Mad Dog" Adair, the notorious loyalist terrorist who was returned to prison after breaking the terms of his early release under the Good Friday agreement.[36]

North Belfast, an economically depressed area, is a hodgepodge of Catholic and Protestant communities that in the past saw more terrorist murders than any other region of Northern Ireland. Both Catholic and Protestant communities share similar experiences with violence and the loss of loved ones as well as social and economic deprivation.

Over the years, however, the Protestant community shrank. Upwardly mobile Protestants moved to new satellite towns around the city in part to escape the intergroup violence as well as the domination of loyalist paramilitary forces. Meanwhile, the Catholic presence grew in numbers, and the new residents pushed for more space. Yet because the neighborhoods in Belfast were divided across religious lines, the government was reluctant to move Catholics into empty houses previously occupied by Protestants.

In divided areas where religious or ethnic violence tears the fabric of society apart, it is difficult to sustain the ties of friendship between members of different ethnic groups. Even interethnic or interreligious marriages may not survive in places of extreme hostility. For others who wish to protect themselves from the violence, they often choose to live in segregated communities. The avoidance of the members of other groups decreases the contact between them and consequently the possibility for conflict or violence to develop. Thus, in many places, "good walls make good neighbors." It is not then surprising that solutions proposed to resolve the conflict over Catholics using the school entrance ranged from closing the school and building a new one inside the Catholic area, to building a wall across Ardoyne Road to separate Protestant houses from their Catholic neighbors'.

Meanwhile, as news of the protest spread around the world and television cameras showed pictures of frightened and screaming girls trying to attend school, Protestants found themselves in the middle of a public relations disaster. Embarrassed Protestant politicians and public officials felt compelled to distance themselves from the protest.

The Catholic community, although clearly having the sympathy of the world on its side, suffered as well. The girls were traumatized by their experience, and many had to seek professional help. Some parents took their daughters out of school and the following year the school's enrollment dropped. In retaliation, nationalist youths attacked buses carrying Protestant schoolchildren past the fringe of the Catholic areas.

In the scheme of things, conflict over the passage to school may seem of relatively minor importance, but it illustrates the anxieties that Northern Ireland's Protestants, mainly of working-class background, feel about their future. They are very much influenced by the changing demographics. Once an overwhelming majority in their country, the population of Protestants has shrunk from 70 percent in the 1920s to around 58 percent in 2002. Moreover, Catholic children now account for 51 percent of all students, from early childhood education to secondary schools. The demographics are of supreme importance in Northern Ireland because by law, residents can use a referendum to decide whether they want to stay with Great Britain or join the Republic of Ireland. (This is not to justify the Protestants' behavior toward the Catholics in Northern Ireland, or the reverse, but to analyze it.)

The anxieties of Protestants have also been heightened by a concern about Northern Ireland's employment picture, as the nation moves toward a service-sector economy that demands different types of skills than in manufacturing. Finally, Protestants see the peace process as eroding their privileges and improving the standard of living for Catholics at their expense. This likely increases their resentment toward Catholics which, in turn, exacerbates their hatred. And in communities like North Belfast with many undereducated youth, few job prospects, numerous paramilitary organizations, and easy access to illicit drugs, violence has been seized on by some as a way to fight "for one's rights." Such feelings of vulnerability and anger have been fanned by such politicians as Democratic Union leader Ian Paisley and other loyalists who from the beginning have opposed any process that might lead to peace.

The real dilemma for multiethnic societies is how to resolve conflicts that arise because one group's gains are perceived as losses by the other. Poverty, instability, and the lack of common goals further promote such views. Unfortunately, the only winners in this game are political leaders who exploit hate to gain riches and power, and to keep themselves in office.

CHAPTER 7
HATE AND CULTURE WARS

A growing number of nations have a population that is multi-ethnic. Of course, even where citizens are racially, ethnically, and religiously homogeneous, conflicts may and do arise. However, in some cases of multiethnic populations, when the presence of ethnic diversity reaches a critical mass, the potential for hate and violence between groups can soar.

For a minority in a multicultural society who identifies with a particular ethnic group, instruction in their native language and inclusion of their ethnic history and culture in the school curriculum are positive ways to maintain a sense of pride in their ethnic community, as well as a way to develop in children a sense of their unique self-identity. Yet support for maintaining the distinctive cultural identity of various ethnic groups—aka multiculturalism—is diametrically opposed to the assimilationist perspective that favors a national standard for culture and language. Wherever ethnic and racial diversity is a fact of life, a debate exists between those who believe that the ethnic and racial mix should be metaphorically like a salad bowl versus those who assert it should be a melting pot. The pluralists argue that various ethnic and racial groups should live side by side, maintaining their separate cultural backgrounds and identities. The assimilationists urge instead that everyone in a society adopt the same clothing, language, gestures, expressions, cuisine, and values. They regard a healthy society as a homogeneous society, eschewing the concept and practice of diversity.

There are many ways to maintain a dominant culture that emphasizes what various ethnic groups have in common, but still addresses their disparate needs in a multicultural nation. In some countries, schools teach in a second language as part of their regular curriculum; in others they set up separate schools for members of various ethnic groups. Instruction in a second language may be permanent; or it may be regarded as a temporary bridge that eases a child into the mainstream of society. The approach to be chosen depends on many factors, such as the size of the ethnic groups, whether school systems come under centralized or local control, and which other problems the country is facing at the time.

We saw that in Northern Ireland, Protestant and Catholic children go to separate schools and that that separation continues to fuel the conflict between these religious groups. What it means to be Irish is often defined by the use of the symbols shared by members of only one community: the color of school uniforms, the use of political flags, the color of curbstones at train stations, church membership, and so on.

The debate about language and school curriculum is often incorporated within the larger question of whether it is possible to maintain a sense of national unity if ethnic or religious groups hold to different cultural and linguistic standards. Because schools play a crucial role in socializing children, the debate about language and curriculum takes on added meaning.

Within the context of the United States it is widely accepted that different ethnic groups have contributed to the creation of a general American culture. Sometimes, however, supporters of the traditional school curriculum have put much of their emphasis on maintaining the English heritage, far in excess of the actual proportion of Americans who claim English descent.

Minority groups want their cultures to be recognized as well. When the traditionalists don't allow for diversity in the school program, the result can be "separate but equal" schools. Of course, "separate but equal" schools in the South predate the inclusion of African Americans into the system. It barred them before they could share their culture. Today, the least flexible traditionalists, when confronted with diversity, attack the public education system, crying out for vouchers for private schools. These vouchers would further erode American national ideas of heterogeneity and equality. They also deprive the country's public schools of sorely needed funding.

The same debate about language and school programs was at the root of intergroup conflict and violence in the former Yugoslavia. Although some historians and analysts of the causes for the breakdown of that country's social order pointed to the "ancient hatreds" among some groups or the "artificial" nature of the state, Yugoslavia was not very different in many important respects from European states with a national cultural identity—such as Germany and Italy— that formed over the last two centuries. Unlike these other nations, however, Yugoslavia was not able to sustain the process of creating a Yugoslavian national identity. Strong ethnic differences, supported by ethnic political government structures, effectively blocked the emerging overall Yugoslavian culture. Long before Yugoslavia fell apart, there was not much that kept its people together.[1]

The creation of Yugoslavia was part of movements rooted within the romantic nationalism of the eighteenth century. Croatian, Slovenian, and Serbian writers and intellectuals were on a quest to create a single nation from a South Slav population separated by language, religion, and culture, but having enough in common to envision the existence of a nation-state.

The leaders of the Yugoslavian movement wished to promote the political and cultural unity of South Slavs who lived under the Austrian and Ottoman empires. They celebrated the uniqueness of Slavic culture and folklore and saw them as distinct from other "foreign" traditions, such as those originating in Germany and Italy.

Most nation-states have adopted one national culture and one dominant language. But in the Yugoslavian case, each of the major ethnic groups that constituted Yugoslavia already had its own well-developed and distinct culture. Thus the country adopted more of a pluralistic cultural context. Its political system, however, was based on a model that recognized the individual rights of its citizens but only as part of their collective, ethnic rights. Thus, the government, in short, supported the maintenance of separate ethnic identities.[2]

Nevertheless, Yugoslavian rulers did not give up on creating Yugoslavian national culture. In the beginning, the task was influenced by the presence of Serbian culture, reflecting its status as the largest ethnic group in the country and the fact that the royal family was of Serbian decent. After the Second World War, the Communist Party came to power and in theory downplayed the importance of maintaining separate ethnic identities. In reality, however, the Communists supported ethnic memberships by organizing political divisions along ethnic lines. As a matter of fact, Yugoslav as a separate census category did not even exist until 1971. Up to then, residents were forced to choose an ethnic category such as Serb, Croat, or Macedonian. And by 1981, some 5.4 percent of the residents of Yugoslavia defined themselves as Yugoslavs.[3]

Although this was obviously not a large percentage of the population, it showed promise of an important upward trend. There were four times as many citizens who identified themselves as Yugoslavs in 1981 than a decade earlier, reflecting an increase in children from mixed-ethnic marriages. These children identified themselves across ethnic boundaries. Another possible reason for the increase in membership in this cross-ethnic category involved constitutional changes in 1974 that transferred power and authority from the federal government to state governments. Only the authority for foreign and monetary policy and the army stayed at the national level. Yugoslavia was thus a federation of six states and two autonomous regions, and the leadership of each state was dominated by members of the largest ethnic group of that area. In Croatia, for example, where more than 75 percent of the residents regarded themselves as Croatian, 8 percent identified themselves as Yugoslav. Most of those who identified with this broader national category were Serbs who sought to escape a minority status among the Croatian majority.[4]

During the 1960s, Yugoslavia had introduced a partially market-driven economy and private economic sectors. But, for years, members of the Yugoslavian government and the ruling party, the Yugoslav League of Communists, resisted making the government democratic, arguing that the multiparty system would inevitably lead to creation of ethnic parties. To insure equal representation of all ethnic groups, members of the governing bodies of the Yugoslav League of Communists and the federal government were chosen by a strict quota system based on ethnic origin. Thus, individuals did not receive any benefit from identifying themselves as Yugoslavs.

When, in 1974, decentralization of federal power occurred, the change did not bring more democracy. Instead, it weakened the power of federal institutions and increased the centralized power of the state, based on loyalties and identities rooted in individual ethnic associations. There was no Yugoslav orientation in the ruling party either. The Yugoslav League of Communists was divided into state-based parties dominated by single ethnic groups. In order to keep itself in power, the Yugoslav League of Communists refused to tolerate political opposition. However, many of the nationalist demands, such as adoptions of more ethnically dominated curriculum, were granted.[5]

Thus, the children of Croatia learned about Croatian literature but were taught very little about the literature of other ethnic groups, and so on. The Yugoslav League of Communists controlled all civic organizations, and no independent organizations were allowed to exist. In this way the party actively prevented the development of independent civic groups whose memberships might have a Yugoslav instead of an ethnic base. Instead of preventing the splintering of the country across ethnic lines, the party and the government created the infrastructure for ethnic parties to take over.

Still, between 1987 and 1990, more than two hundred new political parties were founded in Yugoslavia. They did not emerge through grassroots mobilization, but were mostly established by small groups of public officials or intellectuals, and grew through campaigning. These new parties competed with the Yugoslav League of Communists and among themselves for political power. Although the political rhetoric of the majority of the new parties praised the values of civil society, such as an independent judiciary, freedoms of political organizing and public speaking, and the independence of the mass media, they also emphasized the ethnic distinctiveness of their membership: values of religion, nation, and family over individualism.

It is important to note here the unfortunate role of some writers, academics, and other members of the cultural elite of different ethnic groups who contributed to the disintegration of Yugoslavia. Long before political leaders with nationalistic agendas emerged, they championed the vision of separate and distinct ethnic cultures and questioned the existence of common cultural ties across groups.

The new cultural elites also made attempts to exaggerate differences among ethnic groups by stressing their linguistic differences.

Most of the people in Yugoslavia spoke Serbo-Croatian, a Slavic language with many regional dialects. The new ethnic rhetoric emphasized the distinctiveness among those dialects. Linguists in Croatia worked on elaborating distinct languages that would further separate ethnic groups. New words were "invented," and old words were revived. People who used language "inappropriately" were stigmatized or scorned. Never mind that it was often impossible to know which words were "truly" Croatian or Serbian. Language thus became another symbol of ethnic hostilities.

The lesson to be learned from the devastation of the former Yugoslavia can easily be misunderstood. It was not multiculturalism per se but the "false" multiculturalism that contributed to civil war. Every ethnic group "did its own thing." Many politicians and intellectuals within each state emphasized how little Yugoslavians had in common with citizens outside of their own ethnic groups and how much they stood to lose by uniting at the federal level. Moreover, the mass media, which was composed of newspapers and stations separated by ethnicity, played an important role in promoting the ethnic rhetoric of each group's parties. It also added new words and rules for proper speech that further separated groups.

Although opposition newspapers and radio stations existed, they could not compete with the well-supported official media. As noted earlier, the local television stations, which broadcast images of suffering members of their own ethnic group, never mentioned the suffering of others. News articles contained stories that documented the abuses of "their" people at the hands of others but failed to report abuses tolerated in their own states. What was totally absent from the ethnic rhetoric were examples of peaceful coexistence among Yugoslavia's ethnic groups.

Psychologists, political scientists, and sociologists who study conflicts all agree that how we respond to them will determine whether we can defuse tension and find a peaceful resolution, or whether conflict will be transfomed into violence. The downfall of Yugoslavia represents a case study of how ethnic conflict can escalate into violence when local leaders manufacture an enemy and manipulate a threat to suit their own political ambitions.

The Yugoslavian crisis started in February of 1981 by Albanian students in Pristina, the capital of Kosovo province, who staged mass protests asking for better living conditions, but also demanded autonomy for their province. The Yugoslavian leadership responded by force, sending the federal army and special police units to disperse them. The regime felt threatened by the students' demands, especially by their request for constitutional change. According to the Yugoslavian constitution, a republic can secede from the federation but a province cannot.

Students' demands were motivated by their ethnic awakening and wish for independence. Within Yugoslavia, Kosovo was the least developed region, and was widely regarded by other residents as a "welfare case." In the media, the region was often portrayed as being poorly run, and its leadership was criticized for building public monuments instead of investing in facilities that would spark economic development. Moreover, in the province's newly developed university system, students were more likely to major in literature and history than in more "practical" subjects such as business or engineering.

The Yugoslavian media helped in spreading the negative ethnic stereotypes of Albanians, even if they might have been trying to be sympathetic to their problems, by portraying them as being backward, uneducated, less tolerant of new ideas, and carelessly given to having large families. In addition, Albanians were seen as a source of unskilled cheap labor who could be easily hired for the jobs that nobody else wanted. These negative views of Albanians in general and the Kosovo region in particular fueled the development of young Albanians' nationalism and led to the development of a separatist movement. In their quest for a better life and reputation, young Albanians believed that greater autonomy would increase their ability to run things better. In that respect, their demands were similar to the demands of other nationalistic movements such as those of the Basques in Spain or the Pakistanis in Kashmir, India.

In reality, Kosovo was run by Albanian political leaders who were not very different from the leaders in other regions of the country. They were primarily political leaders and, because the economy was grounded in state control rather than market forces, such leaders were not accountable for economic failure or success. As in the rest of Yugoslavia, being of the same ethnic group was more important than being economically proficient. Thus, as long as Albanian politicians remained loyal to the party, their power was never challenged. But in order to solve Albanians' economic problems, the political regime had to change. It had to become more market-oriented and give greater autonomy to economic enterprises. In other words, Kosovo was in need of an economic, not a political solution. Yet the decision of the Yugoslavian government was to ignore the economic hardships and to respond negatively to students' demand for constitutional change. This downplayed the students' social concerns, such as quality of life issues as well as their high unemployment rate.

Many observers and area specialists believe that this choice of response to the Kosovo crisis was the beginning of the end of Yugoslavia. The irony is that by trying to suppress separatism, the Yugoslavian leaders actually precipitated the dissolution of the country. If, instead, the leaders had tried to reform the political and economic system, the future of the nation might have been different.

In the aftermath of the Kosovo crisis, Serbian media coverage of the Kosovo affair changed as well. Instead of portraying Albanians as backward people, there were more and more articles stereotyping them as dangerous people. After the Second World War, the Albanian and Serbian populations of Kosovo were nearly equal in size. Large numbers of Serbs left in subsequent years and by the 1980s, Albanians were the absolute majority. The Serbian media and Serbian nationalists used this demographic change as an indicator of Serbian oppression by the Albanians. The reason for the Serbian exodus, they argued, was forced migration, the push by Albanians to rid themselves of the Yugoslavian ethnic groups they regarded as outsiders: Serbs and Montenegrins.

In reality, Serbs and Montenegrins were for years leaving the Kosovo region, primarily for economic reasons. As the poorest and mostly rural region, it offered few opportunities for economic advancement. Because Serbs and Montenegrins had extensive family and kinship ties with residents outside of the Kosovo province, they could more easily move to other regions. Within Kosovo, Serbs and Montenegrins were also more likely to be urban dwellers with smaller families.

On the other hand, many young Albanians, just like other Yugoslavs, had spent some time in developed European nations such as Germany, Sweden, and France as guest workers. Albanians would send their remittance back to their rural families, who would in turn try to buy land from their Serbian and Montenegrin neighbors. Although many Serbs were happy to sell their land and move on, there were others who rejected the offers to sell to Albanians. In some instances, they were forced to sell their land by being threatened and harassed by potential buyers. When they complained to the authorities, or asked for protection, their plight and demands were largely ignored.

Stories started to appear in the newspapers "documenting" Serbian suffering at the hands of Albanians. When a Serb was murdered by an Albanian, the story was sure to be given more prominence than when an Albanian was murdered by a Serb. In reality, because Serbs and Albanians often lived in separate communities and did not have much direct contact, most murders and rapes happened within their group, not between the groups. Similarly, all disputes over land, which were common in rural areas, were also played up more as attacks by Albanians on Serbs to get rid of them, than as neighborhood quarrels. The Serbian population, it was argued, lived in fear for their lives in Kosovo. In 1986, the document known as the "Memorandum," was written by the members of the Serbian Academy of Sciences and Arts. It claimed that Serbs were subjected to genocide at the hands of the Albanians as well.[6]

Serbs had suffered enormous human losses during the Second World War. They were killed by Germans as well as by Croatian and Albanian fascists who were brought to power by the German occupation of Yugoslavia. By evoking these sufferings, the members of the Serbian Academy of Sciences and Arts, as well as many other prominent writers and public figures, initiated the dangerous route of frightening the Serbs and portraying them as victims at the hands of their neighbors. They also chastened Serbs for forgetting their roots. Nationalistic insignia started to appear in public places and to be sold on the streets, nationalistic songs flooded the airwaves, and a nationalistic interpretation of Serbian history started to dominate public discussions. The nationalistic awakening of the Serbs had begun.

However, it was not until Slobodan Milosevic became the Serbian leader that these sentiments would become a dangerous political force. The Kosovo crisis played an integral role in the rise of Milosevic, from an obscure and little known Communist Party official to the Serbians most powerful leader. Milosevic accomplished this transformation by being the first Serbian politician to acknowledge publicly the "suffering" of Serbs in Kosovo. He did this in a very public way, involving the manipulative use of television cameras. On April 24, 1987, Milosevic attended a meeting of Serb and Montenegrin political leaders in Kosovo. The meeting took place on the Kosovo Polje, the historical site of the famous battle of Kosovo. In 1389, Serbs had lost the battle against the Ottoman Empire, which symbolized the beginning of Serbian domination by the Turks. The meeting was scheduled to provide an opportunity for Serbian political leaders from Kosovo to address their grievances against the Serbian government for ignoring their plight.[7]

However, fifteen thousand Serbs and Montenegrins showed up outside the building where the meeting was taking place. As the angry crowd gathered, some people started throwing stones at the police. When law enforcement responded with force, the crowd started to chant: "Murderers, murderers!" and "They are beating us!" At that point Milosevic came out and made a statement that was to be replayed on Serbian television again and again for months. "No one is allowed to beat you," he said to the crowd that responded enthusiastically, chanting his name, "Slobo, Slobo." Milosevic then proceeded to give a speech to the crowd in which he acknowledged their suffering and reaffirmed their claim to Kosovo's land.[8]

It turned out that the mass show of angry Serbs and Montenegrins was a staged event, just as throwing stones at the police was a planned provocation by Milosevic supporters. But, what the viewers of the television news saw on their screens were seemingly ordinary residents of Kosovo being attacked by the police and being saved by Milosevic.

In his quest for power Milosevic would use the "Kosovo" card again and again, and would emerge not just as the formal political leader in Serbia but also as a protector of all Serbs, regardless of where they lived. He first turned to squash the opposition to his nationalistic agenda within the Serbian Communist Party. Thus he came to power, not through electoral processes, but by mobilizing his supporters within the party. He exploited the weaknesses of the Yugoslavian political system and used the power of the state-controlled media to his benefit. Thus, the controlled newspapers, television, and radio stations provided 90 percent of all the political and economic information to the Serbs in Serbia. He even turned the respectable and somewhat independent newspaper *Politika* into "the mouthpiece" of Serbian nationalism. Although over time independent newspapers as well as radio and television programs were critical of Milosevic's policies and expressed their concerns over the dangers of nationalism, they were no match for the state-controlled media.

The Serbs were the largest ethnic group in Yugoslavia. The Serbian political leaders had enormous political power before and after the Second World War. However, the Serbian nationalists, politicians, and even many intellectuals succeeded in making Serbs believe that they were the target of hatred by other ethnic groups within Yugoslavia, and later, even the victims of a worldwide conspiracy against them. As Serbs waged war against their neighbors and supported Bosnian Serbian leaders who instigated the death and destruction of hundreds of thousands of Muslim residents, most continued to believe that they were doing it in self-defense, and that those actions were necessary in order to protect themselves from a future threat.

The United States is also not immune to raging ethnic hatred. Ethnic animosity continues to represent one of the thorniest problems America faces. And schools have become a focal point for controversies involving the pluralistic versus assimilationist perspectives. In the United States, the debate about the effectiveness of formal education is increasingly being concentrated on the failure of public schools to educate urban, mostly minority populations. Many black and Latino children are doing relatively poorly on national standardized tests; they are disproportionately represented in special education programs and are dropping out of school at a higher rate than their white counterparts. For many behavioral scientists, these deficiencies indicate that the needs of minority children are not being adequately met in the current public school system. To address such problems more effectively, education experts and practitioners are developing linguistically and ethnically based curricula that reflect better the language and subculture of black and Latino students. However, it should also be recognized that a child who is not indoctrinated in mainstream grammatical English will be at a disadvantage in attending college and finding meaningful career opportunities.

It has always been a major role of education to socialize newcomers to the dominant culture, to introduce them to the American way of life. Assimilation was the major objective of a solid public school education. Today, however, the view that immigrants must be assimilated within American society is being challenged by advocates for an integrated or pluralistic society.

In the area of formal education, the assimilationist versus pluralist debate has involved the value of bilingual schooling. Should minority children be immersed in the English language? Or, should they be permitted to keep a foot in both cultural doors and be taught in English as well as in their original language?[9] From the integration or pluralistic perspective, the school is regarded as a vehicle to help students become fully bilingual and bicultural. In such a society the role of education is to nourish diversity and create opportunities for children to develop their potential, not to see that they become carbon copies of one another.

The major problem in education in low-income areas is the scarcity of resources. Fifty-nine percent of teachers in schools with high percentages of low-income students say they lack textbooks. Only 16 percent of teachers in low-poverty schools issue the same complaint.[10] Because disparities in school spending reflect local wealth, there may be school districts that spend as much as $38,572 per student, compared with $5,423 per student in the poorest district.[11] Minority children are more likely to live in such poor districts. Thus they are less likely than white students to have available more challenging academic courses or advanced placement classes.[12] For Latino students, moreover, state after state is limiting or cutting its bilingual programs. The argument is that children who attend bilingual schooling are not progressing at par with their English-speaking peers. Bilingual education is an easy scapegoat for administrators who fail to provide a quality education for all of their students regardless of ethnic or racial background.

In the Yugoslavian case, we saw how the government paid "lip service" to multiculturalism in its official policy, but in reality promoted "false" multiculturalism whereby various states adopted ethnically specific curricula with no regard for the achievements and rights of the other ethnic groups in the country. Ultimately this attitude coupled with hardships brought by a worsening economic situation—as well as strategies used by politicians seeking power by exploiting ethnic differences—tore Yugoslavia apart.

In the United States we are trying to develop "true" multiculturalism that will recognize the rights of ethnic groups to maintain their own cultural identity, at the same time that we recognize their individual rights as equal citizens of this country. But these efforts are dampened by racial inequality and misunderstanding. Americans believe that bilingual education in general will reduce the ability of immigrant children to integrate themselves within the mainstream of American society. They fail to see bilingual education as a temporary bridge that immigrant youngsters may use in making the transition from their original language to English.

Developing a strong ethnic identity and taking pride in one's own ethnic group are not problematic, if at the same time the rights of other ethnic groups are respected. What destroyed Yugoslavia was the lack of respect for the rights of ethnic groups generally and the development of beliefs fostered by the media and many of the intellectual and political elites that people who are ethnically diverse could not live together in the some country. It did not help at all that in reality they had, for centuries, lived together in peace.

CHAPTER 8
HATE IN POPULAR CULTURE

Don Imus, the popular veteran "shock jock," is famous for his lack of subtlety and his irreverent humor. During a November 17, 2001, interview on CNN's *Larry King Live,* Imus discussed how America should deal with Muslim nations in the aftermath of 9/11: "Do you have any thoughts about fighting during a holiday like Ramadan," Larry King asked, "which is not, of course, a holiday celebrated in the Christian world, but is the major holiday in that world?"

In response to his host, Imus urged that we really should "drop more bombs during this rama-lama-ding-dong or whatever it is. . . . I know it sounds awful, but we should kill them all." Don Imus is hardly the Lone Ranger when it comes to radio personalities who spew such venom over the airwaves. In the political arena, a growing number of disrespectful and bigoted ultra-conservatives and so-called libertarians have emerged as the controversial hosts for popular radio talk shows around the country.

To the delight of a national audience of millions, right-wing talk master Rush Limbaugh has for years castigated feminists, animal rights advocates, and gay rights activists. His antagonism toward drug-addicted individuals changed, however, after he admitted to his own habit.

In August 1994, placing the responsibility for the Waco massacre of men, women, and children on the incompetence of federal agents, G. Gordon Liddy, the radio talk-show host and former FBI agent convicted in President Nixon's botched Watergate break-in, advised a caller: "Now if the Bureau of Alcohol, Tobacco, and Firearms comes to disarm you and they are bearing arms, resist them with arms. Go for a head shot; they're going to be wearing bulletproof vests."[1]

Originating in New York City, Howard Stern's FM talk show has long made a fetish of targeting blacks, gays, women, and the disabled. Stern's "satirical" disparagement of minorities along with his objectifying remarks about women have propelled the contentious talk-show host into the national limelight and his own television show.[2] In April 2004, a threat from the FCC caused six major radio stations to drop Stern's program, not because of his bigotry, but as a result of his crude language and sexual references.

In July 2003, Michael Savage, another popular radio talk-show host, was fired from his MSNBC Saturday night television program *The Savage Nation* for his antigay remarks. Savage had previously ranted and raved about immigrants, affirmative action, and liberal politicians. But his attack on gays was apparently too much for the NBC cable channel to tolerate. In a segment about airline horror stories, a male caller who was apparently gay talked about smoking in the plane's restroom. In response, Savage said: "You should only get AIDS and die, you pig. How's that? Why don't you see if you can sue me, you pig. You got nothing better than to put me down, you piece of garbage. You have got nothing to do today, go eat a sausage and choke on it." Though MSNBC did away with Savage, this is more the exception than the rule.[3]

The popular cultural arts in the United States—its music,

comedy, television, radio programs, and motion pictures—have at times become sources of misinformation for millions of Americans, giving them a distorted picture of reality and at times fostering hatred and bigotry against people who are different.

Since mass culture is entertaining, it has tremendous potential to influence behavior and attitudes. When taking a "soft sell" approach, music, comedy, TV, radio, and motion pictures eliminate the defensive posture of audience members who might otherwise be put off by a message obviously intended to change them.[4] But when their favorite program, CD, or motion picture is manifestly intended to entertain rather than inform or propagandize, members of the audience can more easily let down their guard and accept a message, whether about delicious hamburgers, the need for warfare, or which groups to despise.

Popular culture generates basic data about what our society is supposedly like. It provides us with a source of information—even if it is misinformation—about social reality. It both reflects reality and manufactures its own version of it. According to communication specialist George Gerbner,[5] millions of Americans have completely accepted as fact the televised version of society. Typically viewing several hours of television dramatic series, commercials, and situation comedies daily, they tend to overestimate the proportion of whites, Americans, and males in the world population. In addition, while viewers typically underestimate the number of Americans who live in poverty, they exaggerate their own probability of being personally victimized by violence.

This is precisely the view that the audience "witnesses" every day on network television. Gerbner has long reported that incidents that hurt, kill, or threaten to injure human beings occur in more than two-thirds of all prime-time programs and in nine out of ten weekend morning programs. In television dramatic series, 63 percent of all major characters engage in some type of violent conduct.[6] The exciting climax seems inevitably to involve a bloody fight scene in which a heroic character pulverizes the enemy. Perpetual viewers tend to have an exaggerated sense of fear and mistrust. They are unrealistically concerned about their own personal safety, about crime, and about law enforcement.

The televised representation of minority and majority characters is no more accurate than are televised images of the prevalence of violence. In a more recent study of prime-time network dramatic series televised in 1997, Gerbner determined that only 37 percent of all TV characters were female (females represent more than 51 percent of the US population), less than 18 percent were minorities (blacks, Latinos, Asians, and Native Americans represent at least 28 percent of the US population), less than 6 percent were at least sixty years of age (people age sixty or over represent almost 17 percent of the US population), less than 2 percent were in the lowest income category (some 13 percent of the US population are at or below the poverty level), and only 5 percent had some physical disability (people with a physical disability represent 20 percent of the US population).[7]

If we look only at the racial identity of characters in significant roles, television seems even more biased. In a single TV season, for example, of the twenty-six new prime-time shows, none featured people of color in lead roles that predated Whoopi Goldberg's situation comedy. Moreover, the behind-the-scenes representation of blacks, Latinos, Asians, and Native Americans in television—writing, acting, and producing—is similarly lacking. An NAACP survey found only fifty-five blacks, eleven Latinos, three Asian Americans, and no Native Americans among the 839 writers of prime-time network programs. What is more, the overwhelming majority (83 percent) of the fifty-five African American primetime writers worked on shows with primarily black casts.[8]

Media portrayals of the all-American beauty can put many

African American women at a disadvantage. Just watch TV and see the ubiquitous presence of the blonde-haired, blue-eyed, and skinny role model. (For that matter, anyone over a size 2 has scant chance of a role.)

The humiliation of black Americans caused by media portrayals is more than just skin deep. For example, late-night television programs frequently consist of old motion pictures and TV shows displaying African American characters in such demeaning roles as smiling buffoons, impoverished prostitutes, and submissive servants. Nightly newscasts often feature handcuffed African American men being led to court or to jail for crimes they may or may not have committed.[9]

The lyrics of recordings directed to younger audiences, both black and white, have been a subject of great concern.[10] Some black rap artists through the 1990s expressed an angry antiwhite, anti-cracker, anti-Devil theme. In 1993, for example, Apache in its recording of "Kill d'white People" urged: "Kill the white people; we gonna make them hurt; kill the white people, but buy my record first." In 1995, Menace Clan in "Fuck a Record Deal" said: ". . . kill whitey all nightey long. . . I would kill a cracker for nothing, just for the fuck of it." In 1997, Killarmy in "Blood for Blood" described "snipers hitting Caucasians with semi-automatics heard around the world." In 1998, Paris in "Heat-featuring Jet and Spice 1" observed "a cracker in my way; slitting, slit his throat; watch his body shake; watch his body shake."[11]

Popular rap artists have also expressed an anti-Semitic theme, not only in their music but also in their interviews with the media. Calling himself "Supreme Allied Chief of Community Relations," a member of the rap group Public Enemy (Professor Griff) once told the press that "Jews are wicked. They create wickedness around the globe." Public Enemy subsequently released a single, "Welcome to the Terrordome," in which the Christ-killer anti-

Semitic theme was again espoused.[12] More recently, Menace Clan bragged about stabbing "a fucking Jew with a steeple." Although apologists describe these lyrics as nothing more than hyperbole, the message of hate still gets through to young people.

Nonetheless, rap as the principal musical expression of hip-hop culture has become increasingly mainstream and diverse. Although created by black teenagers on the streets of inner-city neighborhoods as rhythmic stories of violence, drugs, and crime, hip hop has actually replaced rock and roll as the most popular genre of youth music in the United States. Millions of American teenagers—white, black, Latino, and Asian residing in big cities and suburban towns alike—have adopted the uniform of hip hop (including the cap worn backward, baggy pants, and expensive sneakers), use inner-city street slang, and collect CDs recorded by rap artists.[13]

Notwithstanding its bad reputation, much of contemporary hip hop is neither violent nor bigoted; indeed, some is decidedly multicultural and antiracist. The late rapper Tupac Shakur, for example, in his song "I Wonder if Heaven's Got a Ghetto," raps about the scourge of racism and about the need to bring blacks and whites together.[14]

Yet there is also a continuing theme in the "gangsta" strain of hip-hop culture in which racism, misogyny, and homophobia are frequently expressed. White rapper Marshall Mathers, aka Eminem, who raps about despising "fags" and killing women has become an icon among American teenagers, some of whom may too eagerly embrace his message of violence and hate.[15] Listening to rebellious and antisocial rap music may not inspire most youngsters to go out and commit murder, but it does seem to increase their level of anger.[16]

Also during the early 1990s, the lyrics of some "heavy metal" records (loud and guitar-driven rock music) emphasized violence, sexism, power, and hatred. In Motley Crue's song "Live Wire," for example, all of these themes came together in a scene of brutal assault and murder.[17] Moreover, the heavy metal rock band Guns N' Roses sold more than four million copies of "G N' R Lies," whose lyrics were blatantly antiblack, anti-immigrant, and antigay. In "Used to Love Her," the same group attempted to justify violence against women by depicting a young man being incessantly nagged by his girlfriend until he could take it no more and so killed her. Guns N' Roses leader Axl Rose defended his beliefs to members of the press as follows: ". . . he's mad at immigrants because he had a run-in with a Middle Eastern clerk at a 7-Eleven. He hates homosexuals because one once made advances to him while he was sleeping." He uses words like "niggers" because you're not allowed to use words like "nigger."[18]

Much of heavy metal is quite benign in terms of its intended message. Unfortunately, however, the fans of metal, especially its most youthful followers, tend to be unsophisticated with respect to understanding the lyrics of their favorite songs. Their interpretation tends to be literal. They often don't construe the words as hyperbole or metaphor. There is reason to be concerned about the impact of the most bigoted and violent heavy metal on the attitudes and behavior of its audience members.[19]

Into the new millennium, as the popularity of heavy metal has gradually waned, a new, more sinister form of specialized metal music has recently emerged in its place. Known widely as black metal or the satanic metal underground, this latest genre represents the hardest strain of heavy metal, emphasizing cold-blooded murder, hate, prejudice, nihilism, and the unbridled expression of masculine lust. Moreover, running as a general theme through the lyrics of black metal is a preoccupation with eliminating Christianity and its basic tenets from the face of the earth. Support for the virulently anti-Christian (and, in many cases, anti-Jewish) position comes from at least two sources. A number of fans of black metal are followers of Satan whom they praise and honor in their music and their behavior, since he is considered to be the archenemy of Christ. Others cling to ancient pagan rituals and beliefs which were supplanted by a wave of Christian conversions throughout Europe some one thousand years ago.[20]

A closely related genre of music has recently given inspiration to the extremist thinking of the members of racist skinhead groups and white supremacist organizations. Known as "white power" or "hate core" rock, the lyrics preach hate and support acts of violence directed against blacks, gays, and Jews, and they encourage *RaHoWa*, a racial holy war.

White power rock has attained popularity among teenagers around the world who purchase the CDs over the Internet. In Sweden, for example, more than 12 percent of all youngsters admit listening to hate rock. Hate-rock concerts in Germany have attracted thousands of teenagers.[21]

The nation's largest hate-music record label, Resistance Records, is owned by the National Alliance, a white supremacist group that was, until his recent death, led by William Pierce. Pierce's novel *The Turner Diaries*, noted earlier, reportedly inspired Timothy McVeigh in his blueprint to blow up the federal building in Oklahoma City and kill 168 innocent victims.[22] In one hate-rock song entitled "Third Reich," produced by Resistance Records, the lyrics suggest that killing all blacks, Jews, and Roma would feel "darn right."[23] Aggravated Assault's "It Could Happen to You" includes the message: "Krystallnacht to the survivors of the so-called holocaust, we laugh at you." And "Six Million Lies" by No Remorse contains the following Holocaust-denying lyrics:

Did six million Jews really die, or was it just a Zionist lie?
Torture by the Nazis, where's the proof?
Why did they try to cover up the truth?

Scared in case national socialism grew.
Organized lies imposed by the Jews.[24]

In 2001, Resistance Records may have grossed more than $1 million. Despite its continuing popularity with bigoted youngsters, however, the distributor of hate rock has more recently seen a diminishing demand for its CDs. In the wake of the death of its leader William Pierce in 2002, the National Alliance's major source of revenue, Resistance Records, took a serious hit. Visits to its Web site have declined substantially. Sales of Resistance Records' CDs have dropped. Many racist skinheads withdrew their memberships in the organization.

The National Alliance and other hate groups have also begun selling racist and anti-Semitic video games on the Internet. In "Ethnic Cleansing," distributed by Resistance Records, players receive points for killing blacks, Latinos, and Jews. Throughout the game, characters are depicted stereotypically. Monkey and ape sounds play when dark-skinned characters are killed. Jewish characters who are slain shout "Oy vey!"[25]

Even in the mass media, many observers have been critical of the distorted images of minorities. They voice concern that through peripheral learning, Americans are being indoctrinated or reinforced in stereotyped and bigoted views.

As harmful as the domestic impact may be from American entertainment, its worldwide prevalence is regarded as an even bigger menace by those in other countries who seek to defend their language and art from American domination. Citizens of Islamic countries, many moderate nations among them—Jordan, Kuwait, Indonesia, Lebanon, Morocco, Saudi Arabia, Pakistan, Turkey, and Iran—express ambivalence regarding American popular culture. On the one hand, many residents, especially its younger members, say that the West produces enjoyable motion pictures and music.[26]

On the other hand, the same young people believe that Western values have a negative impact on local values, and that American culture is destroying their own culture.

Based largely on their exposure to television programs, motion pictures, and music originating in the United States, residents of Muslim countries see Western culture as immoral and decadent, and accuse it of promoting vulgarity and nudity, inappropriate sexual attitudes, alcoholism, and unacceptable dress and hair-styles.[27] A majority of the residents of Jordan, Lebanon, Morocco, Turkey, Saudi Arabia, and Iran are convinced that modernity, as expressed in Western nations, is fundamentally in conflict with Islamic values.[28]

Many Muslims admire the West's scientific and technological achievements. They also express their respect for the equality enjoyed by people residing in Western societies. But their attitudes turn overwhelmingly negative when Muslims are asked whether Western nations are willing to share their technological expertise with less-developed countries. Most believe that Westerners are unwilling to share their knowledge.[29] They say that Western nations have little respect for Arab/Islamic values and do not treat Arab/Muslim countries with fairness.[30]

In Arab nations such as Saudi Arabia, Kuwait, Jordan, Lebanon, and Morocco, skepticism about the fairness of Western countries seems to be profoundly colored by the image that the United States and other Western societies side with Israel in its conflict with the Palestinians. In the non-Arab Islamic nations of Turkey, Pakistan, Iran, and Indonesia, however, the perception of Western unfairness toward the Islamic world doesn't seem to be very closely connected to confrontations between Israelis and Palestinians. In non-Arab nations, fewer than 25 percent of the residents follow news about the situation in Israel/Palestine. Their negativism is apparently a result of multiple grievances against the United States and a more general belief in the unfairness of Western nations,[31] whose citizens seem unwilling to share their technological advancements or economic resources with the residents of third-world nations.

The same sort of ambivalent feelings about American culture—both popular and technological—can be observed in Muslims who have had some contact with the West. Many living in the Islamic world who have some exposure to the West (through knowing someone who has emigrated to a Western country or having access to the Internet at home) possess a slightly more positive opinion of Western nations than those without such exposure to the West. Still, the impact of contact is not strong enough to make a dent in the largely negative views that Muslims hold of the Western world. Moreover, those with some level of exposure to Western culture are more pessimistic than the general population about Islamic and Western nations ever reaching a better level of understanding.[32]

The reaction of the Islamic world to the tragic events of September 11, 2001, should be understood with reference to the longstanding negativism and mistrust by residents of Muslim/Arab nations. Since 9/11, the Arab and Muslim media have presented a demonized image of Jews, Americans, and Israelis in order to deflect responsibility for the attack on America. Such anti-Semitic and anti-American propaganda has been published in newspaper columns, on Web sites, and on television news programs (including those which are government owned), even in countries claiming to belong to the United States coalition against terrorism. The following is a representative selection.

According to the *Syria Times*, the Israeli government should be considered "terrorist Number One" with respect to its ability to carry out an attack on Washington, DC, and New York City. Moreover, Zionists with "a tremendous influence in the US decision-making circles" can easily accuse others of the terrorist crimes that they themselves have committed.

According to the mainstream *Times of India*, six Israelis suspected of being involved in the attack on America were arrested, confirming "our strong suspicions about the involvement of Israel's Mossad in the ugly crime."

The *Tehran Times* reported the accusations of a Syrian official who claimed having "reliable evidence to prove that the Israelis have been involved in these incidents." The same official also suggested "that no Jewish employee was present in the World Trade Organization buildings on the day of the attack."

As reported by Pakistan's *Jihad Times*, the 9/11 terrorist attacks "were masterminded by an international Zionist organization, 'The Elders of Zion.'"

According to a Jordanian columnist in *Al-Dustour*, "What happened is, in my opinion, the product of Jewish, Israeli, and American Zionism, and the act of the great Jewish Zionist mastermind that controls the world's economy, media, and politics."

A columnist for the Lebanese newspaper *Al-Safir* speculated that the perpetrators of the attack on America may have belonged to "local American militias."

On Abu Dhabi television, one of the most popular stations in the Arab world, Israeli Prime Minister Ariel Sharon is depicted ordering his troops to drink the blood of Arab children.

According to *Al-Maydan*, an Egyptian weekly newspaper, millions of people around the world shouted in joy when they learned that Americans had been hit. "This reaction expressed the sentiments of millions across the world, whom the American master has treated with tyranny, arrogance, bullying, conceit, deceit, and bad taste."[33]

As we have seen, nastiness is by no means associated only with the media in Muslim countries. Many European nations have laws that restrict offensive speech, including words targeted at vulnerable groups. By contrast, the United States has perpetuated a tradition of safeguarding individual rights as codified in a constitutional amendment in which freedom of expression, including speech, is protected. Moreover, unlike in most other countries, there are powerful advocacy groups in the United States such as the American Civil Liberties Union (ACLU), whose mandate requires that it assist in preserving the First Amendment.[34] As a result, American popular culture is free to be as hate-filled and offensive as its producers feel may be necessary in order to attract an audience and beat the competition. This is the price that Americans have to pay in order to ensure freedom of speech, which is worth preserving.

The widespread use of simple and familiar stereotyped images in popular culture both in the United States and in many other countries is in part a result not of religious zealotry but of commercial interests targeting their appeal to a large and diverse audience. A detailed characterization may be boring when it occurs in either a thirty-minute situation comedy or a thirty-second commercial. By contrast, stereotyped characterizations enable mass communicators to frame their messages with the least amount of lost motion, so that audience members can understand what is being communicated with speed and facility.

Economic factors are also implicated in the effectiveness of American popular culture to take over and, in some cases, totally eradicate the local popular culture of third-world countries around the world. Local producers are forced to compete with United States studio films and recording companies with budgets in the tens if not hundreds of millions of dollars. America's promotional budgets far exceed those realistically affordable by local alternatives. In addition, American television programs are dumped on third-world countries by a formula which keys the charge for a particular show to the per capita income of a country. Thus, developed European nations will pay much more than developing nations in Asia, Latin America, and the Middle East. From the

American perspective, we are giving them the same products at bargain rates. But from the point of view of many third-world residents, even those who prefer our products, we are only destroying their cultural identity.

Moreover, multinational corporations will simply not sponsor local artistic or entertainment programs in the third world, even if they garner high ratings. Such companies are interested in allying themselves only with images of consumption, freedom, and youth. Even when American movies and television programs are popular, their overwhelming domination of the media is disturbing. In countries around the world, cultural identities have been to some degree eroded by an overwhelming Western influence that refuses to coexist alongside local culture.[35] Consequently, Americans continue to be regarded not only as the "great entertainers," but also as the "great manipulators."

CHAPTER 9

WHEN THE ECONOMY GOES SOUTH, HATE TRAVELS NORTH

In a classic study published in 1961, Muzafer Sherif and Carolyn Sherif demonstrated the connection between competition and intergroup hostility. Their research took place at a summer camp for eleven- and twelve-year-old boys.[1] After a period of time together, the boys attending the camp were separated into two groups and placed in different cabins. When the boys in each group had developed a strong sense of group spirit and morale, Sherif and Sherif arranged for a number of intergroup confrontations—a tournament of competitive games including football, baseball, tug-of-war, and a treasure hunt—in which one group could fulfill its objectives only at the expense of the other group. Even though the tournament began in a spirit of friendliness and good-natured rivalry, it soon became apparent that negative intergroup feelings were emerging on a large scale. The boys in each group began to name-call their rivals, completely turning against members of the opposing group, even against those members whom they had selected as their best friends when they had first arrived at the camp.

Sherif and Sherif's experiment sheds light on the nature of intergroup conflict and hostility. They showed, in essence, that when the advantages of one group depend on the subordination of another group, then we might expect that intergroup competition will turn ugly. Thus, discrimination may have an economic basis, occurring as the members of one group seek to secure a larger share of the scarce resources of their society.

Economic competition may also help to explain why so many of the citizens of other nations envy and hate Americans. In countries around the world, residents say that they do not trust America. In Pakistan, for example, only 5 percent express a predominantly positive view of the United States. A mere 1 percent report their impression of Americans to be very favorable. A majority of Pakistanis describe Americans as "arrogant," "ruthless," and "conceited."[2]

Authors Ziauddin Sardar and Merryl Davies refer to the American economic influence globally as "the obscene power of hamburger culture."[3] They argue that multinational companies force out of the picture any homegrown products in third-world countries that might have given local residents a sense of personal identity, attachment to their history, and stable relationships. Instead, there is tremendous pressure for local residents to prefer American imported fast food, electronic gadgets, popular music, and television programs.

Thus, there is an impression shared by many that the United States has organized globalization so as to increase its national and corporate wealth at the expense of other nations, especially non-Western societies. That is in contrast to the American viewpoint. Under its free-market philosophy, American capital moves freely, American corporations expand in unfettered fashion, and American products are in demand around the world.[4]

The same competitive forces that create hostility toward the United States also contribute to hostility between groups within the United States. America can easily be characterized as a nation of immigrants. The foreign-born population of America is currently about fourteen million, by far the largest of any country in the world. For centuries, immigration was an essential source of labor for the economic development of the United States. Until the early part of the nineteenth century, large numbers of European newcomers continued to come from England, France, and Germany. These were mostly farmers and artisans who brought their marketable skills and capital in order to seize upon more attractive opportunities in the New World.

But the nature of immigration changed considerably after 1840, when sizable groups of landless peasants from Ireland and Germany arrived in the United States. Lacking resources or skills, most of these immigrants had only their labor to sell and therefore managed to secure only a marginal existence for themselves and their families. The distribution of immigrants throughout the United States was directly related to the presence of opportunities for unskilled labor.

Emigration from Ireland and Germany continued at a respectable level beyond the turn of the twentieth century, at the same time that new waves of immigrants began to arrive. Only a decade later, the same social and economic changes in eastern and southern Europe resulted in an increasing amount of immigration to the United States and elsewhere. Between 1880 and World War I, large numbers of Italians and eastern European Jews entered the United States. Smaller groups of newcomers also arrived from Greece and Romania, and from the Slavic and Baltic nations. Like those before them, most of the members of these immigrant groups were predominantly peasants without skills or money who were forced to enter the lowest levels of the American labor market.

Upon their arrival, these immigrants were faced with the unenviable task of getting work immediately in order to survive. They had little choice because they desperately needed jobs and could not afford to negotiate wages, hours, or working conditions. As a result, many immigrants were exploited by employers who found a willing labor pool for poor pay and miserable working conditions. What is more, a growing prejudice against these newcomers often developed to justify their continued exploitation, keeping them tied to lowly positions in the economic order.[5]

In 1845, the largest group of newcomers was from Ireland; in 1890, it was from Germany. In 1900, they came from Italy, and then from Canada. During the 1980s, most immigrants had their roots in Asia, Latin America, or the Caribbean. By 2002, the newcomers hailed from Mexico, the Philippines, Vietnam, China, Taiwan, South Korea, and India. Smaller numbers also entered the United States from the Dominican Republic, El Salvador, Jamaica, and Iran.[6]

The welcome wagon hasn't always been out for America's newcomers. In fact, immigrant bashing has arisen as a national pastime whenever economic conditions worsen. During hard times, non-alien, "100 percent Americans" have sought to limit competition from "foreigners," and incidents against immigrants have tended to soar.

Thus, the depressions of 1893 and 1907 solidified opposition to further immigration from Italy, setting the stage for the widespread acceptance of stereotypes of Italians as "organ-grinders, paupers, slovenly ignoramuses, and so on."[7] In contrast, Chinese immigrants in nineteenth-century America tended to be regarded as "honest," "industrious," and "peaceful," that is, as long as jobs remained plentiful. But when the job market tightened and the Chinese began to seek work in mines, farming, domestic service, and factories, a dramatic increase in anti-Chinese sentiment emerged. They quickly became stereotyped as "dangerous," "deceitful," "vicious," and "clannish." Whites who felt themselves in competition for jobs accused the Chinese, just as they accused other immigrant groups, of undermining their standard of living.[8]

Economic depression during the 1920s encouraged Americans to reject "Mediterranean-Latin-Slavic people." Based on IQ testing, psychologists of the day testified conveniently that immigrants coming from Poland, Russia, Greece, Turkey, and Italy tended to score lower on intelligence tests than "Nordics." In order to stop a dramatic decline in the level of American intelligence, they argued, it was necessary to limit immigration. More realistically, the opposition to immigration was designed to limit competition for jobs. Hence, the passage of the Immigration Quota Act of 1924.

For the same reason, the Great Depression of the 1930s saw the birth of 114 organizations that spent their time and money spreading anti-Semitism. In addition, the Depression period brought a major increase in activity aimed at excluding all potential immigrants as well as deporting all of recent arrivals. As before, the newcomers were blamed for all of America's economic ills.[9]

During the recession of 1982, anti-immigrant sentiment again gained momentum, as many Americans blamed competition from Japanese manufacturers for massive layoffs in the automobile industry. Detroit was especially hard hit, not only by unemployment but also by hate and violence. In June, a twenty-seven-year-old Chinese American, Vincent Chin, was brutally murdered by an out-of-work Chrysler employee and his stepson who apparently failed to appreciate the distinction between Japanese- and Chinese-Americans.

Chin was spending the Saturday night before his wedding enjoying his bachelor's party in a bar located in one of Detroit's working-class neighborhoods. At first, the two angry strangers shouted at the Chinese American, accusing him of causing their unemployment. Then, the attackers broke a baseball bat over Chin's skull. Needless to say, the Asian American community was outraged when a judge sentenced the two killers to three years of probation and imposed a small fine.[10]

In the history of the United States, some immigrants have served as middleman minorities, exploiting a niche between the dominant group above them in the status hierarchy and impoverished groups below them. Intervening between producers and consumers, between employers and employees, such middleman immigrants have typically played the role of traders, moneylenders, brokers, shopkeepers, and rent collectors. They were frequently resented on both sides of the status hierarchy: From the top, by members of the dominant group who sought to maintain their monopoly on the goods and services they provide and, from the bottom, by subordinate groups whose members felt exploited. During the civil rights movement of the 1960s, the shops and stores of Jewish immigrants in largely minority areas of the city were targeted by black residents who resented the presence of these outsiders in their neighborhoods. In the 1990s, Korean and Vietnamese shopkeepers were similarly targeted by angry Latinos and blacks in New York City and Los Angeles. The upper classes looked down upon all of them.

At the turn of the millennium, as the American economy took an unexpected nosedive, violence perpetrated against newcomers once again increased. As noted earlier, in September 2000, two Mexican immigrant workers were beaten by white men who despised foreigners. One of the Mexican workers was hit on the head with a shovel and knocked unconscious to the ground; the other man was slashed on the neck and wrists with a knife. Two months later, a xenophobic man taunted immigrant workers by spitting on a Mexican flag, then wiping his truck with it, and dragging it in the mud.[11]

After the September 11, 2001, attack on America, hate crimes against Muslims (and anyone who might possibly "look like" a Muslim) increased some 1600 percent over a year earlier, making them the second-most victimized religious group behind Jews.

Many were victims of arson, vandalism, or assault. A few were murdered simply because they wore a turban or spoke with an accent.[12]

Americans are certainly not alone in their opposition to newcomers. The voices of xenophobia and racism have long reverberated throughout European nations, wherever immigration has reached a critical mass. During the 1990s and into the opening decade of the new century, growing numbers of foreigners from eastern European and third-world nations have resettled in Germany, France, England, and the Scandinavian countries. The mix of high rates of national unemployment and immigration in these countries has been volatile; in some cases, hate-inspired violence has spiraled out of control.

In German cities during the 1990s, there were thousands of attacks against foreigners, especially Turks, Africans, and Vietnamese. As noted earlier, in September 1991, for example, six hundred right-wing German youths firebombed a high-rise apartment building that housed foreigners and then attacked two hundred Vietnamese and Mozambicans in the streets of Hoyerswerde. In 2001, a gang of young Germans firebombed the same apartment complex and a nearby Asian grocery store in the city of Rostock.[13]

In France, resentment against its six million Muslim immigrants has spurred the French government to restrict illegal immigration, reflecting public opinion surveys suggesting that 76 percent of all French citizens now believe that there are too many Arabs in their country. Advocating an anti-immigrant and anti-Semitic platform, right-wing extremist Jean-Marie Le Pen, as noted earlier, received 18 percent of the vote in France's 2002 presidential election.[14]

In England, two thousand racial attacks on immigrants occurred over a recent two-year period. Angry Brits spray-painted swastikas on the automobiles of Indian immigrants and murdered an Iranian refugee. Moreover, many English citizens now equate foreigners with terrorists.[15]

Even Scandinavian countries have seen groups that decry the arrival of unprecedented numbers of immigrants. In Norway, a relatively small neo-Nazi skinhead movement has initiated violence against dark-skinned foreigners living there. In Sweden, racist youth movements, as noted earlier, have become more active, using white power rock music to spread their xenophobic propaganda and violence to target their enemies.[16]

Not unlike xenophobia, racist sentiment in the United States has increased and decreased depending on the state of the national economy and on how much the dominant group has stood to lose from the equal treatment of people of color. It is obvious why Southern slaveholders sought to preserve the institution of slavery. They benefited by the availability of essentially free labor. The vast majority of slaves filled the roles of field hands and domestic servants, though smaller numbers were employed as needed in salt works, mines, railroad construction, textile mills, and in other occupations that required specialized skills.

Less obviously, the nearly three-fourths of the Southern whites who were not slaveholders also benefited from slavery. Psychologically, their white skin color designated that they belonged to a superior caste. Economically, the institution of slavery also protected them from black Americans competing with them in the job market.[17]

After the Civil War ended, there was a short period of reconstruction during which newly freed slaves sought some measure of economic and political equality. Hostility against blacks rose precipitously. The Klan responded with a campaign of terror and violence in which many blacks were targeted and lynched. Whites, in direct competition with ex-slaves for jobs, reinforced the myth that blacks were innately unable to do exactly the same skilled work they had performed before emancipation.[18]

In the history of race relations in the United States, whites gained from the presence of institutionalized forms of prejudice. Wherever racism thrived and prospered, whites received higher returns for their work and secured a larger share of goods and services. They got greater incomes, higher employment rates, and higher occupational status.

Moreover, not unlike newcomers to the United States, black Americans were scapegoated whenever economic times were tough. From 1800 to 1930, lynchings of blacks in the South increased when the price of cotton decreased. Apparently, white Southerners who depended greatly on a one-crop economy—cotton—blamed blacks for what bad weather and competition had done to reduce their sales and therefore their incomes.

Split labor markets, where blacks and whites receive lower wages for doing exactly the same work, have often encouraged violence perpetrated by white workers against vulnerable black Americans.[19] Blacks were doubly victimized here; first, for receiving less pay for the same work, and then being assaulted for "taking away" a white man's job because they were cheaper. During the early part of the twentieth century, for example, blacks were systematically excluded from joining labor unions. Eager to lower their labor costs and break the back of union organizers, employers who were faced with striking white workers would hire black strikebreakers in their place. This resulted in raising the hostility of white workers toward their black counterparts. Racial violence frequently erupted.[20]

At the turn of the twentieth century, as a system of Jim Crow segregation became institutionalized, white Southerners expressed their fear of competition from blacks. As one working-class Southerner wrote,

All the genuine Southern people like the Negro as a servant, and so long he remains the hewer of wood and carrier of water, and remains strictly in what we choose to call his place, everything is all right. But . . . take a young Negro of little more than ordinary intelligence, even, get hold of him in time, train him thoroughly as to books, and finish him up with a good industrial education, send him out into the South . . . to take my work away from me and I will kill him."[21]

Such attitudes continue to shape people's relationships and to fuel conflict over scarce resources within the United States and abroad.

Remnants of the Berlin Wall, once used to divide communist East Berlin from capitalist West Berlin, now preserve the memories of events from Germany's past, including its Nazi era. (Photo by Jack Levin)

The broad perspective shown here emphasizes the beauty of Rio de Janeiro's landscape while obscuring the poverty of millions of Brazilians who live on the side of hills and mountains in Havalas or shantytowns entirely lacking in municipal services. (Photo by Jack Levin)

The Wailing Wall and the Dome of the Rock stand in proximity to one another, but the coexistence of Jewish and Muslim historical sites in Jerusalem now depends on a military presence. (Photo by Myron Lench)

Every July, Protestant Orangemen parade through Catholic neighborhoods, sometimes provoking widespread violence between the groups. (Photo by Wilfred Holton)

Muslims and Christians in Bulgaria's capital city of Sofia remain at peace while the former Yugoslavia's ethnic groups have experienced years of brutal violence. (Photo by Jack Levin)

Once a thriving marketplace for Christian, Jewish, and Arab merchants, Jerusalem's Old City no longer attracts large numbers of tourists. (Photo by Jack Levin)

Because of recent attacks on Jewish residents, Berlin's police were forced to place barricades in front of this Jewish restaurant. (Photo by Jack Levin)

The Israeli military patrols an area outside of east Jerusalem. (Photo by Jack Levin)

This statue of a woman in Belfast, Northern Ireland, represents the concerns of women in Northern Ireland, regardless of their ethnicity. (Photo by Wilfred Holton)

CHAPTER 10
MANUFACTURING HATE

When radical Muslims attacked the World Trade Center and the Pentagon on September 11, 2001, and slaughtered thousands of innocent people, the residents of nations around the world—even many citizens of Muslim countries—understood completely the hatred that welled up in Americans. The lives of some three thousand civilians—Christians, Muslims, and Jews—were taken without warning in an instant. Tens of thousands of relatives and friends mourned the loss of their loved ones. Millions of Americans who had no personal connection with the tragedy still identified with the victims of 9/11, donating their money, their blood, and their time at Ground Zero.

September 11 was a major turning point in American history. It illustrated in the most tragic way that a single situation of catastrophic proportion can change the thinking of an entire people, regardless of their earlier personal attitudes, feelings, and beliefs. In truth, a situation does not even have to be a catastrophe in order to serve as a turning point. All it needs is enough symbolic value.

During the 2000 presidential election campaign, just after Gore announced his selection of Senator Joseph Lieberman as his running mate, anti-Jewish comments appeared in chat rooms and online message boards around the Internet. On racist Web sites, organized hate groups warned about having a Jew in the White House and about the ZOG (Zionist-Occupied Government) being ready to take over the country.[1]

In a press release e-mailed to his followers, Matthew Hale, the twenty-nine-year-old leader of World Church of the Creator, expressed his happiness about the choice of Lieberman, asserting that "it brings the pervasive Jewish influence on the federal government out in the open so that people can see what we anti-Semites are talking about."[2]

In a message to a mailing list of American Nazi Party members, Tom Metzger, who heads the white Aryan Resistance out of Falbrook, California, suggested that the election of the Gore-Lieberman team would be but the first step for "Jewish masters" who want to remove Gore and install the "first Jew president of the most powerful and bloodthirsty corporate empire in world history."[3]

Some black leaders also expressed an anti-Semitic theme. Speaking on a radio program to black voters in Dallas, Lee Alcorn, president of the local NAACP, warned them to be suspicious of "Jews at that kind of level" whose primary interest is to amass personal wealth rather than make decisions that would benefit the country.[4] Nation of Islam leader Louis Farrakhan suggested that Lieberman would have "dual loyalty" to both the United States and the state of Israel.

Almost any excuse brings hatemongers out of the woodwork, but the state of affairs in the Middle East has had an especially profound impact on increasing the number of anti-Semitic acts around the world. In October 2000, as the violence between Israelis and Palestinians began to escalate, Jews around the world increasingly became targets of abuse, assault, and harassment. In the United States alone, the number of anti-Semitic acts reached a peak, some

259 incidents occurred over a thirty-day period,[5] more than occurred later during the entire six-month period prior to September 11. Similarly, the Israeli army occupation of West Bank towns during the spring of 2002 brought a sharp rise in anti-Jewish attacks around the world.[6]

Such episodes illustrate what hate-crime experts Paul Iganski, Barry Kosmin, and Robert Wistrich argue is a new Anti-Semitism, originating in the growing tensions in the Middle East as reported in a blatantly anti-Jewish Muslim and Arab press. The new Anti-Semitism is linked to Muslims or Palestinian sympathizers, both Islamic and non-Islamic, who have pushed to the hilt their revised version of the worldwide Jewish conspiracy. They argue that Jews control Washington, DC; Jews are responsible for 9/11; all Jews support the state of Israel at the expense of the Palestinian cause; and Jews are the enemy of Islam.

The residents of nations around the world have recently experienced the anxieties and ambiguities of major transitions. For millions of migrants, a new life in a new land—the United States, Europe, or Latin America—has meant giving up traditional, time-tested ways of living in favor of accepting the uncertainties of a different cultural milieu. For millions of eastern Europeans, the "great change" from Soviet-style communism to free-market democracy has left a structural void, causing individuals to be left to depend on their own devices, creating an entirely new social order. And for millions of Americans, rapid technological change has left gaping holes in the rules and regulations that previously held sway. Moreover, the uncertainties left by the September 11 attack on America and the wars in Afghanistan and Iraq have added a new, more ominous element to perceptions of security and safety, not only for Americans, but for Europeans, Asians, Africans, and Middle Easterners as well.

When anxiety and anomie prevail, and people are desperate to make sense of a senseless situation, conspiratorial thinking thrives and prospers. During the 1980s and 1990s, driven by economic hardships in rural areas of the United States and publicized fiascos involving federal law-enforcement agencies in Waco, Texas, and Ruby Ridge, Idaho, members of civilian militia groups in a number of states became convinced that the federal government was controlled by communists; "one-world order" types who favor reducing political, social, and economic barriers between countries; and the United Nations. Some also blamed what they referred to as ZOG—Zionist-Occupied Government. The so-called Patriot Fax Network transmitted to its militia members around the country a series of articles tracing the origin of a Jewish conspiracy to the kingdom of Khazaria, in what is now southern Russia, in the eighth century, which lasted for some 250 years. The Patriot Fax Network accurately reported that the pagan Khazarian king decided to convert to Judaism. Soon afterward, other Khazarians decided to follow their esteemed leader, resulting in the Jewish religion being adopted by the majority of his subjects.

This is the point in the story of Khazaria that turns from fact to unsubstantiated legend to complete fiction. In the Patriot's version of the story, when the Khazarian kingdom was eventually invaded by Russian soldiers, Jewish subjects either were forcibly baptized or fled to Hungary, Ukraine, Lithuania, Belarus, Slovakia, Romania, Poland, and other parts of Russia.[7] According to the Patriot Fax Network, most European Jews can trace their ancestry back to the Khazarian kingdom, making them converts to the religion rather than descendents of figures in the Old Testament. Moreover, this group asserts that for more than one thousand years after the dissolution of Jewish Khazaria, the former Khazarians instilled in their children a secret plot to amass tremendous wealth and political power, in order ultimately to take over all of the countries on Earth.

The Khazarian story has at least a couple of benefits for militia groups looking to blame Jews for their miseries. First, they can claim they are not anti-Semitic, only anti-Khazarian. Second, because they argue that most European Jews can trace their ancestry back to the tiny kingdom of Khazaria, the Patriots lay the groundwork for a racial rather than a religious theory of Judaism.

Throughout history, when basic anxieties spread through an area, Jews have been particularly targeted by those looking for supposed conspiracies. Their unfamiliar religious rituals and language, their marginal position in society, coupled with their relative political and economic successes, have made dominant members of the population, Christian and Muslim alike, very uncomfortable. During the Middle Ages, Jews were widely believed responsible for poisoning the wells of Europe, thereby causing the epidemic of Black Plague that swept across many European cities. Circulating among the masses were rumors about secret conferences of rabbis where strategies for subjugating and exterminating Christians were discussed. *SCAPEGOATS*

In the early twentieth century, Russians claimed to have uncovered the *Protocols of the Elders of Zion*, an allegedly secret document—later determined to be a total fraud—claiming to detail a worldwide Jewish conspiracy to control the world's resources. Actually, the *Protocols* was penned by members of Czar Nicholas II's secret police in 1903, and based on an anti-Semitic tract published in France around the same time. The *Protocols* claims to have documented a meeting of Jewish elders in Switzerland in 1897, where they conspired to destroy Christian civilization. For most of the twentieth century, the *Protocols* was employed as a pretext for eastern European pogroms (massacre of Jews) and later as a cornerstone of Nazi propaganda including Hitler's *Mein Kampf*.[8]

Jewish conspiracy has been a theme in the contemporary world as well. Matthew Hale's white supremacist organization known as the World Church of the Creator expresses disdain for blacks, Latinos, and Asians who it considers to be subhuman, at the same level as animals. But the hate group reserves its greatest vitriol for the Jews; they are regarded as power-hungry characters who have exploited Christianity as a tool of deception to nurture a popular mindset that will ultimately allow them to take over the world.

Similarly, some Muslims have recently revived the Jewish conspiracy theme to deflect blame for the attack on America away from the Islamic world and onto Jews. As we suggested earlier, many residents of Muslim countries have been unwilling to accept the notion that 9/11 was perpetrated by any fundamentalist Muslims, including Osama bin Laden. Instead, they attribute the attack to the CIA, the White House, Israel, and Jewish influences within the American government.[9]

In a speech at an Islamic summit, Malaysian Prime Minister Mahathir Mohamad argued in October 2003 that the "Jews rule the world by proxy," meaning that they are able to get others, for example, Christians, to fight and die for them. He explained that Jews were able to survive two thousand years of prejudice by inventing human rights and democratic ideologies to make it appear that persecuting them would be wrong. Mohamad's speech received a thunderous ovation from the Islamic sheiks, prime ministers, presidents, and kings in attendance. Some were important allies of the United States.[10]

Muslims are certainly not alone in their conspiratorial notions about 9/11. The French editor of the monthly *Mainenant*, Thierry Meyssan, recently wrote a runaway best-selling book, translated from French into English, German, Spanish, and Arabic, in which he argued that the attack on America was actually a plot designed by the Bush administration to discredit Islam and to justify the invasion of Afghanistan. In Germany, Andreas von Bulow, a former cabinet minister, authored a book that claimed no plane had crashed into the Pentagon. The damage was actually caused by a bomb that had been planted inside the Pentagon by a set of Western conspirators. One in five Germans now believes that the United States government carried out the September 11 attacks.[11]

It is breathtaking just how quickly public opinion can be turned around as a result of a persuasive episode or series of episodes. During World War II, Japan was our enemy; afterward, it became our staunch ally. Before the dissolution of the Soviet Union, Russia was the "evil empire" in the eyes of Americans. Since the early 1990s, Russia has been widely considered our friend. Prior to United Nations negotiations leading to the war in Iraq, most Americans regarded France as a close ally. Since then, many Americans aren't so sure. Some have even renamed french fries "freedom fries" and have boycotted French wines. During the 1950s and early 1960s, many Americans held an image of the English as stodgy, stuffy, and conservative. The typical Brit was pictured on the streets of London wearing a derby and a cane, dressed in a dark three-piece suit, holding a black umbrella, and entering a black taxi. Once the Beatles, Elton John, and the Rolling Stones became world renowned in the late 1960s and 1970s, however, the stereotyped image of the conservative Brit quickly dissolved and was transformed into an image of someone "cool," even avant-garde.

Three kinds of threatening situations—threats to life, economic well-being, and values (both religious and secular)—have historically provided the underlying basis for committing acts of hate violence against outsiders. The most obvious circumstance leading to an aggressive response is one that is life threatening. The survival instinct provoked the aggressive stance of Americans in the aftermath of 9/11, which resulted in our wars in Afghanistan and Iraq, and our warnings to countries in the "Axis of Evil."

Of course, human beings have the capacity to construct their own reality, even when it means exaggerating or creating a threat to their survival. Our use of terminology can reflect and dramatically shift our thinking about a topic. A "suicide bomber" from the Israeli perspective who sacrifices his own life in order to blow up dozens of innocent civilians—men, women, and children—may be considered a heroic figure among militant Palestinians who are fighting for statehood—"a martyr for Islam." A "terrorist" in Northern Ireland who randomly selects a Protestant police officer to shoot in the head may be seen as a "freedom fighter" by certain IRA Catholics.

The attack on America has left an indelible mark in the minds of most Americans. A majority continues to say that September 11 had a greater impact on this country than any other event of the last four decades, including the assassination of President John F. Kennedy, the end of Soviet Communism, or even the Vietnam War. Almost three out of four Americans still support tightening immigration restrictions against Arabs and Muslims. And a national poll taken in 2002 discovered that a large minority of Americans has become phobic about terrorism. Avoiding large crowds and national landmarks, they are suspicious of people of Arab descent. Some twenty million Americans now refuse to fly, but, as noted earlier, millions more are terrified when they do. And because of 9/11, many Americans have bought guns or have cancelled their vacation plans abroad. September 11 continues to be on our minds and in our hearts and affects our decisions.[12]

Following the 9/11 attack, Americans have been vastly more willing to accept a preemptive strike against another country. We were told that al Qaeda had orchestrated the attack on America from their headquarters in the country of Afghanistan. It was explained that the political/religious Taliban leaders had provided a safe haven for organized terrorists, including Osama bin Laden, and that it was necessary to dismantle the terrorist training camps and other terrorist activities before the members of al Qaeda had a chance to strike again.

It could therefore be argued that our involvement in Afghanistan was a responsive war—a war of survival—targeting those members of al Qaeda and their political sponsors in the Taliban who were responsible for the attack on America. No such argument can easily be made, however, for the war in Iraq. There was no credible evidence that Saddam Hussein was, in any way, connected with terrorist groups.

If anything, radical Muslim fundamentalists saw themselves in conflict with Saddam's secular government. If anything, the war in Iraq likely diverted our national resources from efforts to root out the remnants of Osama bin Laden's al Qaeda terror network.[13] According to former secretary of state Madeleine Albright, the chaos in the aftermath of the Iraqi war may actually have enabled terrorist groups to begin operating among the Iraqis. In other words, our attack on Iraq actually encouraged terrorism to develop there.

According to *New York Times* columnist Paul Krugman,[14] the Bush administration persistently claimed that Saddam Hussein was somehow linked to al Qaeda, illustrating the larger point that the Iraq war was just one phase in the fight against terrorism. Yet Greg Thielmann, who formerly served as an intelligence officer with the State Department, revealed in the aftermath of the war in Iraq that US intelligence personnel repeatedly claimed that such a connection existed, at the same time that they suppressed evidence that Saddam had no "meaningful connection" with al Qaeda.

This is not to say that our war in Iraq could not be justified on other grounds. Clearly, the American position was that Saddam was a tyrannical dictator personally responsible for the massacre of thousands of his own citizens. He had earlier invaded another nation, Kuwait, and then led his own country into pervasive poverty and world condemnation. Hussein despised Western nations and had possessed weapons of mass destruction—whether nuclear, chemical, or biological—that he could have used on the

United States if indeed they were still there. Moreover, Iraq holds more than 112 billion barrels of oil—the world's second-largest proven reserves—and contains 110 trillion cubic feet of natural gas. Factoring in all of these reasons for going to war, Sadam Hussein may have presented an intolerable presence to the United States.

Except in a political sense, however, the only rationale for our war in Iraq that was almost impossible to justify was to link Saddam with terrorism. Clearly, the anxiety generated by 9/11 created a groundswell of popular support for attacking Iraq. Yet, US troops found no evidence in that country to confirm the administration's allegations of connections between al Qaeda and Saddam Hussein's regime. According to Magnus Ranstorp, the director of the Centre for the Study of Terrorism and Political Violence at the University of St. Andrews in Scotland, Bush exaggerated Iraq's contribution to Middle Eastern terrorism.[15] Senator Edward M. Kennedy went even further, suggesting that administration officials relied on "distortion, misrepresentation, a selection of intelligence" to make the case for linking Saddam Hussein to the terrorist threat.[16] The Bush administration, however, claimed it received faulty intelligence. Almost two years after the attack on America, even as American ground forces were facing daily guerrilla attacks on the streets of Iraqi cities, the American people continued to see a connection between the war on Iraq and the war on terrorism. According to a *Washington Post* survey, nearly seven in ten Americans believed it likely that Saddam Hussein had been personally involved in the September 11 attack.[17]

Before, during, and after we attacked the country of Iraq, President Bush repeatedly referred to the war on terrorism as a reason for striking the Iraqis.

In December 2002, Bush argued that: "The war on terror also requires us to confront the danger of catastrophic violence posed by Iraq and its weapons of mass destruction."[18]

Making reference to the need to disarm Saddam Hussein, the president asserted, "The gravest danger we face in the war on terror is outlaw regimes that seek and possess nuclear, chemical and biological weapons."[19]

In announcing that combat operations in Iraq had ended, Bush told the American people that "The battle of Iraq is one victory in a war on terror that began on September the 11, 2001—and still goes on."[20]

Speaking with the press on July 23, 2003, in the Rose Garden after Saddam's sons were killed in a firefight with coalition forces, Bush again suggested that Saddam Hussein's regime had "promoted terror abroad."

In his address to the nation on September 7, 2003, President Bush referred to Iraq as "the central front in the war on terror."

Threats to the economy or to values shared by a group of people can sometimes seem as intolerable as threats to a group's physical survival. Throughout history, nations have gone to war to protect their religious values and rituals against those they regard as intruders. Religious groups have waged war in order to capture cities and buildings that have important religious symbolism as well as to convert a population, voluntarily or not, to their religion or cause. Nations have attacked other countries for economic reasons. And groups of vulnerable individuals have been persecuted during periods of economic instability and depression.

Just after 9/11, President Bush spoke to the American people about the need for a "crusade" against terrorism. In all likelihood, he intended to emphasize to the American people, if not the entire world, that the War on Terrorism represented a serious threat to the well-being of Western democracies, requiring a Crusade-like response.

In the West, the term *crusade* is often used to denote a concerted collective effort—a movement or campaign for some important cause whether diseases such as cancer or Alzheimer's, racism or sexism, corruption, crime, or terrorism. For the most part, there is no longer implication of a religious meaning. And even where the definition includes a religious motivation, it evokes images of chivalrous knights in shining armor driving the infidels out of the Holy Land.

For Muslims, however, the term *crusade* conjures up cultural memories of the massive attacks by Roman Catholic soldiers against Islamic nations beginning in 1095 CE, resulting in the slaughter of hundreds of thousands of non-Christians—Muslims and Jews alike—and the temporary seizure of Jerusalem.

From across the Muslim world came condemnation for the president's use of the term *crusade*. Osama bin Laden immediately seized on Bush's faux pas to mobilize Islamic radicals. A statement attributed to bin Laden referred to the American military response to 9/11 as "the new Christian-Jewish crusade led by the big crusader Bush under the flag of the cross."[21]

This image was reinforced by Muslims on many occasions in the aftermath of 9/11 by noting links between the Bush administration and the Christian right as well as the Republicans' Bible Belt constituency. In addition, though Jews suffered as much as Muslims during the course of the original Crusades, the support of the United States for the state of Israel became a reminder that Christian crusaders had stolen the Holy Land. From this perspective, moreover, the same infidels were now invading one Muslim nation after another—first, Afghanistan and then Iraq, where American soldiers were seen attending Christian religious services in proximity to Islamic sacred shrines.[22]

On the Christian side of the ledger, the call for "jihad" in the Islamic world after 9/11 made Christians and Jews very worried. It suggested that the September 11 Attack on America was but the opening salvo in a much longer series of terrorist battles, if not an all out holy war, against the West.

Actually, jihad is not necessarily a declaration of war against the Judeo-Christian world, although some extremist groups in the Middle East—for example, Islamic Jihad—have adopted the most militaristic and violent version of the term. The Islamic word "jihad" means "striving," primarily with reference to the efforts of an individual Muslim to achieve a higher moral standard. Also included under the rubric of jihad are activities of a legal, diplomatic, economic, and political nature aimed at improving the welfare of society and humanity in general. At the extreme, Islam does not exclude the use of force in response to evil, but only if other alternatives prove to be ineffective.[23]

The term *jihad* dates back to the Middle Ages. During this period, Christian crusaders had attacked Muslim lands. In response, Islamic men everywhere were called to wage a holy war against the infidels. By the end of the Crusades, the Muslims controlled the Middle East, Northern Africa, and part of southern Europe. Post 9/11, many Westerners hear "jihad" and think that New York City (hit already) or Los Angeles will soon be hit.

Religious identity is but one of the important characteristics that divides humanity. Intergroup violence frequently also has an economic basis that may be obscured by patriotic speech making or moralistic justification. The Japanese December 7, 1941, attack on Pearl Harbor was the launching point for the American involvement in World War II. To understand the rationale for the attack, it is important to examine the economic forces that were unleashed years earlier between the United States and Japan. Through the 1920s and 1930s, the international competition became increasingly contentious. Over the decades, Japanese industry depended more and more on imported raw materials and fuel. Its manufacturing base continued to expand in dramatic fashion, as did its share of overseas markets—at the expense of American industry. Moreover, the Japanese economy continued to grow through much of the Great

Depression. Between 1932 and 1941, its manufacturing and mining production almost doubled, while that of the United States declined.

By 1939, the United States had already imposed strict economic sanctions on the Japanese. Having few natural resources, Japan depended heavily on importing its raw materials. A year later, the American government introduced a licensing system for exporting petroleum and scrap iron to Japan. Then, in July 1941, the United States froze all Japanese funds in the country and suspended all trade. England and Holland immediately followed suit. Japan was left with some eighteen months of petroleum reserves.[24] The Japanese responded by going to war.

Similarly, the seeds of discontent leading to Germany's entrance into World War II may have been sown in the economic hardships associated with losing World War I. Signed in June 1918, the Treaty of Versailles specified that Germany be demilitarized and occupied by the Western allies for fifteen years. Also by treaty, Germany lost 13 percent of its territory containing 12 percent of its population, three-quarters of its iron industry, and one-fifth of its coal. The Treaty of Versailles established an Allied Reparations Commission whose mandate was to set the amount of war-damage payments that Germans would pay to the Allies.

During the 1920s, German agriculture began to fail, causing a food shortage. Coal and steel production had fallen dramatically. Moreover, reparations for World War I were set at 132 billion gold marks. Many Germans refused to work, under the assumption that any money they earned would go to the Allies. By November 1923, the value of the mark had plummeted to 4,200,000,000,000 marks to the dollar. Though the economy later recovered somewhat from the sanctions imposed by the Treaty of Versailles, opposition to reparations grew as larger numbers of the Germans responsible for the war died and their progeny resented having to make payments for what their parents' generation had done.

In the 1930s, Hitler was able to harness the economic resentment of the German people in building his Third Reich and gain widespread cooperation in carrying out the "final solution." Many German citizens who had felt themselves unfairly mistreated by the international community now benefited in a material sense from the confiscation of Jewish property.[25] Furniture and personal belongings were auctioned to the highest bidder, and tens of thousands of Jewish apartments were taken over. In addition, the exclusion of Jews from lucrative occupations had the effect of reducing competition for well-paying jobs.[26]

In addition, many people are often afraid of conflicts and try to minimize them, avoid them, or ignore them. Although conflicts are a normal part of our existence, they frequently leave us feeling threatened, afraid, or less valued by other people. They are caused by many factors, such as competition for scarce resources between individuals and groups, unequal treatment of one group by the other, or competing value systems that threaten our understanding of the world.

The manufacturing process involves more than just creating an enemy to hate or a conspiracy to attack. Powerful elements in society can also actually help determine which members of society belong to the in-group or the out-group. Their personal identity is subsumed by this group label. Indeed, individuals may not always have 100 percent control over how others define them. In the United States until recently, being black was regarded in law and social custom as possessing an ancestor who was black. Thus, given the "one drop of black blood" standard, even someone who had light skin, blonde hair, and Caucasoid physiognomy could still be considered black, not white. Under many state laws, some overturned as late as the 1980s, the choice of a marriage partner would have been restricted to someone black. Moreover, even today, the standard remains intact, at least informally. Golf pro Tiger Woods, who is of mixed racial ancestry, is routinely referred to by television commentators as the "great black golfer."

The imposition of a group identity is well known to Barbara Principe. The seventy-year-old Principe received a bizarre phone call from a lawyer she didn't know. Attorney Gary Osen was calling about Principe's late father, a German immigrant who ever since migrating to the United States had eked out a living as a chicken farmer in New Jersey.

Like her father, Principe had long considered herself to be a practicing Christian who held strong religious convictions and regularly attended church services. So she was shaken by what Osen had to say. He explained that her father had actually been born into a wealthy Jewish family that owned one of the largest department store chains in Germany. When the Nazis gained power in the 1930s, he was forced to give up his fortune and to leave the country with his wife, a son, and Principe, then only six years old. In 1939, her family fled first to Cuba and then to the United States.

In the process, Principe's father left behind not only his worldly possessions, but also the Jewish religious identity that the Nazis had singled out to brand him an enemy of the state. Hoping to avoid the stigma inherited from his family's Jewish identity, Principe's father had anglicized his last name, referring to himself as Wortham rather than Wertheim. He decided to shed what had been a troublesome identity, to say the least.

Principe realized that Hitler would never have recognized her own Christianity. To the führer, Jewishness was a genetic affliction, not a voluntarily chosen set of religious beliefs, transmitted biologically from one generation to the next. (In Jewish law, it too is passed on genetically, not through choice.) Her father had been afflicted with the Jewish disease; therefore, Principe would have been regarded as just another member of the Jewish *race*.

In the United States, however, after a period of reflection,

Principe was able to maintain her Christian identity. "My mother wasn't," Principe indicated. "She was Aryan. She had no Jewish in her at all." At the same time, Principe decided to seek restitution for her family's financial loss during the Holocaust.[27]

On the one hand, viewing Jewishness as a racial condition that is transmitted from generation to generation might ultimately benefit Principe economically. Of course there is no Jewish "race" in terms of racial categories. On the other hand, regarding Jewishness as a religion provides her with a choice. It makes it possible for her to continue to consider herself a Christian. From her point of view, then, she makes the most out of both definitions.

Principe's "Jewish" identity illustrates an important point. If those in power say that we are Jewish, then we are Jewish with respect to the consequences that that identity has for our lives. In Nazi Germany, Principe's father and she would have qualified for the gas chamber. Defining Jewishness genetically, Hitler identified anyone with a Jewish parent as being Jewish. An individual's current religious practices and beliefs were, from his point of view, thoroughly irrelevant. Thus, a practicing Christian could easily have protested all the way to a death camp, where he would have been incinerated like any other "Jew." And just in case there could be perceived some ambiguity as to his religious identity, the Nazis could easily have affixed a yellow star to his clothing or a tattoo to his arm.

Jews aren't the only group of human beings to be "racialized." Cabdrivers in Northern Ireland like to tell tourists that the only arguments about color they will hear revolve around the many shades of green covering their beautiful hillsides. Race is never an issue in Northern Ireland, because almost every resident is white.

At the same time, religious and political differences dominate Northern Ireland's physical, social, and economic landscape. There are Catholic and Protestant towns, neighborhoods, proper names, schools, pubs, colors, and graffiti. If the curbstones outside a train station are marked red, white, and blue, you know you have entered a Protestant town; if instead you see green banners flying, you are among Catholics. If you hear someone refer to the country as "Northern Ireland," he's probably a Protestant unionist; if he says "North of Ireland," then he's more likely a Catholic nationalist. If you come across schoolchildren wearing orange uniforms, they are probably Protestants; if their uniforms are green, then they are likely to be Catholics.

Of course, Americans don't have to cross the Atlantic in order to observe intergroup hostility and violence. We have our own, albeit racial, version of the Northern Ireland conflict in our own backyard. The parallels are striking, so much so that the troubles in Northern Ireland might serve as a mirror of our own past, if not a foreshadowing of our future.

Not unlike Catholics and Protestants in Northern Ireland, black and white Americans remain segregated in almost every aspect of everyday life: neighborhoods, schools, and workplaces. In America, we haven't needed to develop symbols of segregation such as uniforms, banners, and curbstone markings because we have always had the more reliable indicator of skin color to be able to locate the other—the enemy.

And even though black and white differences overshadow the American landscape the way that religious differences dominate the life of Northern Ireland, most white Americans go about their business never giving a thought to racial issues, except in the most superficial way. As in Northern Ireland, there is an illusion of normalcy that makes many Americans believe that everything is just fine with respect to intergroup relations. They are totally shocked when some extraordinary event occurs—such as the events surrounding Rodney King or O. J. Simpson—in which the depth of the divide between the races becomes temporarily clear. White Americans are surprised that so many of their black counterparts believe that whites plot against them, specifically, that nationwide restaurant chains add a secret ingredient to sterilize black men; that beverage companies are owned by the Ku Klux Klan; that the government's so-called War on Drugs was actually an excuse to incarcerate large numbers of young black men; and that the US military conspired to infect Africans with AIDS.[28]

And, not unlike the residents of Northern Ireland, those Americans who are most affected by race—the poor, the disaffected, and the alienated—are also the very Americans who are the least capable of making changes in the quality of race relations. At the same time, many wealthy and powerful Americans continue to distance themselves from the issue or consider it a nonissue.

Black and white Americans have long stereotyped one another in unflattering ways. In the United States, we tend to think of race as one of the most significant characteristics that an individual can possess. Thus, we too often look first at an individual's skin color and racial physiognomy, and second at the content of his or her character.

It may seem somewhat more surprising that the residents of Northern Ireland also stereotype one another, and in physical terms that one might associate only with race. Many Northern Irelanders claim that Protestants are taller than Catholics and have more space between their eyes. They claim also that Catholics have shorter foreheads and larger genitalia.

Northern Ireland is a homogeneous society in which Protestants and Catholics share history, culture, and genetics. Almost everybody in Northern Ireland is Christian and can trace their roots back to the same part of the world. Yet, when it comes to the images they hold of one another, they might as well be talking about race.

In order to justify the butchery and the bloodshed, the people of Northern Ireland have apparently racialized their conflict. French philosopher Jean-Paul Sartre once wrote that if the Jew did not exist, the bigot would surely invent him. In Northern Ireland's war without end, the same can be said for the radical Catholic and the reactionary Protestant.

CHAPTER 11
ORDINARY PEOPLE;
EXTRAORDINARY COURAGE

Those who intervene to help a victim may do so at some risk to their personal well-being. Consider the costs to someone who comes to the rescue of the victim of a street crime. At the very least, they may run the risk of being inconvenienced, for example, by being late for an important appointment or by having to serve as a witness in a lengthy courtroom hearing. Even worse, they may suffer physical injury or even death as, for example, in an attempt to stop an assailant or a mugger.

When the state is the perpetrator, the stakes for intervening to assist victims may require extraordinary courage. During the 1930s and 1940s, the citizens of Germany and Nazi-occupied European countries who aided Jews by concealing them from German soldiers exposed themselves to the possibility of paying the ultimate price. In one Ukrainian village, for example, an entire family including husband, wife, and their three children were shot to death by the Nazis for sheltering a Jewish woman.[1]

There are other minor costs or discomforts in helping someone who is regarded as unpleasant or unworthy—someone a witness might otherwise go out of his way to avoid—for example, a homeless man who falls to the pavement, someone who is disfigured or physically disabled, or a person from another race or religion. If we are uncomfortable being around someone in trouble, we may be less likely to go out of our way to intervene on his or her behalf.[2] Moreover, if we sense that someone has created his own troubles, we are even more likely to ignore his plight. This may explain why a sick man carrying a cane who collapses on the subway is offered more help than a drunk who carries a bottle and smells of liquor.[3] Minorities are frequently different in socially significant ways from the dominant group. They may be stigmatized by virtue of their skin color, religious beliefs, dress, or national origin. And they are often stereotyped culturally as deserving their fate, based on the belief that they come from inferior heredity or culture.

Finally, those who intervene to help others feel some personal responsibility to do so. Ironically, the presence of other bystanders may make an individual feel less personally responsible and therefore less likely to give his assistance. Social psychologists John Darley and Bibb Latane refer to this phenomenon as diffusion of responsibility.[4] If your car breaks down on a crowded highway, hundreds of cars may pass by without stopping to help you. The thinking seems to be, surely someone else will come to the rescue. If you break down on a lonely country road, however, the first person who passes may stop to lend a hand.

Darley and Latane's results are interesting, because they highlight the important influence of the group on an individual's moral decision making; but such studies also tend to downplay those extraordinary individuals who come forward to rescue victims even in large crowds, mobs, and other gatherings. Under the most unfavorable conditions—when many normal people have easily justified their bystander status—it is almost always possible to locate at least a few genuine heroes who render a broad range of support, care, and protection to their fellow human beings in need. Not unlike hate, empathy and altruism are learned behaviors that can be shaped and developed by the institutions of our society, to the extent that they foster respect for individuals who are different. Situations make a tremendous difference, but so do the traits learned by members of society as they develop and mature into functioning adults.

It is true that millions of German citizens stood by in silence as enemies of the Nazi movement—Jews, Roma, Poles, gays, and the disabled—were sent to death camps. But there were also some striking exceptions. According to sociologist Samuel Oliner,[5] rescuers possessed an exceptionally well-developed sense of personal responsibility to relieve the pain and suffering of others. They believed strongly that persecution of innocent people was unjustifiable. And they saw their parents as virtuous individuals who were accepting of others, even those others who differed in terms of religion, ethnicity, or social status. Their parents had taught them the importance of helping others without expecting to benefit in return. Rescuers were angered when others were harmed. They had friends from diverse ethnic groups and felt themselves as having a good deal in common with human beings generally.

Years ago, researcher Peter London[6] interviewed German Christians who during World War II had helped rescue Jews from their Nazi persecutors. He found three characteristics which were shared by many of these good Samaritans. First, they tended to be adventurous types who had previously taken considerable risks with their personal safety. All of them now risked their lives in order to save the lives of German Jews who would otherwise surely be apprehended by the Nazis and sent to death camps for extermination. Second, most were socially marginal people who hadn't really fit well into the mainstream of German society or who themselves had been victimized in the past. Third, like Oliner's subjects, most of the rescuers had at least one parent who served as a model of altruism and respect for others, an intensely moralistic mother or father with whom the good Samaritan strongly identified.

Both London and Oliner agree that concern for others varies widely depending on the availability of a role model for goodness and decency in the life of an individual. Subsequent studies similarly found identification with a moral parent among civil-rights activists of the 1960s (called Freedom Riders), many of whom had given up their homes and jobs for the sake of playing an active role in civil-rights causes.[7] Moreover, psychologist Michael Barnett and his colleagues discovered the same modeling of a moralistic parent among college students who were extremely concerned about the welfare of other people.[8]

Yad Vashem, the Holocaust Memorial Complex in Jerusalem, was established in 1953 by the Israeli government to commemorate the six million Jews who were slaughtered during the Second World War. In addition to honoring the victims, however, the memorial also recognizes acts of courage by non-Jews who helped Jews to escape Hitler's death camps. The Avenue and the Garden of the Righteous Among the Nations is the part of the complex that consists of two thousand trees containing the name plaques of these good Samaritans as well as another seventeen thousand name plaques engraved on the walls that surround the garden, also honoring individuals for their heroic deeds during the war.[9]

One of the plaques in the garden contains the name of the Japanese consul-general, Chiune Sugihara. At the beginning of the Second World War, when many countries including the United States refused to help Jews escape persecution in Europe, Sugihara rose to the occasion and saved the lives of thousands of Polish Jews by granting them transit visas through Japan on their way to two Dutch colonial islands, Curacao and Dutch Guiana, where formal entrance visas were not required. When some Polish refugees discovered the legal loophole, they came up with a plan to escape from Hitler's Europe. However, they could succeed only with the cooperation of Japanese, Dutch, and Soviet consuls. The Dutch consul, Jan Zwartendijk, secured the permission of his government to stamp refugees' passports with entrance permits, and the Soviet consul agreed to let refugees pass through the Soviet Union if they also had a Japanese transit visa.[10]

When the Japanese government denied his request for permission to grant visas, Sugihara had to make a difficult decision: whether to disobey his superiors or to betray his samurai honor of helping people in need. Sugihara's conscience prevailed, and for twenty-nine days, he and his wife, Yukiko, worked tirelessly writing and signing visas. He stopped only after he was transferred to Berlin. As the story goes, he was still writing visas as his train was pulling out of the station. As a last gesture of Sugihara's goodwill, he gave his visa stamp to a refugee who promised to continue issuing visas. Most of the Polish Jews who were lucky enough to be granted a transit visa ended up in Shanghai, where they stayed until the end of the war. For his disobedience, Sugihara was dismissed from the Japanese Foreign Service and lived in obscurity until he died in 1986. But just before his death, he was recognized for his deeds as "Righteous Among the Nations" by the Yad Vashem. It is believed that there are today more than forty thousand Jews who owe their lives to his acts of courage.[11]

Varian Fry, an American editor from New York, went to France, where she established a French relief organization, the American Relief Center, that succeeded in saving two thousand Jews by providing them with forged documents and safe passage from Nazi-occupied France.[12] Similarly, Englishman Frank Foley who served as a passport control officer in the British Consulate in Berlin saved thousands of Jews by issuing them visas for Palestine, or by providing them with false documentation to flee from Germany.[13]

Following Yad Vashem's example, and in order to recognize individuals for their heroic deeds during wartime, Gabriele Nissim, an Italian historian and essayist of some repute, founded the Garden of the Righteous, a nonprofit organization with branches worldwide.[14] One such garden is being planned for Sarajevo, Bosnia, and Herzegovina. Similar to Yad Vashem in Jerusalem, the concept is for each planted tree to represent a person who risked his or her own life in order to save the victims of prosecution, terror, and violence during the Bosnian war. The founders also have planned to build a Museum of the Righteous in order to collect and preserve the testimonies of those survivors whom the righteous have protected.[15]

The director of Sarajevo's Garden of the Righteous is Dr. Svetlana Broz, cardiologist, journalist, essayist, and the granddaughter of Josip Broz Tito, the former president of Yugoslavia. In addition, she wrote the book *Good People in an Evil Time* in which she recorded ninety stories of how Muslims, Croats, and Serbs helped one another escape death and violence unleashed by the war. Although many of these stories document horrible atrocities, they also offer amazing stories of humanity, decency, and courage. For example, one Muslim survivor explained how his neighbor, a Croat, risked his life to prevent his capture by Croatian military forces. When the Muslim warned his neighbor that his act of courage could easily get him into trouble with authorities and reminded him that he had daughters to take care of, the neighbor replied: "It is because of my daughters. Our children grew up together. For the rest of my life I'd never be able to look them in the eye if I didn't help you now."[16] Similarly, a Muslim woman recounted how her Serbian neighbor who helped her escape certain death was later brutally murdered as a result of his humanitarian actions. In yet another testimony a Serbian soldier recalled how he was saved by a Muslim military unit after having been wounded and left to die by his Serbian comrades.[17]

Such stories inform us that there are certain ordinary people who rise to the occasion when called upon to act in a compassionate and unselfish manner. In such moments, ethnic and racial differences are of little importance. For the good Samaritan, an honorable death is far more important than a dishonorable life.

Although ordinary individuals have been known to make an extraordinary difference, their impact tends to be severely limited by the scope of their personal influence. Knowing this, many altruistic and courageous men and women have banded together in small groups, social movements, and common causes. By acting jointly, they greatly increase the effectiveness of their efforts to rescue victims of atrocities.

For example, the organized efforts against slavery in the United States involved the participation of countless honorable people who formed the abolitionist movement. The most famous was the so-called Underground Railroad that carried thousands of slaves to their freedom in Canada, Mexico, and the Caribbean islands. Although not literally a railroad, the movement used the imagery of a train to capture the courageous efforts of African Americans and their supporters as they helped fugitive slaves escape the inhumane conditions under which they lived. The movement was in essence a loosely connected system of escape routes from slave states in the South. Its most active members were former slaves who risked their lives and freedom to help other slaves to escape. Harriet Tubman, one of the most famous former slaves, for example, traveled back and forth from the North to the South at least nineteen times, guiding more than three hundred slaves to freedom. African Americans were also helped by whites who supported the abolition of slavery and provided blacks with safe houses along the way, as well as money for supplies and food.

The secrecy of the Underground Railroad makes it hard to document the activities of individuals who participated in its operation. It is clear, however, that the railroad was a movement that brought together members of different ethnic, religious, and racial groups to oppose what they believed to be morally wrong. These courageous individuals risked their lives, possessions, and freedom to do the right thing.

The antislavery movement in Texas was supported by an influx of German immigrants, especially during the 1840s and 1850s, whose political, philosophical, and religious views made them not just opposed to slavery, but also compelled them to actively fight against it.[18] Many of these immigrants settled in rural Guadalupe County and towns such as New Braunfels and Fredericksburg. Although most German settlers in Texas supported the Confederacy, there were also many who opposed it and refused to fight on the side of the South during the Civil War.[19]

Altruistic Europeans similarly joined together during World War II in order to reduce Hitler's body count. In August 1943, for example, one heroic man from Denmark heard rumors that the Nazis intended to round up Danish Jews and transport them to death camps. In coordination with his friends on the police force, he organized a group effort to carry Jews in police cars and taxis down to the harbor, where they were ferried to Sweden and freedom. As a result, seven thousand Danish Jews escaped with their lives.[20]

John Rabe, a German businessman living in Nanking, China, worked tirelessly along with his like-minded associates to save thousands of Chinese civilians during the Japanese Imperial Army's six-month siege of the city in 1937–1938. During that period of time, in an invasion known as the Rape of Nanking, hundreds of thousands of Chinese were raped and killed by Japanese soldiers. Although a member of the Nazi Party, Rabe was shocked by the atrocities he observed. Most of the members of the Chinese government and other foreign nationals had already escaped from Nanking prior to the arrival of the Japanese army, but hundreds of thousands of vulnerable residents of the city remained.

Using Hitler's name and his own German status as an ally of Japan, Rabe was able to secure the permission of the Japanese military command for the establishment of an "international zone,"a safe haven for Chinese citizens trying to escape the brutal assaults. Together with other Western residents of Nanking, including other German citizens who decided to remain in the city, Rabe refused to abandon the people he loved in their time of need. It is believed that more than 250,000 people were saved during the four months that the "international zone" was in existence.[21]

On occasion, an entire people has been honored by Yad Vashem as Righteous among the Nations. One such example is the French Protestant village of Le Chambon during World War II. The Chambonais hid Jews in their homes, sometimes for a period of four years, and assisted them to escape to Switzerland. Their spiritual leader, Pastor Andre Trocme, and his wife, Magda, argued that it was their duty to assist their Jewish neighbors, "the people of the Old Testament," in need. Trocme, upon learning of the deportation of Jews from Paris in July 1942, delivered a sermon to his parishioners in which he accused the Christian Church of cowardice in its apathetic response to the plight of Jewish victims of the Nazis. He urged his congregation to provide shelter to any Jew in need. As a result, some five thousand Jews were sheltered from the Nazis.[22]

When ordinary people put aside their differences to work collectively, they can accomplish remarkable humanitarian feats. In October 2000, when Serbian strongman Slobodan Milosevic was ousted, at least one hundred thousand people poured into central Belgrade's Republic Square as a demonstration against the dictator's turbulent thirteen-year rule. What had started years earlier as an inconsequential protest movement of college students known as Otpor (the Serbian word for "resistance") ultimately became a powerful political force that, in profound and pervasive respects, changed Serbian society.

Otpor started as a movement of a few student activists in 1998 who were fed up with Milosevic's regime and wanted to get rid of him. Otpor was not a political party; it did not have a leader; and its members did not support any of the existing political parties. Lacking either an office or supplies, they relied on cell phones for communication. Their political strategy was based on using peaceful resistance, civil disobedience, and grassroots mobilization.[23]

Otpor became more visible after the NATO bombing of Serbia in 1999. Their symbol, the clenched fist, started to appear everywhere. Members started to pass out leaflets critical of Milosevic, and to organize events that looked like entertainment but, in actuality, carried an anti-Milosevic message. For example, during a lunar eclipse the members of Otpor set up several telescopes on the Belgrade streets, which instead of showing a moon eclipse, showed an eclipse of Milosevic.

Over time, Otpor's messages became more and more political. On January 13, 2000, the group organized an outdoor party to celebrate the Orthodox New Year. Thousands of people came to listen to popular music and to have some fun. After midnight, however, the organizers turned off the special New Year's lights to highlight the darkness in which Serbs live. They also read the names of Serbs who were killed during the "Milosevic wars." The night concluded with the message that there was no reason for a celebration until they had deposed Milosevic.

Most Otpor members were young people, eighteen to twenty-four years old. They came of age during the 1990s and were disturbed by the downslide in the quality of their lives and lack of prospects for the future. In order to reclaim their lives and create a better future for themselves and their families, they joined Otpor and worked on organizing protests and demonstrations in their communities with the clear message that Milosevic had to go. As a grassroots organization, Otpor had members in all cities in Serbia and many layers of leadership. In that way, it was hard to destroy the organization; police could not possibly arrest them all.

Otpor also received the support of organizations outside of Serbia. The United States Foreign Aid Office, the Soros Foundation, and the member states of the European Union provided them with the resources to buy equipment and staff their office in Belgrade. The outside support also allowed them to get Internet access which became the major tool of communicating among its members, as well as for securing recruits.

As Otpor gained in numbers and became a more visible force, the Milosevic regime began to take the movement more seriously. It started its attacks by accusing Otpor members of being terrorists, neofascists, drug addicts, and criminals, or lackeys of the United States. The regime also cracked down on the organization and arrested its most visible members. Otpor responded by organizing large demonstrations in front of the prisons, demanding the release of their arrested members. The members were joined by their parents and other residents of their cities.

The most important contribution of Otpor was its ability to mobilize opposition parties in Serbia and to get them to create a coalition that could successfully challenge Milosovic in forthcoming presidential elections. The democratic opposition in Serbia was created by eighteen parties that agreed to support Vojislav Kostunica, a lawyer and the leader of a small opposition party, as their candidate. The survey conducted by US pollsters had shown that Serbian voters were desperately looking for a reason to vote against Milosevic. Up to then, none of the opposition parties had given them effective enough alternative candidates. Opinion polls suggested that Kostunica had the best chance of being elected.

Otpor and the democratic opposition in Serbia organized five major presidential campaigns in support of Kostunica in order to prevent the Milosevic regime from cracking down on them. They also anticipated that the regime would try to steal the election. Thus, they trained over thirty thousand people to be observers in about ten thousand election places. In order to prevent Milosevic from manipulating election results, the opposition organized a communication system for recording and transmitting the results of the vote.[24]

In 1996, Milosevic lost the municipal election and promptly used his power to annul it. Thousands of Serbs took to the streets but were not able to reverse the decision. Slogans such as *Gotov je* (He is finished) and *Slobo, Ubi se i spasi Serbiju* (Slobo, save Serbia; kill yourself!") started to appear everywhere.

As predicted, Vojislav Kostunica won the presidential election. The opposition immediately went public with the results. Milosevic, however, was not ready to accept his defeat. He declared that no candidate had won more than 50 percent of the vote, and thus that there was a need for a runoff election. But Serbs had had enough of Milosevic. Protests started immediately throughout Serbia. Seventeen thousand workers from the Kolubara mines went on strike. They were joined by taxi drivers and bus drivers in cities all over the country who blocked streets and brought life to a standstill. Public disobedience lasted ten days. On the tenth day, convoys of cars from all over Serbia began streaming toward Belgrade. Along the way they confronted the police who had built barricades along the roads to stop them from reaching Belgrade. The police did not, however, defend those barricades, so convoys of citizens, after removing them, continued toward the city.[25]

Opposition leaders made sure that protesters did not use violence against the police. As hundreds of thousands of Serbs marched toward the parliament building, it became clear that the police and the army would not defend Milosevic's regime. They simply could not oppose so many people. Moreover, their own children were among the protesters. In the end, Milosevic was forced to accept defeat and step down. Only two people died, one of a heart attack and another in a traffic accident.[26]

Today, Milosevic has been brought to justice and is facing the War Crime Tribunal in The Hague. Who would have predicted in 1998 that groups of students using nonviolent means of protest would succeed where the power of NATO's military forces had failed in toppling the tyrant?

CHAPTER 12
COOPERATION AND COMMUNITY ACTION

A local Brookline, Massachusetts, gas station is owned and oper-
ated by Israeli immigrant Shimon Cohen. He doesn't run the
station by himself, but employs Mohammad from Afghanistan,
Sher from Pakistan, Kamal from a Palestinian village on the West
Bank, and Nelson from Cape Verde. These five men, who might
under a different set of circumstances avoid one another at any cost,
instead work together on a daily basis, bound by an economic
interest that cuts across their ethnic differences. Over time, they
have learned to trust and rely on each other. But in order to keep
their relations in good standing, they avoid discussing politics.[1]

Social psychologist Gordon Allport[2] argued early on that prejudice was largely a result of ignorance—a lack of shared experience
and knowledge. From this point of view, in order to overcome hate,
the members of opposing groups need to engage in activities that
allow them to gain mutual understanding. This approach became
known as the *contact theory of prejudice*, according to which
increased interaction between members of different groups tends to
decrease the hostility between them.

Of course, not every form of contact leads to improved intergroup relations. During the 1970s, black and white Boston children

were bused to schools outside of their own neighborhoods in order to comply with a court-ordered desegregation plan. Much attention was given to how these youngsters would get to school; little attention was paid to what they would do together when they reached the classroom. The hostility of parents to the desegregation plan was transferred to their offspring. Their children were given almost no guidance in getting along with peers who were different in racial and social-class terms. In the end, the contact between black and white students only reinforced their bigotry. For too many, hate prevailed.

For interaction to work in a positive direction, it needs to be: (1) personal and sustained; (2) involve a cooperative venture; (3) be conducted in a framework of official institutional support; and (4) guarantee equal status between the groups. It is in the process of finding the characteristics we share with other people that we gain opportunities for agreement, conciliation, and the resolution of group conflict.[3]

An appropriate example is provided by the experience of black and white soldiers in the United States military. When in 1948 President Harry S. Truman integrated the army by executive order, he started a process of institutional change that brought white and black soldiers to work cooperatively together on the same tasks toward the fulfillment of shared objectives. Not just contact, but the experience of working together provided them with the opportunity to see one another as human beings as well as fellow soldiers. The interdependence that developed between them made it possible to successfully wage war. The best armies are those in which soldiers work together as a strong unit. Not only did these soldiers fight together against a common foe, but in doing so, their attitudes toward their group's members of other races consequently improved. Today, the US Army remains as the most racially integrated sector of American society.

One of the biggest problems for the United States has long been how to improve its race relations. Hate and bigotry that exist as a consequence of racism can undermine efforts to create a more inclusive society. We saw previously how stereotypes about poor African Americans result in their being feared and further marginalized. To resolve such tensions we need strategies that address problems experienced by the residents of poor neighborhoods who seek to improve their quality of life. One of the most important issues is crime reduction in the inner cities of America. The success of the Boston crime-fighting strategy, we believe, offers a possible model for the nation. It suggests strongly that racially and socially diverse segments of a community can put aside their differences and work together in an effective coalition.

Similar to other large cities, Boston crime soared during the period from 1986 on, reaching its peak in 1990 with 152 homicides.[4] Fear of crime became so pervasive that residents were afraid to go outside after dark. Some put their children in bathtubs rather than in beds in order to protect them from stray bullets.[5] The impoverished neighborhoods of Dorchester, Roxbury, and Mattapan were especially hard hit. As a result of white and middle-class flight to the suburbs and joblessness caused by a decline in industrial production, minority residents became concentrated in these Boston neighborhoods. The exodus of whites who had had ties to local political and economic institutions also led to a decrease in the collective efficacy of local residents to address neighborhood problems.

As morale in the city hit rock bottom in the early 1990s, it was apparent to everyone that something had to be done. What followed was a mobilization of community groups, probation officers, teachers and parents, church leaders, judges and government officials, and business leaders who in partnership with the police created a multipronged strategy to address crime by targeting youthful offenders. The Boston strategy was based on a focused enforcement effort under which the most violent offenders were arrested and sent to prison, while other young and poor African Americans were given help to overcome their poverty.

Traditionally, Boston's police had had a dysfunctional relationship with black community members. But in the aftermath of the Carol Stuart murder in 1989, things went from bad to worse. Looking for the murderer (who turned out to be Carol Stuart's husband), the police used aggressive, even unconstitutional, search tactics whereby they stopped and frisked all black men in proximity to the crime scene. For the minority residents of Boston's poor neighborhoods, the lack of trust between police and residents was a major issue. Residents were seen by the police not as victims, but as potential criminals. The police became regarded by many black Bostonians as an army of occupation rather than as community defenders of the peace.

In the aftermath of the highly visible exposure of illegitimate police tactics, the mayor appointed a commission that investigated the work of the local police and suggested changes that would lead to the appointment of a new police commissioner. The new leadership adopted a community policing strategy which was more decentralized, proactive, and directed toward solving neighborhood problems than the traditional police model. For example, their community policing approach involved the public not just in identifying the local problems, but also in suggesting solutions for them. By encouraging personal contact, law enforcement intended to develop trust between police officers and community residents, especially those living in high crime areas of the city.[6]

In order for this model to work, however, community leaders' attitudes toward police had to change as well. After gang violence spilled into a local black church in May of 1992, local religious leaders realized that they could no longer ignore the violence.

Together with African American clergy who were already active in working with young men on the streets, they founded an organization known as the "Ten Point Coalition."[7] Eventually this coalition grew to the point where it attracted not only local religious leaders, but also leaders from the suburbs. More importantly, the coalition inspired diverse segments of the Boston community in schools, businesses, and families to get involved.

The coalition's main objective was to develop a plan for mobilizing resources for addressing youth problems such as drug abuse and gang involvement by mediating potential conflict, developing economic alternatives to drug dealing, and working with social service agencies and community organizations to offer services to at-risk youth and children. However, the coalition's most important decision was to develop a working partnership with police, probation officers, and other members of the criminal justice community in Boston.

The community and the police thus agreed that the most dangerous youthful offenders had to be incarcerated, whereas youngsters with the potential to change would be offered alternatives to gang activities such as job training, access to jobs, after-school programs, basketball leagues, cultural enrichment programs, and services such as drug counseling. The goal of these programs was to provide young people with skills and opportunities that would make crime-related activities less attractive. Moreover, the Ten Point Coalition leaders continued to monitor the police carefully for any signs of excessive force or brutality.

As a part of their preventive policy, the police also started paying more attention to quality-of-life issues. Public safety was seen as an important element of satisfaction among residents of the community. Addressing issues such as loitering, trash removal, and violation of city codes contributed to improving the social order at the local level. As residents felt safer in their neighborhoods, they also felt more satisfied with their everyday lives. Less fearful residents participated more in local affairs, which had the result of increasing informal social control.

From 1995 to 2001, Boston's safety ranking among the fifty largest cities improved from twenty-eighth to fifteenth.[8] Reported violent crime and attempted crimes went down from its high of 2,380 per one hundred thousand residents in 1990 to 1,250 in 2001.[9] The number of homicide victims decreased, from 26.5 per hundred thousand in 1990 to eleven in 2001. Juvenile murder dropped from thirty-nine committed in 1990 to three perpetrated in 1998.[10]

What was truly remarkable about the Boston model is that it was not only effective in decreasing violence. Many other places succeeded as well. Boston was effective even though it never depended on increasing the prison population. Between 1995 and 2002, the incarceration rate for the United States rose 27.2 percent, but it decreased in Massachusetts by 14.2 percent.[11] The Boston model also strengthened the sense of community in the city: Nearly 80 percent of Boston residents felt "very safe" or "somewhat safe" being out alone at night as well as trusting their neighbors and feeling that they could rely on them for help.[12] And yet reports of police brutality plunged.

The fundamental tenet of the Boston strategy to counteract violence in the city was a collaboration among a wide range of civic and public organizations and agencies—a coalition of black and white Bostonians working closely together for a mutual goal. Rather than confront one another, the police and the community— both white and black— moved together to establish a mutually supportive relationship.

Many programs in societies around the world have been designed to bring people of different ethnic backgrounds together in a spirit of cooperation. The majority of schools in Northern Ireland, for example, although segregated along religious lines, take part in some cross-community activities. Protestant and Catholic youngsters put aside their differences long enough to interact across groups.

Known as "peace-building work," many social service agencies have developed offices for community relations that sponsor various activities, programs, and projects to overcome divisions within society and promote reconciliation between divided parties. An interesting example of developing activities to encourage intergroup cooperation is the organization known as Playing for Peace, founded by Sean Tuohey, an American from Washington, DC. The major goal of this organization is to bring together through the sport of basketball children from opposing sides in areas of major conflict.

Through his organization, Tuohey and his colleagues have already worked with more than ten thousand children in South Africa and two thousand in Northern Ireland to develop intergroup basketball clinics and tournaments. He chose basketball because the game was not claimed by either racial group—black or white—in South Africa or either religious group—Protestant or Catholic—in Northern Ireland. The clinics usually begin with children's free play, at which time they often remain with their own group. However, the formal part of the training is based on getting youngsters to work in mixed groups. As a result, children's excitement for the game often overshadows their differences. After playing for a while, many see only their common humanity.[13]

Another example of the power of cooperation comes from the recent media obsession with reality TV. In April 2002, the most watched current affairs program in Great Britain, *Tonight with Trevor McDonald*, aired a story featuring four Catholic and four Protestant contestants from Northern Ireland who had responded to a newspaper ad calling for volunteers to appear on the television program. All eight were put on the Isle of Man for a week, where a television crew filmed their interactions as they lived together. They participated in mixed-group activities that had been developed by a psychologist, including cooking dinner and solving puzzles in cross-religious pairs and holding roundtable discussions on some aspect of life in Northern Ireland.

The outcome of their activities and discussions was somewhat puzzling. On the one hand, the participants did not have any problem relating to each other as they worked on accomplishing their tasks together. They cooperated in completing jigsaw puzzles and preparing meals; they even bonded over common interests, such as two smokers from opposite groups who shared the details of their addiction and commiserated with one another on the difficulties of giving up the habit.

On the other hand, the after-dinner discussions between Protestants and Catholics quickly revealed the depths of their sectarian differences. During the debates, members of each group tried to advance their own interpretation of the conflict and past events in Northern Ireland with little regard for the position of the other side. After the nightly discussion was over, however, the contestants resumed their intergroup activities, such as playing games and cooking, with ease. It was surprising to producers of the television program that Protestant and Catholic contestants in group activities and ordinary conversations related to each other so well as individuals and were able to develop friendly relationships without changing their opinions about the conflict per se.[14]

This would not be surprising to some critics who argue that the impact of contact between groups can be superficial in nature. Instead, they suggest the use of single-identity work, consisting of educational projects and role-playing programs that engage their participant members solely from one side of the divide. The groups first work separately on developing their members' self-confidence and skills needed in successfully resolving conflicts in general. The participants of those groups can also explore and affirm issues that are related to their own cultural identity. Then, when the members gain enough confidence and skill, they can work with members of opposing groups to address the causes of conflict in their societies and develop possible solutions.

Television can be a powerful tool for preparing groups to cooperate. *Sesame Street*, a popular children's program in the United States produced by the Children's Television Workshop, has as one of its goals to promote tolerance and respect for diversity among American children. In 1999 the show's producer created an Israeli-Palestinian joint television program in Arabic and Hebrew to promote peaceful coexistence. The reasoning was as follows: If children can learn appreciation and respect for diversity at a young age, they may be less likely to develop negative attitudes when they are older. Television programs like this complement other methods of promoting tolerance toward others.

Contact between the opposing groups is not enough, as we've seen, to overcome the hurdles of hate. Another limitation of the contact hypothesis is that individuals may benefit in an economic sense from hate and bigotry as noted earlier. Groups often have unequal power in society. Prejudice justifies one's position of power and allows one group to claim more resources for itself. In Brazil, for example, residents of different racial groups easily interact with each other and even show genuine human warmth toward each other. Still, racism makes it hard for black residents to enjoy the same political, social, and economic opportunities that whites have.[15] In Northern Ireland, some Protestants are not eager to give up their advantaged economic position, even when they number Catholics among their friends.

It seems that the best way to decrease hate and bigotry between the members of groups in deeply divided societies is to integrate their social institutions. What limits healthy contact between the opposing sides is that they live in segregated communities, go to segregated schools, and often even work in segregated workplaces. Many small villages and cities are so ethnically homogeneous that it is possible for residents to live their lives in relative isolation from others who are different. In large cities, however, one is less likely to find homogeneous communities. There is more room for accommodation of diversity, but also for hate violence. Reducing social conflict by means of contact between groups is far from fool-proof. In some instances, the interaction may actually reinforce the stereotypes that the members of one group hold about the other.

Education can play some role, however meager, in developing respect for differences and in learning skills for peaceful conflict resolution. In the 1960s under pressure from young people, Germany started to examine critically its history as part of the school curriculum. Antiwar sentiment among young Germans increased. In Northern Ireland, although most schools there are segregated, the experience of their few integrated schools is encouraging. Some students actually break down the barriers between themselves and fellow students to interact across religious lines. Others adopt a "live and let live" attitude toward students from the opposing group. The existence of integrated schools at all shows that Catholic and Protestant children can at least potentially learn together.

Notwithstanding such successes, few researchers continue to assert that the substance of formal education represents a powerful instrument for the reduction of hate and hostility between groups. In a 1969 study in the United States, sociologists Gertrude Selznick and Stephen Steinberg found an inverse relationship between anti-Semitism and amount of education, a relationship that could not be explained by differences in social class.[16] Yet results claiming to show the impact of education on hate are extremely difficult to interpret and may demonstrate only that the educated members of our society have learned to express their prejudices publicly in subtle, more sophisticated, ways—especially on the paper-and-pencil questionnaires generally employed by social science researchers. Moreover, historical examples simply fail to support the connection between education and intergroup hate. The residents of Nazi Germany, for example, represented one of the best-educated populations in the history of the world, yet bigotry and violence prevailed.

Rather than examine the content of education, it may be useful to analyze the structure of schooling. Behavioral scientists have long recognized that the structure of American education depends on strategies that reinforce academic and athletic performance: Students tend to be encouraged to exceed the achievement levels of classmates and friends. Competition is emphasized, while personal improvement tends to be ignored. Being the best you can be is less important than doing better than the rest of the class. High schools in the United States give each student a number as his or her placement standing. Learning that competitive skills are highly valued, they have their competitive edge for interpersonal comparisons (for example, "grading on the curve" and percentile scoring). But it is not only academic achievement that pits one student against another. At the high-school level and again in college, there is also intense competition for popularity, status, financial assistance, organizational budgets, internships, jobs, and acceptance by the more prestigious colleges.

As we have seen, enclaves of peace and tolerance allow for areas in which the members of various groups put aside their differences to cooperate rather than compete. Where intergroup relations work in a positive way, there is almost always a large degree of interdependence. In some cases, members of different groups cooperate formally in political leadership and organizational memberships. In other cases, members of different groups become close friends and neighbors. In either case, they find that people who are different from one another need one another. They cooperate, collaborate, encourage, and support. Rather than treat one another as the enemy, they depend on each other as allies and friends.

In an early study, social psychologist Elliott Aronson and his associates[17] created what they called a *jigsaw teaching technique*, whereby fifth graders participated in a small experimental classroom. Each child was sorted into a racially integrated learning group and given a piece of information that had to be shared with classmates in order to put the puzzle together. The key ingredient was that students in the learning group were forced to depend on one another in order to complete their group project and to receive a grade. They were interdependent in two ways: first, students were purposely structured around the goal of getting a good grade in the class, so that when one student gained, all of them gained. Second, their efforts were shared, so that they had to work together in order to achieve their goal. They taught one another; they shared information with one another. Cooperation rather than competition was their only means for achieving a good grade in the course. After using his jigsaw method for a period of six weeks, Aronson measured any changes in the attitudes of students toward one another. As compared with children in traditional competitive classrooms, fifth graders in his jigsaw groups liked their black and white classmates better, had more positive attitudes toward school, had better self-esteem, and performed just as well on their exams.

Even outside the classroom, working toward a shared goal has been known to bring together disparate members of a community. In the aftermath of the vicious 1998 murder of James Byrd in Jasper, Texas, the community's reactions showed social responsibility. The three white supremacists who were eventually convicted of Byrd's murder—John King, Lawrence Brewer, and Shawn

Berry—had beaten the African American hitchhiker until he was unconscious, and then chained him to their pickup truck and dragged him down the road for more than two miles to his death. Investigators discovered a Ku Klux Klan manual among the possessions carried by one of the assailants; and two of them had white supremacist body tattoos depicting the Confederate Knights of America. The killers were definitely ardent admirers of the Klan and used white supremacist propaganda and proudly identified themselves with white supremacy symbols of power.

Given the history of racism in the Deep South, it might seem that the brutal murder of a black resident in a small and impoverished southern town would precipitate a melee or a riot. Yet, rather than divide the community on racial grounds, the murder of James Byrd actually served to bring the black and white residents of Jasper together. In the aftermath of the slaying, townspeople reported going out of their way to cross racial lines in greeting residents and feeling a new street-level friendliness toward members of the other race.[18]

Just as in many other southern communities, blacks and whites in Jasper had not always been sympathetic toward one another.[19] The legacy of Jim Crow segregation continued to color the informal relations between blacks and whites, keeping them apart in their everyday lives. One issue which had long symbolized the community's struggle with race relations was the town's cemetery, where a fence down the middle separated whites buried on one side from blacks buried on the other. After Byrd's murder, however, the town came to an agreement to integrate its cemetery. Many residents of Jasper, black and white, joined together to pull out the posts and tear down the fence.[20]

The political leaders in Jasper had strong credibility among both its black and its white residents. The local government had long been racially integrated. Black residents who comprised 45 percent of the town's population occupied the position of mayor, two of the five city council positions, and the directorship of the Deep East Texas Council of Governments. In addition, school principals and the administrator of the largest hospital were black. Even in the almost total absence of interracial friendships, blacks and whites in Jasper had developed a tradition of cooperating at a formal level.

Jasper's leadership inspired new areas of reconciliation and nonviolence. The community's white sheriff went out of his way to encourage confidence among black residents in the aftermath of Byrd's slaying. Within twenty-four hours, he had arrested two suspects and then immediately requested the assistance of the FBI. Moreover, Jasper's local 6,000-watt radio station kept residents informed in an evenhanded way about developments related to the murder and the trials, ensuring that racially dangerous rumors and anxieties never had an opportunity to spread.[21]

Jasper, Texas, represented a source of community pride for black and white residents alike; all of them felt a common bond to the town that transcended racial differences. Even extremists on both sides of the racial ledger were genuinely embarrassed by the cruelty and sadism of James Byrd's murder. They seemed to unite across racial lines against the very strong stigma imposed on their community by members of the outside world. Interracial unity was possible because many of the town's formal organizations had already brought together representatives of both groups who were accustomed to working together.[22]

In divided communities where intergroup violence can and often does rip apart the fabric of social relations, it is difficult to sustain ties of friendship between the members of different racial or ethnic groups. Even intergroup marriages may not survive in places with extreme hostility, because of the absence of support from either side. In order to protect themselves from violence, people often choose to live in segregated circumstances. The avoidance of the members of other groups decreases the contact between them and consequently the possibility for conflict to develop. Thus, in many places, walls make good neighbors.

The historic divisions between blacks and whites in Jasper, Texas, all but eliminated any chance that its residents would, in the short term, establish friendships across racial lines. The "glue" that held together the community consisted of a sharing of formal leadership functions that made residents, regardless of their racial background, feel a sense of identification with Jasper rather than with only the white or only the black segment of the town. Thus, a precedent for interracial cooperation had long existed.

Even in deeply divided societies like Northern Ireland, where terrorism continues to threaten the residents in everyday life, there are examples of interpersonal contact across group lines. Catholics and Protestant may live in segregated neighborhoods, but some of them drink in the same pubs or share the use and management of some of the same local facilities and programs.[23]

In general, middle-class communities seem to be more likely to have cross-ethnic clubs or religious organizations whose activities cut across religious barriers than the communities where poor people live. In middle-class communities residents often actively participate in organizations such as golf and tennis clubs, business organizations, and cultural clubs that address their common social, economic, and cultural needs and concerns for the community at large.

One such community in Northern Ireland is Dunville.[24] In this community, a common infrastructure allows Catholics and Protestants to coexist, and consequently to protect themselves from communal violence. Dunville's middle-class residents own their homes in integrated neighborhoods. Also, Catholic business families are actively involved in the commercial life of the town and are engaged in mutually beneficial relationships with Protestant businesses. It is not contact per se, but a common interest in maintaining their business success that has led Catholics and Protestants there to negotiate potentially divisive issues such as the routes of political demonstrations in order to keep the peace.[25]

The members of both religious groups in Dunville share local shops and offices. Both Catholics and Protestants, for the most part, use the same local pubs, clubs, and recreational facilities as community amenities. Although the local newspaper supports a Protestant, unionist agenda, it makes an effort to also reach a Catholic audience by reporting Gaelic football matches and is consequently read by Catholics as well. The existence of business ties across groups has led to the development of affective relationships among some of the residents who have participated in, across religious lines, each other's christenings, marriages, and wakes.

Interdependence between groups can help to inoculate a community against hate violence. Even in the war-torn relationship between Israelis and Palestinians, pockets of peace and tolerance exist where members of the conflicting groups have worked together in harmony and peace. Such a relationship was present in the experiences of a modern Israeli Jewish settlement known as Kibbutz Metzer, a collective farm that was founded in 1953 by middle-class Argentinian Jews, who had fled the rule of Juan Perón to build a utopian egalitarian community on Israeli soil. Their leaders were not looking to promote violence between Arabs and Jews. They sought to be good neighbors and friends.[26]

Then, on November 10, 2002, the brutal murder overnight of five members of Kibbutz Metzer by a Palestinian gunman shocked the residents of this Jewish settlement into recognizing the harsh reality of ethnic conflict in the wider society. The victims included a mother and her two young sons, who were shot to death while she was reading them a bedtime story. One of the children was sucking on his pacifier when he was gunned down.[27]

In the early years, the founders of Kibbutz Metzer relied on nearby Arabs for the basics of their survival. For example, their closest Arab neighbors in Maisir village allowed the Jewish settlers to share a pump for drawing their water. In return, Kibbutz Metzer's nurse assisted the Maisir villagers with their healthcare needs. By the time of the atrocity in 2002, the residents of Metzer and Maisir were permanently sharing a common water source.[28]

Over the years, cooperation and friendship between the five hundred members of Kibbutz Metzer and their Arab neighbors increased generally. Palestinian children visited the kibbutz to play football and see the farm animals with their Jewish friends. Arab parents attended the weddings and funerals of their Jewish neighbors. Members of the collective farm strongly supported the establishment of an independent Palestinian state.

After the attack on the Jewish settlement, Arab residents of Maisir village paid condolence visits to families of the victims. Members of Kibbutz Metzer held a meeting to come to grips with the terrorist attack. They lit candles and visited the scene of the tragedy.

The kibbutzniks finally came to the conclusion that peaceful coexistence was the only effective path to Israeli security. Rather than incite calls for revenge, the killings only reinforced in the minds of members of the kibbutz the need to maintain friendly relations with their Arab neighbors. The Palestinian residents of Maisir Village concurred.

Of course, members of the kibbutz were hardly able to control the reaction of Israeli and Palestinian leaders in the larger scheme of things.

The al-Aqsa Martyrs Brigades, the military branch of Yasser Arafat's Fatah faction, claimed responsibility for the deadly attack.

Israeli military officials warned that they would retaliate for the murders.

Speaking in English to the international media, Arafat condemned the massacre. But in an Arabic broadcast, he justified the attack as retaliation for Israel's shooting of two terrorists who were in the process of committing a suicide bombing.

Israeli government spokesperson Avi Pazner rejected the Palestinian condemnation and placed the blame on the Palestinian Authority.

Israeli Defense Minister Shaul Mofaz said that he would seek government approval for a military response.

And then, Israel retaliated by taking over the West Bank town of Nablus, arresting at least thirty Palestinians, and raiding the Tukarem refugee camp, not far from Kibbutz Metzer.[29]

Reactions to the murders at Kibbutz Metzer highlight the limitations that small groups of extraordinary individuals can expect to have on a conflict that originates in the larger society. Peace and tolerance are not likely to spread to the larger group unless the major differences of a political and economic nature can be resolved. At the same time, the experiences of Kibbutz Metzer provide a glimmer of hope in what at this juncture has become an increasingly dark and disappointing state of affairs in the Middle East.

CHAPTER 13
WOMEN AS PEACEMAKERS

Throughout history, women have resisted oppression. Even in Germany during the Second World War, a movement of women defied Hitler's final solution. In February 1943, in an attempt to rid Berlin of its Jews, the Gestapo arrested some ten thousand Jewish residents. Among them were two thousand Jews who were married to German women. When their wives heard of their husbands' detention, they went to the collection center demanding their release. Day after day, the women gathered in protest, withstanding the Gestapo's acts of harassment, intimidation, and threat. In response to a vigil lasting seven days, the Gestapo feared the possibility of further public outrage and decided to let the men go.[1]

Community-based movements and organizations provide an important base for developing cooperation and strengthening civic participation between opposing groups. In societies divided by ethnic conflict, some groups led by women have represented a significant resource for building peace. Women's organizations have typically fallen outside the main institutional spheres and have thus enjoyed greater flexibility in practice because of their outsider's status.

Thus Palestinian and Israeli women have had a far easier time meeting and discussing peace issues than have men. Bat Shalom, Israel's National Women's Peace Organization, is one such group that promotes peace. The members come from neighboring Palestinian villages and Jewish kibbutzim around the town of Nazareth. Their primary activity is facilitating the connection between women from both sides in order to explore the possibilities for peaceful coexistence. Members also organize several cultural and educational events alternating the location between villages and kibbutzim.[2] There are other peace organizations in Israeli, such as Gush Shalom and Ta'ayush (a word in Arabic that means "living together," "life in common"). Many of their actions are oriented toward strengthening relationships between Arabs and Jews. They have sponsored activities such as paving a road or building a playground in a Palestinian village, or bringing food and medicine to villages that are under military blockade. Even though the current political situation makes it nearly impossible for such groups to continue their work, their members continue to be committed to the peace process.

At least at the local level, women's groups such as these are apt to behave in a less bureaucratic manner and to value keeping their diverse memberships together over adhering strictly to a set of founding principles or procedural rules. One such example is the Center for Women War Victims in Zagreb, Croatia. Founded in 1993, its central function was to provide financial help to refugee women from Bosnia. It was soon obvious, however, that the organization also needed to offer counseling as well as political and moral support to its female clients.

The work of the center then became complicated by an outbreak of violence between Croatian and Muslim forces in Bosnia. The Muslim refugees became enemies of the Croatians. Thus the center found itself fighting for refugee women's rights and preventing their deportation.[3]

Certain characteristics of grassroots organizations, nonprofit organizations, and nongovernment organizations give them an advantage in peacemaking activities. Being independent of government, such groups have more inclusive and flexible structures, providing the basis for their members to learn how to cooperate and compromise. Therefore, women can and often do bring everyday human relations' skills into peacemaking organizations, allowing them to build on each others' connections as they interact in their communities.

Organizational activities, among all members, are essential to the process of creating a sense of community that goes beyond the one-sided emphasis on one group over the other. They also deal with the community at large. These activities might include initiating after-school programs, conducting conflict resolution classes, and doing charitable work. The group dynamic that results puts the emphasis on the connectedness of its members, their everyday needs, and their interpersonal relationships, rather than on obtaining political positions for the individuals involved or on enhancing their personal status. This approach strengthens women's ties to the community and further builds their social, and potentially political, networks. But it also may mitigate against their being nominated to fill positions of institutional power when these become available. Being regarded as not totally loyal, they are often locked out of formal political and economic roles within the group, but they also make the most of their informal roles across groups.

Although community-based organizations used to be on the margins of society, they are increasingly being seen as vital players in shaping civil society.[4] Similarly, because women's organizations have less access to official resources, their members have learned to make creative use of available resources. Women invest in the social and friendship networks available to them through their organizational affiliations to gain information, know-how, and support. These networks allow for grassroots mobilization and coalition-building in times of crisis.

Some of these organizations also use as resources women's traditional roles and cultural positions in society, family, and community. Especially in Latin America, women have been able to tap into cultural and religious images of the Virgin Mary in order to create a political space from which to claim their human rights. In Argentina, the Mothers of the Plaza de Mayo and the Grandmothers of the Plaza de Mayo have not only shown tremendous courage in the face of danger, but have also broken a conspiracy of silence by exposing the hypocrisy of a military junta that would pose as the defender of family and tradition.[5] Also, in Israel and Yugoslavia, Women in Black's silent presence on the corners of the major streets made it all but impossible for their fellow citizens to ignore the deleterious consequences of war. Sometimes women just meet to listen to each other's story, to recount the terror that they experienced, or to discuss the rage that they feel over what happened to them and their families. Thus, they become sounding boards for each other.

A good example of women organizing for peace building is Women's Support Network in Northern Ireland.[6] This organization consists of a network of community centers that were established in the 1980s in the Catholic and Protestant working-class neighborhoods of Belfast. Through the network, women saw an opportunity to have their voices heard and their interests expressed in the peace process, state policy, and international-funding programs.

The impetus for the development of community centers in Northern Ireland came from two sides: the community development movement and the women's movement. For a long time, women have experienced poverty, have suffered from sectarian and domestic violence, and have felt politically marginalized—because of their gender—across religious lines. Thus the goal of the centers was to use community development strategies to address problems that women faced whether Catholic or Protestant.

The centers started by first providing women from opposing groups opportunities to get to know one another better and to break down misconceptions that they might have held about members of the opposing group. They also worked on broadening women's understanding of differences in general in order to create a more accepting environment. They were aware that to bring women from opposing sides together, it was important first to show inclusion and respect for all people involved. Therefore, they built a democratic governing structure that gave all women an equal voice. Their motto: "What you think, say and do is more important than what you 'are.'"[7]

It is worth noting that most of these activities had an instrumental goal. As one of the participant's stated, women came together not out of friendship, but "because a common goal or common cause was stronger than the fear of personal risk involved in moving out of safe familiar territory and across onto enemy terrain."[8] In many instances, the connection was their shared concern for women and children, their distaste for violence, and their common poverty and marginality.

As more and more women participate in gender-based intergroup networks, they make outside contacts which create space for dialogue among women who find themselves on opposing sides of ethnic conflicts. During troubled times, Kosovo and Serbian women were able to engage in a dialogue because they were members of such networks and because they shared a feminist framework of understanding. Similar examples can be found among Somali women of different clans, Hindu and Muslim women in India, and Jewish and Arab women. As Radha Kumar[9] reports, networks of women are often the only ones that can survive the devastation of civil society in civil war. During conflict in the former Yugoslavia, women's organizations continued to cooperate and share experiences and strategies as they dealt with increases in violence brought by the war. They provided counseling and medical services to rape victims across ethnic lines. They also created alliances among other peace and human service organizations in order to push for recognition of rape as a war crime.

In many instances, women work hard to prevent violence. For example, in one Indian city where some angry Muslim youths wanted to attack Hindus, Muslim women formed a human chain outside the mosque where the youngsters had been attending a prayer meeting. Their intention was not only to prevent young people from going on a rampage, but also from clashing with the police. The women were members of a grassroots organization containing both Muslim and Hindu members that worked on addressing social problems faced by both ethnic communities. The women worked together to address poverty, to create schools and vocational programs for young people, and to provide loans and training for women who sought to start their own businesses.[10]

What helps resolve conflict and prevent violence? The existence of civic connections across ethnic and religious lines seems to create a more democratic social context and infrastructure in which women and men have room for action to address communal tensions in a constructive way. Sociologists and political scientists refer to these resources as *social capital*. The presence of social capital—networks and existence of common norms—makes it possible for community residents to act together effectively to address their shared goals.[11]

Women's organizations may lead, in several ways, in contributing to the peace and stability of their society. The first contribution involves the choice of issues they address. Women-led organizations emphasize the importance of addressing problems that affect the well-being of all residents at the local level such as community development and the provision of local services. They also create spaces for residents from opposing sides to sit down together and talk. By bringing essential issues to community meetings, they give people a chance to come together, to exchange ideas, and to forge relationships. Over time these interactions lead to the creation of shared community norms and goals, and allow for the development of trust between disparate community residents. The existence of shared norms and trust, in turn, facilitates the creation of networks that can serve as a basis for social, civic, or political activities that are crucial for democratic participation.

The second contribution involves the democratic decision-making process. Women-led organizations, like many other community-based groups, seem to put more emphasis on the inclusion of all members in the decision-making process. Collaborative leadership is the opposite of the male model in which elected office is on the career path to individual advancement.

The third contribution derives from women's smaller investment in conflict. While war disrupts the lives of both men and women, to some men it also offers new career opportunities. They might become leaders of military or paramilitary organizations, engage in smuggling operations, or secure new positions in provisional governments. As soldiers, of course, men are more likely than women to die in battles. Yet women and children may even be at greater risk, representing a large number of civilian casualties. Since the Second World War, 80 percent of all casualties have been civilians.[12]

A potential settlement agreement often jeopardizes these new endeavors for some men, whereas in periods of armed conflict, women suffer a disruption of services, a shortage of necessary resources, the loss of men's contributions to the household, as well as an ever present and agonizing concern for the safety of their children. Because, in general, they do not have access to the opportunities to gain from war, they will again be less likely to invest themselves personally in the conflict. Therefore women, in most cases, have been more receptive to seeking peaceful solutions to conflict and to turn to compromise and cooperation as tools to achieve them.

The fourth contribution of women-led organizations is that women's participation in these organizations can increase their economic and political role, which leads to greater gender equality. This is important because societies that have greater gender equality are less likely to engage in military conflict. However, the problem for women is that in peacetime they are often pushed back into their homes and out of the more public roles that they have assumed during an armed conflict. To assure that hate and violence do not reappear, it is therefore of the utmost importance that progress toward tolerance and peace be institutionalized over the long term. Also, it would be productive to instill mechanisms in the government that will ensure that women will continue to participate.

Thus, women's organizations represent a significant component of peace-building and peace-sustaining activities. They often add to the establishment of civic institutions in societies that have been engaged in fighting and bloodshed for many years. In order for peace, reconciliation, and coexistence between people of different ethnic groups to work, women and men have to also rebuild their communities so that residents have jobs, children can safely go to school, and normal social activities can resume.

CHAPTER 14
SOCIETIES THAT RESIST HATE AND VIOLENCE

As we have seen, the emergence of a good Samaritan, someone who is willing to risk his life to rescue vulnerable victims, is in part an individual phenomenon, rooted in the personality character- istics and family influences of that person. In addition, however, the willingness of an ordinary person to assist those being persecuted depends just as much on the characteristics of his community and his society. The impulse to act honorably tends to be realized in a population where there is a history of tolerance in the culture that can be taught from one generation to the next; the leadership does not see any benefit to promoting or sustaining intergroup violence; the victim's group is not regarded widely as posing a threat to sur- vival, values, or the economy; and interdependence between groups exists, either formally or informally.

The absence of such social factors explains why relatively small numbers of German Christians came forward to rescue their Jewish neighbors from Hitler's final solution. First, instead of a tradition of tolerance, there were numerous precedents in German history for rampant anti-Semitism. During the seventeenth and eighteenth cen- turies, Jews held only a marginal position in the social structure of the larger German society, having no citizen rights or legal protections and being widely despised and persecuted by the German people.[1] Anti-Semitism had long been part of German culture.[2]

Second, Hitler's regime benefited greatly by holding Jews responsible for all of Germany's economic woes. Anti-Semitism was exploited by leaders who were able to locate a vulnerable scapegoat in their midst. They were able to convince ordinary German citizens that the Fatherland would be far better off by eliminating the Jewish enemy.

Third, German Jews were widely regarded as a threat to the economy. The concentration of Jews in commerce and finance as well as in upper-middle-class professions was seized on to target Jews as a menace to the economic well-being of the nation. Moreover, religious Jews and Jewish immigrants from eastern Europe looked different, emphasizing the social and cultural gap between them and their Christian neighbors.

Finally, Christians and Jews lived side by side, but few were close friends. Many Jews resided in predominantly Jewish neighborhoods and attended Jewish schools. In addition, the concentration of Jews in certain areas of the economy assured that few would have cooperative relations with non-Jews.

At the other end of the continuum is the eastern European nation of Bulgaria. It has long demonstrated a collective inclination to choose peace and tolerance over hate and violence. Most obviously— notwithstanding its proximity to the former Yugoslavia, a potentially explosive ethnic mix, and an impoverished economy— Bulgaria represents the only country in the Balkans that has escaped serious internal conflict. Moreover, Bulgaria has a track record of ethnic tolerance that dates back at least to its Nazi alliance during World War II, when the Bulgarian people resisted Hitler's efforts to send Bulgarian Jews to death camps. Of course, Bulgaria has also had its share of ethnic conflict (for example, with Turks and Roma), but it has also managed, in most instances, to resolve its hostilities in a peaceful manner.

In 1943, the citizens of Bulgaria, whose own king was a staunch ally of the Nazis, saved the lives of almost fifty-thousand Jewish citizens who awaited the trains that would have carried them to the death camp Treblinka. The Bulgarian King, Boris III, had already sent eleven thousand Jews from occupied territories to their death, but his Bulgarian subjects would tolerate no more.

Thanks to the presence of Nazism, by 1943 there were no longer Bulgarian Jews in places of importance, and none in the assembly, press corps, diplomatic corps, officers' corps, state police apparatus, teaching corps, or civil service. Yet influential Christian groups in society—the physicians and lawyers, the academics and writers, and the church leaders—confronted the government many times in order to fight with complete commitment against anti-Jewish measures.[3]

Those Bulgarians who participated in public affairs sought to use whatever influence they had. They wrote letters of protest, made numerous telephone calls, and engaged in debates in the assembly. The Union of Lawyers vociferously cited an article in the Bulgarian constitution, in which all individuals were regarded as equal under the law. The leadership of the Bulgarian Orthodox Church pointed to the "words of our Savior in whose eyes all are children of one heavenly Father."[4] The Bulgarian Writers' Union reminded Bulgarians of their own victimization under the Turks. Assembly members emphasized the suffering of the victims, that they were surely to be transported not to labor camps, but to their certain death.

Most important, Bulgarian Christians organized at a grassroots community level to convince the leadership of Bulgarian society that its Jews should not be deported. There were protests from influential bishops in the Bulgarian Orthodox Church and from the professional organizations of doctors, lawyers, and authors. A bill was introduced in parliament by its vice president to ignore Hitler's decree.

Yet the impetus for tolerance originated in the minds and hearts of ordinary people. Many average Bulgarian Christians chose to wear the yellow Star of David, a symbol that was required by law of its Jewish citizens to wear in order to identify them for deportation. Many average citizens tore down Nazi flags flying from public buildings. Many others risked their lives to protect Jewish Bulgarians from anti-Semitic gangs.

Never seeing them as constituting a personal threat, average Bulgarians simply could not conceive of their Jewish friends and neighbors as evil wrongdoers and did not understand Hitler's struggle against the Jewish population of Europe. First, like their neighbors, the Bulgarian Jews were dispersed throughout the social structure. Many had low-paying jobs and lived in poor Bulgarian neighborhoods. Unlike their counterparts in other European countries, very few Bulgarian Jews were moneylenders, bankers, or owners of large businesses. The Bulgarian Jews didn't cluster around upper-middle-class professions such as doctors, lawyers, professors, or reporters. Instead, they held socioeconomic positions much like their Christian and Muslim counterparts, playing roles in a wide range of occupations including small-grain merchants, retail tradesmen, maids, pushcart vendors, laborers, authors, poets, factory workers, dentists, composers, pharmacists, artists, engineers, and musicians.

Second, though maintaining their religious identity, the Bulgarian Jews were structurally and culturally assimilated, having many intimate friends and acquaintances among their Christian and Muslim neighbors and looking almost exactly like other Bulgarians. Hasidic Jews did not exist; most Jews did not wear yarmulkas (skullcaps), eat Kosher food, or attend Saturday services; only rabbis wore beards. Jews didn't live in ghettos. All of them—even those who were familiar with Ladino, the Judeo-Spanish dialect of their ancestors—spoke Bulgarian. In sum, for many Bulgarians, the

Jews "were like everybody else." Thus, in terms of socioeconomic status and cultural values, Bulgarian Jews were hardly regarded as a threat to the population of Christians and Muslims.[5]

The absence of any Jewish Bulgarians in formal organizations during the critical period when their fate was being negotiated precluded the possibility of Christians and Jews cooperating in any formal sense. Thus, it required a grassroots community movement to convince the leadership of Bulgarian society that its Jews should not be deported, and they came through.

According to Jacky and Lisa Comforty in their documentary film *The Optimists*, Bulgarian Christians, Muslims, and Jews had lived side by side for hundreds of years, prior to Nazi Germany making its influence felt across Europe. Through the centuries, religious groups in Bulgaria coexisted in relative peace, friendship, and harmony. As depicted in *The Optimists*, for example, Mordechai Arbel, one of the almost fifty thousand Bulgarian Jews who escaped Hitler's final solution, articulated just how much Jews and Christians crossed ethnic lines in their friendships: "Actually, I didn't know who was Jewish and who was not Jewish because the non-Jewish friends participated actively in the Jewish holidays and we participated very actively in the Bulgarian holidays. So we knew that in this and this house, they do it the Bulgarian way, and in this and this house they did it the Jewish way. But the company was mixed, and there were no real differences." A Jewish Bulgarian woman in the film added, "Most of my girlfriends were Bulgarian Christians and they treated me like a sister. There was no isolation from society. On the contrary, you felt embraced by society."[6]

The Bulgarian example is especially meaningful because it illustrates that human beings *are* able to confront and organize against even horrific cases of hate and violence. Actually, the fact that the Nazis had to work so hard to separate Jews from non-Jews shows that hate toward this minority was not natural among the masses, but orchestrated from the top. First, the Nazi government had to distinguish who was a Jew and who was not, and then to develop laws and regulations that effectively separated the two groups. It was not some kind of inborn instinct, but widespread fear of punishment that kept people from interacting with each other. At some point in the process of eliminating Jews from their society, Christian Bulgarians declared that "enough is enough," and rebelled against the dictates of Nazi authority.

Cooperative formal relations between Bulgaria's Jewish and Christian populations would have been all but eliminated by Hitler's decrees restricting Jewish participation in the political and economic life of the nation. Saving Bulgarian Jews from the Nazis depended almost exclusively on the power of friendship and neighborliness that was both authentic and profound.

The conflict between Hindus and Muslims in Kashmir, India, has made ethnic violence in this South Asian country highly visible to observers around the world. The Hindu-Muslim cleavage widened dramatically after the separation of Pakistan from India in 1947 and continued to grow through the 1990s. Although limited to certain areas, the ethnic riots that have periodically broken out in Indian communities have resulted in great losses to both life and property. In addition, rioting has spawned a rise of nationalistic political parties that have further radicalized the Hindu and Muslim local populations.

In his research in India, however, Ashutosh Varshney[7] was able to identify certain Indian localities in which residents successfully resisted the push toward intergroup violence. He attributes the absence of violence between Hindus and Muslims in such communities to the existence of formal ties between residents who come from different ethnic or religious groups in order to pursue a variety of shared goals. These formal ties are forged through civic organizations which occupy the space between the government and private family life in promoting public activities and common interests. Although friendships are important for maintaining integrated communities, Varshney argues, it is formal intergroup organizations that are more effective because of their greater resilience to outside threats. These formal ties are, moreover, substantially absent from those communities in which intergroup violence has occurred on a large scale.

In Calicut, a town in the southern state of Kerala, for example, Hindu, Muslim, and Christian residents live in integrated communities which are connected by their joint participation in formal organizations such as business groups, labor unions, professional associations, as well as social and cultural organizations. Calicut's Muslim population represents about 37 percent of the town's population, and over the last twenty years has made steady progress in joining the town's middle class. Muslims in Calicut have a strong ethnic identity. But this identity has not led to the development of separatist political activities. On the contrary, the Muslim League is a partner in local government and is able to use its position to provide benefits for its constituency such as state pensions for Muslim clerics and contracts for Muslim businessmen. The Muslim politicians in Calicut benefit from the stability of their community and are thus less likely to use divisive nationalistic strategies to create animosity.[8]

Muslims, Hindus, and Christians in Calicut have many points of cooperation in both formal and informal settings. In a survey conducted by Varshney, 83 percent of respondents reported that they eat with members of other religious groups in social settings, 90 percent reported that their children play together, and 84 percent reported that they visit each other regularly. In addition, the residents of Calicut participate across religious lines in activities of many civic organizations and associations such as trade associations, Lions and Rotary Clubs, and reading and art clubs.

Calicut's economy is based on merchandise trade, and most of the traders and workers belong to one of the many trade associations and trade unions in the community. Historically, relationships among merchants were based on trust and did not require formal contracts. The trade associations have members from all religious groups. For example, in 1995, eleven out of twenty-six trade associations registered with the Federation of Traders Associations had Hindu, Muslim, and Christian officeholders: If the president of the association was from one community, the general secretary was from another.[9] Similarly, the members of the largest trade unions come from all religious groups. They might join political organizations within their own ethnic group, but when it comes to protecting their labor rights and wages, they join the organizations that they think will represent them best.

One of the explanations for the existence of interdependence between Muslims and Hindus in Calicut is that the caste differences among residents were perceived by Hindus as more important than their religious differences. Because it was historically organized around issues of social justice, the political life of Calicut allowed Hindus and Muslims to forge common bonds around shared social and economic interests. The Muslims were seen by Hindus as another caste that was put down by the upper-crust Brahmins. Caste divisions thus overshadowed religious divisions. (Of course, this could be seen as its own form of prejudice.)

When religious tensions in the wider society reached Calicut, the residents were able to resist taking a "divide and conquer" political and economic stance by creating city-level peace committees that focused on what was viewed as good for the community as a whole. The political leaders of both groups, Muslims and Hindus, joined these committees and helped maintain peace. Moreover, the peace committees managed ethnic tensions by becoming a source of accurate information to counter any rumors circulating in the town that might otherwise have threatened the peace. Such formal organizations became a forum for everybody to speak up and express their anger. All the major players had a sense of participation on an equal footing; and they provided links all the way down to the neighborhood level.[10]

Locating societies that have managed, in the midst of violence, to maintain peaceful relations between opposing groups is by no means an easy task. Very few exemplars exist in the historical record. Yet there are some significant exceptions—societies where ordinary residents have ignored the violence that surrounds them to live in peace and harmony with their neighbors who are different from them.

We recognize that the effectiveness of contact depends on the quality of the interaction between groups. Not all forms of contact bring peace. Indeed, bringing warring parties together in a spirit of competition only emphasizes that they are opponents rather than allies and that the differences separating them might never be bridged. It is much more effective for reducing hate and violence to bring the group members together so that they can cooperate in the pursuit of shared objectives. In the case of Bulgaria, Christians and Jews were interdependent emotionally as good friends and neighbors. In Calicut, India, Muslims and Hindus depended on one another as members of integrated civil organizations and commerce. In both instances, the vulnerable group was not considered a threat but an asset to the entire community, and not seen as an opponent for scarce resources but a valuable ally.

CHAPTER 15
ENDING HATE AND VIOLENCE

Ordinary citizens, in general, don't support a policy advocating hate and violence based purely on their abstract notions regarding members of another group. They ask themselves: How will this policy or program affect my close friends and neighbors, the people in my life whom I love and care about? How will this policy or program affect my economic well-being? If this policy is passed, will my family gain or lose?

We suggest that peace in the midst of intergroup violence is most likely to be achieved and maintained in the presence of the following four factors: (1) a history of tolerance in the culture of the groups involved; (2) a leadership that does not see benefit in promoting intergroup violence; (3) a widespread belief that the groups do not necessarily pose a threat to one another; and (4) interdependence, either formally or informally.

In explaining the incredible rescue of some fifty thousand Bulgarian Jews from the Nazis in 1943, French intellectual Tzvetan Todorov[1] refers to the "fragility of goodness." He suggests that moral and heroic behavior won out in Bulgaria thanks to a tenuous chain of events. Even one important ingredient missing from the chain—a different response from leadership, a perception that Jews were a threat, cultural anti-Semitism, or lack of friendships between Jews and Christians—might have spelled doom for Bulgaria's Jewish population.

During World War II, the fragility of goodness was also made clear in America's treatment of its citizens of Japanese descent. In the aftermath of Japan's December 1941 attack on Pearl Harbor, the American government responded by forcing Japanese Americans to give up their jobs and live by a 6 AM to 6 PM curfew. They were also restricted to traveling within five miles of their homes. Then, in 1942, many Japanese Americans were forced into internment camps. More than two-thirds of them were not immigrants but American citizens who were nevertheless regarded as a security risk based solely on their Japanese ancestry. Using Executive Order 9066 as a legal foundation, the federal government gave as its rationale the fact that the United States was at war with Japan and simply could not afford to permit disloyal Americans of Japanese descent to sabotage the war effort. It did not seem to matter that there was no evidence of Japanese disloyalty.

Cultural bigotry was only part of the story of sending Japanese Americans to internment camps. Knowing that they would be gone for a period of time, many were willing to sell their houses and personal property in a few days for next to nothing. Real estate agents eagerly bought up the land left by farmers of Japanese descent. White Americans could have helped their Japanese American neighbors by offering to help rent the homes instead of letting them be sold, but few made the effort. Though many white Americans recognized the injustice of forcibly moving an entire group of people, only a small number had the courage to speak out against government policy.[2]

Discrimination against Japanese Americans was widespread on mainland America. In Hawaii, however, Japanese Americans were treated in a much more humane way. Unlike their counterparts in

California, residents of Hawaii were oriented toward peace rather than conflict. Their multiracial, multicultural population had accumulated a history of tolerance. Many of their leaders did not see a political benefit in removing their Japanese American neighbors. Moreover, Hawaiians of Japanese descent were not widely regarded as posing a threat. Furthermore, Japanese Americans were seen as providing an important economic function that would have been sorely missed in their absence.

From the beginning of the war, the local military commander, the business community, the mass media, and ordinary long-term Hawaii residents refused to label their fellow Americans of Japanese descent as a danger to security. In that way they were distancing themselves from the official government view championed by Navy Secretary Frank Knox who accused Japanese American residents of Hawaii of being the "fifth" column that made an attack on our shores possible. Although an investigation by naval intelligence and the FBI did not find any evidence to support his claim, Knox recommended on December 19 that all Japanese aliens from the islands be interned on the mainland.[3]

But this was not to be. In order to calm the population, General Delos Emmons, the military governor of Hawaii, gave a radio address in which he declared, "No person, be he citizen or alien, need worry, provided he is not connected with a subversive element." What happened next is an example of how leadership can make a difference in how we respond to crisis.

General Emmons was a man of integrity. He had a good grasp of local conditions and was aware of Japanese Americans' loyalty to the United States. During the attack on Pearl Harbor, Japanese Americans were active in civil defense and gave blood for the wounded. Some two thousand Japanese Americans fought enemy planes as part of the US Army troops' station on the island.[4] When in January of 1942, the War Department requested the evacuation of Japanese Americans from Hawaii, General Emmons contested the order as dangerous and impractical. "How can you evacuate 100,000 people without straining military recourses which were needed to protect the islands?" he argued. "And if the islands are in danger, we should first evacuate more than 20,000 white civilian women and children who live there."[5]

On the grounds that Japanese labor was "absolutely essential" for the rebuilding of the military base, Emmons also fought the War Department order from February 9, 1942, to dismiss all Japanese workers employed by the army. In the end, a compromise was reached whereby General Emmons ordered the internment of 1,444 Japanese out of a population of 158,000. This number sharply contrasted with the size of the Japanese American population from other Pacific Ocean states such as California, Washington, and Oregon where more than one hundred thousand Japanese Americans were sent to internment camps.[6]

General Emmons's leadership clearly made the difference. However, he was also helped by the fact that other important leaders on the Hawaiian Islands supported his actions. For example, the president of the Honolulu Chamber of Commerce called for just treatment of Japanese residents. He suggested, "There are 160,000 of these people who want to live here because they like the country and like the American way of life. . . . The citizens of Japanese blood would fight as loyally for America as any other citizen. I have read or heard nothing in statements given out by the military, local police or F.B.I. since December 7 to change my opinion. And I have gone out of my way to ask for the facts."[7]

In addition, local newspapers and radio stations refuted rumors about Japanese disloyalty and criticized federal government policies against Japanese Americans. Police Capt. John A. Burns and the head of the FBI in Hawaii, Robert L. Shivers, also spoke publicly in defense of the loyalty of Japanese American residents.

It is easy to attribute Hawaii's approach to Japanese Americans to the islands' self-serving economic interests. Hawaii's 158,000 Japanese represented 37 percent of Hawaii's population, as compared to California's ninety-four thousand Japanese Americans, representing 1 percent of the population of the state.[8] The economic life and military defense of Hawaii would have been seriously threatened if its Japanese population had been removed. But the Japanese were also well integrated into the life of the islands, and not only in an economic sense. They had a long history of peaceful coexistence and cooperation with Hawaii's other ethnic groups.

After the Japanese American internment camps were closed in 1946, redress efforts were very slow to develop in any substantial way. The Japanese American Evacuations Claims Act of 1948 compensated Americans of Japanese descent who were able to document their property losses. But it took until 1976 for the president of the United States, Gerald Ford, to admit that the World War II evacuation of Japanese Americans had been indefensible. In 1988, Pres. Ronald Reagan signed into law the Civil Liberties Act which made possible the assignment of reparations to Japanese Americans who had been personally and directly harmed by government action. Appropriating federal funds for these reparations took two more years. In October 1990, Pres. George H. W. Bush issued the first redress checks for $20,000 to surviving internees.[9]

Most people who have survived internment, war, genocide, ethnic cleansing, or other forms of state-induced violence need to reach closure for what has happened to them during traumatic times. For survivors, the truth is important because by perpetrators' accepting responsibility for their atrocities, they are also acknowledging that their acts were wrong. By recognizing the humanity of the people they have harmed, victims are able to regain their dignity.

In many cases where intergroup violence has been resolved, forming a Truth and Reconciliation Commission is the only way that victims can gain information of what altogether happened and to come to terms with the past. The first country to form such a commission was South Africa. Covering the period of South African history from March 1, 1960, to May 10, 1994, the commission was chaired by Archbishop Desmond Tutu, a well-known and respected religious figure in South Africa who in 1984 received the Nobel Peace Prize.[10] It took the members of the organization more than two years, from April 1996 to July 31, 1998, to hear testimony from twenty-one thousand victims of apartheid.[11] The commission dealt with human rights violations and with requests for reparations and amnesty. It received over seven thousand applications for amnesty that came from members of the police, black militants, and white right-wing activists. Over forty-five hundred applications were rejected and 125 were granted (the rest are still under investigation).[12]

The goal of the commission was not to punish people, but to expose their role in crimes committed under apartheid. When it publicized its report the most important finding turned out to be the role of the South African state in protecting the power and privilege of the white minority. The commission showed how state policy led to the dehumanization of black residents, as government ceased to regard them as fellow citizens. Instead, they became enemies of the state, making the atrocities committed against them appear to be legitimate. The state, however, did not do it alone but was supported by a complacent media and business enterprises.

Not all people who lost members of their families or were themselves victims of violence in South Africa sought revenge. Most of them simply wanted to know why they were subjected to inhumane treatment, what happened to their loved ones, and who was responsible for making decisions that led to their suffering and loss. Reparation was important, because even though it could not help them replace who or what they had lost, it could help them to rebuild their lives.

Ending hate and violence is always a worthwhile pursuit, but it is not the end. Once a peace agreement has been signed and residents seek to make the transition back to the normalcy of civilian life, they must still confront the past in order to rebuild trust and understanding among themselves as well as to prevent another outbreak of violence in the future. However, it is hard for people to come to terms with the truth. As we saw earlier, the government and the media have often been involved in manufacturing an enemy by encouraging the development of stereotypes that are hard to dislodge. Thus it is essential for the state and the media to accept responsibility for whatever role they played in perpetrating hate and violence.

In Bosnia and Herzegovina the organizers of the Truth and Reconciliation Commission seek to provide a forum for the victims to tell their stories. The War Crime Tribunal for Bosnia deals only with a fraction of the cases. And as victims come forward, expressing a need to be heard, the commission will provide them with the place to do so. In addition to reviewing atrocities, however, the Bosnian Commission will also collect stories of cross-ethnic support and cooperation. We should never forget the injustices, but we should also never ignore the stories of courage and heroism.

People everywhere have the potential for committing evil on a massive scale. They, however, also have the potential for goodness and compassion. Because hate and violence lead to the destruction of human dignity, societies that have been fortunate enough to resolve their major conflicts still have to work on reestablishing not just the rule of law but also the dignity of victims. Societies frequently struggle over how much to acknowledge about what happened during a particularly dark period in their history. Moreover, there is no clear consensus as to how to employ the law in helping victims, on the one hand, and in prosecuting those who participate in violence or give orders for others to do their bidding, on the other. It is clear, however, that an acknowledgment that crimes were committed can help restore the human dignity of victims and help speed their psychological and spiritual healing.

EPILOGUE:
THE MODERN MADNESS OF HATE

It is frequently difficult to locate the grounds for optimism about prospects for peace. In the Middle East and Northern Ireland, there is more a record of intolerance and hostility between groups than there is any historical precedent for peace. The number of casualties of civil war and terrorist violence can make average citizens desperate for security and safety. Yet the warring forces can also produce a larger and more intransigent group of extremists.

Between Israelis and Palestinians, for example, a cycle of violence and retaliation over the last few years may have made a peace treaty more attractive to many clear-thinking people in the mainstream of political thought; but deadly suicide bombings in Israeli cities and military incursions into Palestinian territory have also strengthened the hold of extremist groups on both sides. The difficult question, at this juncture, is how to turn the violence around, how to stop it in its tracks, so as to give peace a chance, or at least some hope to take root. Certainly, it would be naive to depend on any historical voices of tolerance to bring the warring parties to the peace table. At this point, even the power of the United States has made no discernible difference.

By contrast, Northern Ireland's Catholics and Protestants seem to have turned the corner in their quest for a peaceful settlement of their differences. On Good Friday, April 10, 1998, after thirty years of bloody warfare in which more than three thousand people lost their lives, the two sides negotiated the Belfast Agreement, which established a legislative assembly based on Protestants and Catholics sharing power. This ended the Republic of Ireland's claim to Northern Ireland, and provided for the release of paramilitary political prisoners.

The Belfast Agreement represents the most significant opportunity for peace since the partition of Ireland in 1921. Since its endorsement in 1998, the level of everyday terrorism in Northern Ireland has significantly declined. At the same time, the agreement has not resulted in a total and lasting peace. Fringe organizations, opposed to the peace process, have continued to cause some degree of trouble. In 1998, for example, twenty-eight people were killed when a five hundred-pound bomb, planted by a dissident republican paramilitary group, exploded in Omagh. There have been a number of other deadly terrorist acts since then. Moreover, paramilitary groups on both sides have thus far refused to hand over their weapons.[1]

Roger Mac Ginty's research on violent conflict in deeply divided societies such as those between Catholics and Protestants in Northern Ireland and between Israelis and Palestinians in the Middle East shows that most of the terrorism is carried out by paramilitary organizations that engage in low-level violence, similar to the most destructive and violent kinds of hate crimes. Although particular violent incidents are actually part of the wider conflict, they are perceived by victims as though they constitute individual and isolated hate attacks aimed exclusively at them.[2]

The control of acts of hate in deeply divided societies is based on a high degree of ethnic segregation. Because residents live in sharply delineated areas, there is little daily contact between warring parties of a cooperative or friendly nature that might have reduced the sanctioning of hate and bigotry. Yet, under the threat of violence, segregation may also reduce the vulnerability of residents, at least in the short term. This is apparently the rationale for the Israeli government's plan to construct a fence to divide Israel from the West Bank.

An important factor in controlling acts of hate in the midst of ethnic conflict is that paramilitary organizations commit most of the violent episodes. Intergroup hostilities are frequently regulated by nonstate militant organizations, whose leaders do not regard these abominations as the most efficient way for realizing their goals. Indeed, reliance on an unsystematically carried out agenda of hate attacks could, from a paramilitary perspective, even be counterproductive because they can be interpreted as individual and personal rather than as a part of a political process.

Mac Ginty argues, however, that hate crimes increase when the prospects for peace become a real possibility. We could apply his observation to all acts of hate. Because a primary motivation for ethnic violence is to instill fear, there is often an intensification of the violence meant to exacerbate the fear of political change as long as the process of peace negotiations continues. Hate crimes then become part of a political strategy. Their timing is deliberate, often coinciding with major political developments. Mac Ginty warns that an inflated governmental response to these isolated incidents may give the groups engaged in hate crimes more of the legitimacy they crave.[3] Among the Palestinians, recent retaliatory strikes by the Israeli military have apparently enhanced the credibility of the most militant groups.

Israelis and Palestinians continue to regard one another as a major threat. Each side takes a zero-sum view; and there is reality behind the perception. The amount of land available is finite; the number of Israelis and Palestinians is growing. Considering land alone, the loss of one side is automatically the gain of the other. This thinking takes on tremendous importance when Jewish settlements are built on the West Bank.

Yet there are many other ways in which the connection between Israelis and Palestinians could be turned into a mutually beneficial relationship. Land is not the only significant consideration in the Middle East, though it has had tremendous symbolic importance. One has only to have visited Arab merchants in Old Jerusalem selling menorahs and mezuzahs to the Jewish tourists prior to the Intifada to recognize the economic potential in cooperation between Arabs and Jews. These same Arab merchants have been put out of business by the recent wave of violence and would welcome the return of tourism.

The case of Kibbutz Metzer illustrates the possibility of the state of Israel and an independent Palestinian state becoming trading partners to their mutual advantage. Residents of the kibbutz and their Palestinian neighbors shared sources of water and assisted one another in terms of healthcare. There are many important areas of economic vitality, agriculture, education, tourism, and healthcare where the opposing sides could conceivably cooperate, but only under conditions of peace. In this case, interdependence would help assure that Israelis and Palestinians never resume their conflict.

We focused earlier on the resentment in other countries fostered by America's advantaged economic position in the process of global trade. In some cases, American products have simply pushed out and eliminated the much weaker competition within developing nations, whether for hamburgers, motion pictures, television programs, or CDs.

Yet there are also examples of trade between the United States and Arab nations benefiting both sides. America's free trade agreement with Jordan has resulted in the value of Jordan's exports to the United States jumping from $16 million in 1998 to $412 million in

2002. The increased trade produced some thirty thousand new jobs for Jordanians. The same trade agreement is responsible for increasing United States exports to Jordan from $306 million in 2000 to more than $339 million in 2002.[4]

The United States has played an important role as a third party in the Northern Ireland conflict, effectively pressuring the extremists on both sides to give up their obstructionist tendencies.[5] Unfortunately, the American influence in the Middle East has failed to produce a similar breakthrough, perhaps owing to the fact that the United States is widely perceived in the Muslim world as lacking in objectivity and favoring its Israeli ally. The actual facts of the matter haven't seemed to make much of a difference with respect to encouraging peace. Given the larger history of animosity between Muslims and Western nations, America is frequently perceived as the untrustworthy enemy of the Islamic world. Mutually beneficial trade agreements between the United States and a broader range of Muslim nations might at some future date increase American influence in the process of establishing Middle East peace. Until then, the American contribution to a Middle Eastern peace is quite limited.

For now, important Israeli and Palestinian leaders have been stymied in their efforts to end the fighting. The tendency has been to take the politically expedient and popular route as opposed to the effective but possibly unpopular strategy for achieving a lasting peace. On both sides, there are extremists who fear losing their political clout if peace were to come to the region. And their perception has some reality: Their prestige and power last only so long as the conflict continues. Peace would simply make them irrelevant. Unlike their counterparts in Northern Ireland, the parties in the Middle East have not been able to find a way of bringing the leaders of terrorist and militant groups into the peace process. Yet this may be the only way in which such organizations would attain peace.

At this point in time, Israel's official policy entails retaliating for suicide bombings specifically against members of Palestinian terrorist organizations and their political wings. Yet bombing innocent civilians in restaurants, buses, and nightclubs, on the one side, and assassinating military and political extremists, on the other, have only produced more extremists among Palestinians and Israelis who are unwilling to compromise toward the elimination of tension and conflict in the area. On October 4, 2003, nineteen people lost their lives when a female suicide bomber blew herself up in the Maxim restaurant located in the Israeli port city of Haifa. Ironically, Maxim restaurant was for thirty-seven years a symbol of peaceful coexistence, being jointly owned by a Jewish family and an Arab family. The twenty-seven-year-old bomber from the West Bank town of Jenin had been an apprentice lawyer and a dedicated daughter and sister who never expressed any obvious interest in furthering radical Islamic causes. Her motive? To get even for the death of her twenty-three-year-old brother and her thirty-one-year-old fiancé, who four months earlier had been shot by Israeli soldiers in their search for Islamic Jihad terrorists.[6]

Those negotiating for an end to the Northern Ireland conflict were able and willing to include the leaders of extremist paramilitary groups (illegal armies) in the peace process. The Irish Republican Army and its political wing, Sinn Féin, on the Catholic side and the Loyalist paramilitary groups and their political wings, the Progressive Unionist Party and the Ulster Democratic Party, on the Protestant side, had been responsible for decades of bombings, shootings, racketeering, and other forms of intimidation. Now they all play an integral role in the process of peacemaking.[7]

Northern Ireland has other advantages as well. For one thing, the threat between Protestants and Catholics is more narrow and focused than in the Middle East, where vast religious differences get confused with economic and political inequality. The "troubles" in Northern Ireland represent conflict within society, not between societies. Israelis and Palestinians have fought for land. Northern Ireland's Protestants and Catholics already share the same geographic area, even if they have been miles apart in socioeconomic and political terms. Moreover, unlike those involved in the Middle Eastern conflict, the opposing parties in Northern Ireland may differ in terms of their religious denominations, but they share a stake in their common Christianity. The threat is therefore much more economic than it is religious. The same cannot be said of the Middle East.

The longer the tension between democratic and antidemocratic tendencies is allowed to go unresolved, the less likely is any chance to come up with a peaceful and democratic solution. The lengthy conflicts both between Northern Ireland's Catholics and Protestants and between Israelis and Palestinians have greatly eroded prospects for building trust on opposing sides. In addition, there are large and difficult political and economic issues still to be resolved. Under any circumstance, a lasting peace will only be achieved by reducing the profound hostilities that have developed over the last few decades of warfare.

Major conflicts continue around the world. Hate maintains itself in relations between groups of people who see one another as the enemy. Yet, contrary to popular beliefs, there has actually been a sharp decline in new ethnic wars. Moreover, most such conflicts get resolved not through large-scale physical confrontation but by means of a political process involving accommodation and negotiation.[8] It should be noted, in addition, that the success of strategies for the avoidance of warfare depend also on the ability of national governments and their legal systems to recognize early enough the presence of hate crimes as precursors of worse things to come and to develop strategies to address hate before it turns violent.

In the meantime, the violence between Palestinians and Israelis rages on. Many people of goodwill around the world wonder whether the brutal hate violence in the Middle East has simply gone too far ever to be transformed into a lasting peace. Not only has the violence escalated but so has the hatred.

Yet recent changes in Northern Ireland provide some degree of optimism for those who are ready to give up on the Middle East. Until recent years, Protestant and Catholic paramilitary groups managed to kill thousands of innocent civilians in numerous terrorist acts. Many observers were totally convinced that peace was a totally elusive goal for the residents of Northern Ireland, that they would indefinitely live under the threat and reality of hate and violence. Even allowing for the setbacks that have plagued the peace process there in recent years, the reduction in violence between Catholics and Protestants in Northern Ireland would have been unthinkable a few years ago. Peace now seems within the grasp of ordinary citizens.

APPENDIX

FLAG-WAVING AND ATTITUDES TOWARD ARAB AMERICANS

Gordana Rabrenovic, Jack Levin, Janese Free,
Colleen Keaney, and Jason Mazaic

*The Brudnick Center on Violence and Conflict,
Northeastern University*

In the aftermath of the September 11 attack, the American flag came to life with renewed vigor and augmented meaning. From a sociological perspective, the "Attack on America" illustrated in a contemporary context that there is a much deeper significance attached to the American flag than just national politics. In a sense, if we view it in terms of the great sociologist Emile Durkheim, the flag is a "collective representation." It represents a transformation of collective and sacred values and sentiments into a physical object.[1]

Sociologist Robert Bellah's[2] characterization of what he called "American civil religion" emphasizes that American society has been regarded by its citizens as "the promised land." Throughout the calendar, there are important days of "worship"—Memorial Day, the Fourth of July, Presidents' Day, and Flag Day—when flag-waving assumes the stature of a religious ceremony. Indeed, the sacred nature of the national flag is reflected in the fact that many Americans are more than willing to exclude the intentional destruction of the flag from the purview of First Amendment rights.

In our own recent study, we sought to measure both the quantity and quality of flag-waving as an expression of a renewed sense of patriotic sentiment. Specifically, we asked: Are Americans who displayed flags following the September 11 attacks more likely to approve of the nationalistic objectives of the United States, as measured by their support for the government, military, and the country as a whole? Are those Americans who hung flags more likely to have xenophobic attitudes toward Arabs? And are Americans who displayed American flags, or images of American flags, in a location that can be personally identified with them (i.e., directly on their clothes, such as pins, ribbons, buttons) more likely to express strong nationalistic attitudes and more negative attitudes toward Arabs than those people who displayed their flag in a location that was less personally identifiable (i.e., on a house or in an office)?

The results reported here were based on telephone interviews with a randomly selected national sample of 391 adults, of seventeen years and older. The data were collected approximately four to five months after 9/11 in January and February 2002 by researchers at the Brudnick Center located at Northeastern University in Boston.

The interview schedule consisted of fourteen questions asking the subjects about issues of patriotism, flag displaying, nationalism, and attitudes toward Arabs since the September 11 terrorist attacks. The initial three questions asked respondents about their participation in displaying a flag (where, when, and so forth). The next section elicited responses concerning their reasons for choosing to display or not to display a flag. The following series of questions asked respondents to report their feelings toward Arabs as possible terrorists. The remaining questions collected relevant demographic data relating to age, income, race, education, political affiliation, voting participation, and income. Incomplete surveys were not used in the analysis and that left us with 388 complete surveys.

For the descriptive variables investigated in the study, one can be 95 percent confident that the maximum error attributable to sampling is plus or minus five percentage points. Each interview lasted approximately three minutes.

Fully 60 percent of the participants in the study reported displaying a flag at the time of the interview. This is a substantial increase from prior to September 11 when, of the same group, only 21 percent of residents displayed the flag.

The most common location for hanging a flag was close to home. Nearly 50 percent of the participants stated that they currently had a flag displayed in the yard or on the outside of their house or apartment. Nearly 30 percent (114) of the respondents had placed it on their automobile. The third most popular location (27 percent or 104 participants) was on personal clothing. Just behind having a flag on a piece of clothing, 26 percent or 103 participants stated they had a flag currently displayed somewhere inside their home. The least popular venue to place a flag was at the office with only 13 percent (51 participants) displaying it in this location.

Of the respondents currently displaying a flag, the overwhelming majority reportedly sought to express their nationalistic sentiment. More specifically, 92 percent indicated they did so "to support our troops in Afghanistan" or "to symbolize America's strength and power," 85 percent indicated they did so "to support our government," and 88 percent stated they displayed a flag to "show national unity against the enemy." Unexpectedly, however, some 95 percent—the largest number of respondents—stated that they were displaying the flag not for nationalistic reasons alone but to "support victims of September 11th and their families."

In an analysis of respondents' attitudes toward Arabs, a significant relationship was found between displaying a flag and whether the respondent would "support holding Arabs and detaining them when necessary for investigation purposes," "would keep an eye on Arabs in public places," and "would support questioning Arabs as long as necessary at airports." On all three questions, flag-wavers were significantly more likely than their non-flag-waving counterparts to support measures that singled out Arabs for security purposes.

Questions measuring the more extreme attitudes toward Arabs —"I would agree violence is permissible if an Arab appears to be un-American" and "I would exclude Arabs from my country"—did not show significant differences between flag-displayers and non-displayers. Indeed, even though 18 percent of all respondents expressed agreement that violence was permissible, only 8 percent reported agreeing that Arabs should be excluded from the country.

The respondents who displayed the flag on their clothing were significantly more likely than those displaying the flag in other venues to report wanting to "keep an eye on Arabs in public places," "to support questioning Arabs as long as necessary at airports," and "to support holding Arabs and detaining them when necessary for investigation purposes." Interestingly, the expected values differed significantly from the actual values of those people wearing a flag on their clothing versus those who did not on one of the two questions on the extreme ends of the scale of attitudes toward Arabs: "I would exclude Arabs from my country." However, no significant differences were found between location on clothing and agreeing that "violence is permissible if an Arab appears to be un-American." NUKE' EM ALL

When examining nationalistic attitudes and displaying the flag on one's clothing, respondents wearing a flag versus those who did not were significantly more likely to state they were doing it "to support our government." There was not, however, a significant difference for "support our troops in Afghanistan" or "symbolize America's strength and power."

We did not find any significant differences among respondents' attitudes based on their socio-demographic characteristics nor on their place of residence.

Flags are generally understood as the primary, and most readily available, means of displaying nationalistic and patriotic sentiments. A recent example is the 2002 Fifa World Cup. In a celebration of their victory, Brazilian players draped themselves in the Brazilian national flag. This act served as a visible sign of their national pride and it was replicated by thousands of other Brazilians across the world.

Flag-waving instantly produces a sense of identity and belonging to a particular group. As such, it is not surprising that many Americans immediately put up flags in the aftermath of what many considered one of the most tragic attacks in our country's history. Surprisingly, however, the most pervasive reason reported for displaying a flag was humanitarian and not nationalistic—to express sympathy for the victims of September 11. At the same time, we believe, the vast majority of respondents also expressed a more forceful message by displaying the flag—that of an unquestioned belief in the righteousness and strength of the actions of the government, military, and nation in general.

A review of the scholarly literature on nationalism and patriotism, particularly on how these concepts relate to a general tendency toward prejudice and xenophobia, reveals a gap in research on what role flag-waving may play in this process. As an easily recognizable symbol of nationalistic sentiment, one might expect to find evidence for the idea that flag-wavers are more likely to fully support the actions of their government and military. However, the subject is more frequently covered in the nonacademic literature.[3] An exception to this lack of attention in the scholarly literature is Putnam, who found an increase in levels of trust and confidence in the government after September 11, which were "no doubt partly the result of a spurt of patriotism and 'rally round the flag' sentiment."[4]

The "War on Terror" waged by the US government depends

upon the sense of fear and insecurity felt by many Americans after the terrorist attacks. Residents of New York City, for example, report striking differences in their response before and after September 11 on the question of "how safe they feel compared to four years ago." In the poll conducted by the *New York Times* and CBS News from August 5 to 12, 2001, 58 percent felt safer than four years ago (66 percent for whites, 48 percent for blacks, and 54 percent for Hispanic). In the same poll conducted from June 4 to 9, 2002, 38 percent of residents felt safer today than four years ago (both whites and blacks reported the same rates of safety, 38 percent, while the Hispanic rate was 48 percent).[5] This fear as well as retaliation was used to justify the government's military operations in Afghanistan and interventions in other countries suspected of supporting al Qaeda soldiers or their sympathizers.

The same sentiment also breeds "a negative nationalism"[6] whereby we assume that "the world is a zero-sum game where our gains come at another nation's expense, and theirs come at ours."[7] This is in contrast to "positive nationalism," which assumes that when a country's citizens are provided for, they are more likely and willing to reach out to address the needs of the global community. Negative nationalism targets those within a country's borders who appear different or threatening, somehow, to that country's way of life. These groups usually include immigrants, foreigners, and ethnic minorities. The Justice Department reports having investigated 350 reports of crimes against people of Middle Eastern or south Asian origin since September 11. Such attacks range from alleged threats and vandalism to assaults and bombing plots. Similarly, although residents of New York City reported improvement in racial relations since September 11, residents of Middle Eastern or south Asian origin reported a new sense of alienation and fear.[8] The social distance between black and white residents seemed to shrink, but only at the expense of another group whose members became the target of hostility. In the aftermath of the events of September 11, Americans waving the flag in support of their country and its war efforts also seemed to be supporting suspicious and less tolerant attitudes toward groups they identified with terrorism, in particular those of Arab descent.

Many Americans felt that displaying American flags in the aftermath of the attacks was a way for them to create a sense of national community and shared mourning. As one woman in Seattle said, "I felt this intense sense of unity with everyone else in America. It's just your way of saying 'I'm here. I'm with all of you.' It's like this little internal bond."[9] Some expressed frustration in the weeks afterward because they felt there was so little they could do to help. Hanging a flag may have been a respectful and accessible way to mourn those who were lost and to support their families and loved ones. This action may have led to a greater identification with the victims and yet an increase in fearful feelings and anxiousness. As a result, the collective action of hanging flags gave many Americans a much-needed sense of security and protection under the powerful symbol at a time of anxiety. At the same time, the increased fearfulness may have also heightened the general atmosphere of "negative nationalism" and xenophobia.

We found that people who display the flag on their person (for example, a flag pin on their clothing) held stronger nationalistic feelings and stronger negative sentiments toward Arabs than those displaying the flag elsewhere. This finding logically follows from sociologist Erving Goffman's notions of front-stage and backstage performances. His concept of the *personal front* refers to "the items [of expressive equipment] that we most intimately identify with the performer himself and that we naturally expect will follow the performer wherever he goes. As part of the personal front, we might include: insignia or office or rank; clothing; sex; age."[10] During the 1960s, for example, certain hairstyles and dress were found to be associated with left-wing political attitudes. After September 11, it was the flag that communicated a message of personal patriotism. The personal front is far more intimate than displaying a flag on a house, on a car, or in an office where it might be difficult, if not impossible, to identify a particular individual as patriotic.

These attitudes toward the flag, however, should not be confused with the commercialization of the flag as a symbol of patriotism. Although, we believe, our survey captured the spontaneous use of the flag by many respondents, the flag is also being used since the attack on America for selling all sorts of products. The American flag can also be found on T-shirts, socks, and dresses. For the athlete, the flag may indicate patriotism; for the seller, it's likely commercial.

The use of the flag for commercial purposes dates back to the Civil War. According to journalist Adam Piore,[11] "After hundreds of thousands of war deaths, the flag became an emotional symbol to a nation in mourning—and was exploited by pitchmen for everything from whisky to widgets."

In the aftermath of September 11, Americans apparently felt the need to express their patriotism. Our results suggest that a majority of them chose to do so by displaying an American flag. Several comments were made and recorded during the phone interviews expressing participants' patriotic feelings. One respondent suggested that he was displaying the flag to show his "commitment to democracy," while another suggested that she was "lucky to be an American." We determined, in fact, that large numbers of Americans who put up flags were trying to convey their support of the government, military, and the nation overall. Nonetheless, the primary reason Americans gave for displaying flags after the attacks was to support the victims and their relatives, with an overwhelming 95 percent of respondents answering in that way.

In addition to increased nationalistic sentiment, Americans

were understandably feeling a sense of fear and uncertainty about their national security and the possibility of future terrorist attacks. While we had initially expected to find a connection between this nationalism and intolerant attitudes, it seems that Americans' primary concern was for shoring up their sense of public safety. If, in the process of creating a better sense of security, Arabs happened to be singled out for questioning or investigation, many Americans thought this was the best option—even if regrettable. At the same time, our findings suggest that lashing out violently against Arabs or excluding them from the country did not necessarily ensure that Americans felt safe after September 11. Relatively few of our respondents, with or without flags, voiced support for committing violence against Arabs or excluding them altogether. It seems that Americans are opting for infringement of certain civil liberties in favor of a better sense of public safety, but there are limits as to just how far they are willing to go in this regard.

Although the current study was able preliminarily to address the relationship between flag-waving and nationalistic attitudes as well as attitudes toward Arabs in the post–September 11 period, future research may be needed to elaborate and expand upon this initial survey. It should be noted that the connection between flag-waving and support for government policy seems to have weakened since the invasion of Iraq. Apparently, Americans can still be enthusiastic about our flag but still question the direction of government policy.

The wording of certain questions on the survey caused some confusion for respondents. Some respondents mistook our questions about the American flag as pertaining only to a flag hung on a flagpole, when—in fact—we were interested in any representation of the American flag (stickers, decals, pins, bumper stickers, and so forth). This confusion may have caused an underrepresentation of Americans who answered "yes" to displaying a flag.

Interviewers also reported that respondents had trouble understanding what was meant by the questions asking about support for "holding Arabs and detaining them *when necessary* for investigation purposes" and support for "questioning Arabs *as long as necessary* at airports." It seems that use of phrases such as *when necessary* and *as long as necessary* led some respondents to believe there may have been a legitimate reason for the questioning or detaining and, therefore, they were more likely to support it.

Finally, and more generally, it might be that because whites, females, and older individuals (fifty years and older) were overrepresented in our survey, we did not find any differences in response based on respondents' socio-demographic characteristics and location of residence. In order to avoid this in any future research, we recommend conducting the phone interviews at varying times of the day to be able to obtain a greater diversity of respondents.

Unfortunately, we were not able to compare and contrast patriotic and nationalistic attitudes before and after the events of September 11, which would have allowed for a deeper level of analysis. But this is one of the major pitfalls of the social sciences, just as it is hard to predict the occurrence of major terrorist attacks on home soil. We feel, however, that this study provides insight into the state of patriotism and prejudice in the United States following the events of September 11.

The study also brings a critical question to mind. The United States is a country of much diversity, where people from all over the globe have congregated to form a nation. What impact then might future wars have to inspire hate and prejudice, when—regardless of what nation America is attacking—we transfer that aggression to certain citizens in our own homeland?

This question becomes particularly important when considering wars such as the current offensive in Afghanistan and Iraq. As we have seen through the present study, negative racial attitudes are being generalized to all Arabs, even though we were at war with Afghanistan. We have witnessed entire ethnic groups being affected by prejudice and hate, even when they have literally no relationship to the war or the terrorist attacks. In fact, in some cases they may have supported America's war against terrorism. The difficulty, then, is how to combat hate and prejudice when feelings of nationalism and patriotism run so high that people and nations are considered "either with us or against us." Under such conditions, those who are defined by the state as "against us" then come to serve as an amorphous scapegoat toward whom hate and violence can be directed with impunity.

SUGGESTED READINGS

Abelmann, Nancy, and John Lie. 1995. *Blue Dreams: Korean Americans and the Los Angeles Riots.* Cambridge, MA: Harvard University Press.

Anti-Defamation League Backgrounder on Anti-Semitism in the United States, August 10, 2000.

Adorno, Theodore W., E. Frankel-Brunswick, D. J. Levinson, and N. H. Sanford. 1950. *The Authoritarian Personality.* New York: Harper and Row.

Allport, Gordon W. 1954. *The Nature of Prejudice.* Reading, MA: Addison-Wesley.

Ancheta, Angelo N. 1998. *Race, Rights, and the Asian American Experience.* New Brunswick, NJ: Rutgers University Press.

Anti-Defamation League. 1997. *Vigilante Justice: Militias and Common Law Courts Wage War Against the Government.* New York: ADL.

Aronson, E., and S. Patnoe. 1997. *The Jigsaw Classroom.* New York: Longman.

Barnett, Victoria J. 1999. *Bystanders: Conscience and Complicity during the Holocaust.* Westport, CT: Praeger.

Bar-Zohar, Michael. 1998. *Beyond Hitler's Grasp: The Heroic Rescue of Bulgaria's Jews.* Avon, MA: Adams Media Corporation.

Beck, Aaron T. 1999. *Prisoners of Hate: The Cognitive Basis of Anger, Hostility, and Violence.* New York: HarperCollins.

Blee, Kathleen. 2003. *Inside Organized Racism: Women in the Hate Movement.* Berkeley: University of California Press.

Brook, Kevin Alan. 1999. *The Jews of Khazaria*. Northvale, NJ: Jason Aronson.

Brown, Roger. 1986. *Social Psychology: The Second Edition*. New York: Free Press.

Browning, Christopher R. 1992. *Ordinary Men*. New York: HarperPerennial.

Brustein, William. 1996. *The Logic of Evil*. New Haven, CT: Yale University Press.

Cockburn, Cynthia. 1998. *The Space Between Us: Negotiating Gender and National Identities in Conflict*. London and New York: Zed Books.

Efron, Noah, J. 2003. *Real Jews: Secular Versus Ultra-Orthodox and the Struggle for Jewish Identity in Israel*. New York: Basic Books.

Elder, Larry. 2000. *The Ten Things You Can't Say in America*. New York: St. Martin's Press.

Ezekiel, Raphael S. 1995. *The Racist Mind: Portraits of American Neo-Nazis and Klansmen*. New York: Viking Press.

Fishbein, Harold D. 1996. *Peer Prejudice and Discrimination*. Boulder, CO: Westview Press.

Fox, James, and Jack Levin. 1996. *Overkill: Mass Murder and Serial Killing Exposed*. New York: Dell.

Franklin, John Hope, and Isidore Starr. 1967. *The Negro in 20th Century America*. New York: Vintage.

Gambino, Richard. 1977. *Vendetta*. New York: Doubleday.

Goldhagen, Daniel Jonah. 1996. *Hitler's Willing Executioners: Ordinary Germans and the Holocaust*. New York: Basic Books.

Gordy, Eric, D. 1999. *The Culture of Power in Serbia: Nationalism and the Destruction of Alternatives*. University Park: Pennsylvania State University Press.

Halpern, Thomas, and Brian Levin. 1996. *The Limits of Dissent: The Constitutional Status of Armed Civilian Militias*. Amherst, MA: Aletheia Press.

Hamm, Mark S. 1994. *Hate Crime: International Perspectives on Causes and Control*. Cincinnati, OH: Anderson.

Hilberg, Raul. 1992. *Perpetrators, Victims, Bystanders: The Jewish Catastrophe 1933–1945*. New York: HarperCollins.

Iganski, Paul, and Barry Kosmin. 2003. *A New Antisemitism?* London: Profile Books.

Jacobs, James B., and Kimberly A. Potter. 1998. *Hate Crimes: Criminal Law and Identity Politics.* New York: Oxford University Press.

Jenness, Valerie, and Kendal Broad. 1997. *Hate Crimes: New Social Movements and the Politics of Violence.* New York: Aldine De Gruyter.

Karl, Jonathan. 1995. *The Right to Bear Arms.* New York: Harper.

Katz, Fred E. 1993. *Ordinary People and Extraordinary Evil.* Albany: State University of New York Press.

Keen, Sam. 1988. *Faces of the Enemy.* New York: Harper and Row.

Kovel, Joel. 1971. *White Racism: A Psychohistory.* New York: Vintage Books.

Kurspahic, Kemal. 2003. *Prime Time Crime: Balkan Media in War and Peace.* Washington, DC: United States Institute of Peace Press.

Lamy, Philip. 1996. *Millennium Rage.* New York: Plenum Press.

Levin, Jack. 2002. *The Violence of Hate.* Boston: Allyn and Bacon.

Levin, Jack, and Jack McDevitt. 2003. *Hate Crimes Revisited.* Boulder, CO: Westview Press.

Milgram, Stanley. 1974. *Obedience to Authority: An Experimental View.* New York: Harper and Row.

Olzak, Susan. 1992. *The Dynamics of Ethnic Competition and Conflict.* Stanford, CA: Stanford University Press.

Orizio, Riccardo. 2003. *Talk of the Devil: Encounters with Seven Dictators.* New York: Walker & Company.

Sardar, Ziauddin, and Merryl Wyn Davies. 2002. *Why Do People Hate America?* New York: Disinformation Company.

Schuman, Howard, Charlotte Steeh, Lawrence Bobo, and Maria Krysan. 1997. *Racial Attitudes in America.* Cambridge, MA: Harvard University Press.

Selznick, Gertrude J., and Stephen Steinberg. 1969. *The Tenacity of Prejudice.* New York: Harper Torchbooks.

Sherif, Muzafer, and Carolyn Sherif. 1961. *The Robbers Cave Experiment: Intergroup Conflict and Cooperation.* Norman: University of Oklahoma.

Sniderman, Paul M., and Thomas Piazza. 1993. *The Scar of Race.* Cambridge, MA: Harvard University Press, Belknap Press.

Staub, Ervin. 1989. *The Roots of Evil: The Origins of Genocide and Other Group Violence.* Cambridge: Cambridge University Press.

Temple-Raston, Dina. 2002. *A Death in Texas.* New York: Henry Holt.

Todorov, Tzvetan. 1999. *The Fragility of Goodness.* Princeton, NJ: Princeton University Press.

Turner, Patricia A. 1993. *I Heard It Through the Grapevine.* Berkeley: University of California Press.

Varshney, Ashutosh. 2002. *Ethnic Conflict and Civic Life: Hindus and Muslims in India.* New Haven, CT: Yale University Press.

Wachtel, Baruh Andrew. 1998. *Making a Nation, Breaking a Nation: Literature and Cultural Politics in Yugoslavia.* Stanford, CA: Stanford University Press.

Wachtel, Paul L. 2001. *Race in the Mind of America.* New York: Routledge.

Watts, Meredith. 1997. *Xenophobia in United Germany.* New York: St. Martin's Press.

Weiss, John. 1996. *Ideology of Death: Why the Holocaust Happened in Germany.* Chicago: Ivan R. Dee.

NOTES

CHAPTER 1: IN THE AFTERMATH OF 9/11

1. Anti-Defamation League, "September 11 and Arab Media," ADL Web site, November 26, 2001, http://www.adl.org; Gallup Organization, December 2001–January 2002, http://www.gallup.com.

2. Gallup Organization, March, 1, 2002, http://www.gallup.com.

3. Ibid.

4. Vivienne Walt, "The Dichotomy of Sept. 11," *Boston Globe*, September 11, 2003, p. A6.

5. Ibid.

6. Jack Levin and Jack McDevitt, *Hate Crimes Revisited* (Boulder, CO: Westview Press, 2003).

7. James A. Fox and Jack Levin, *The Will to Kill: Making Sense of Senseless Murder* (Boston: Allyn and Bacon, 2004), p. 155; Associated Press, "LAX Gunman's Apartment Searched," July 5, 2002, http://www.ap.org.

8. Levin and McDevitt, *Hate Crimes Revisited.*

9. Gallup Organization, February 2001, http://www.gallup.com.

10. Ibid., February 2002.

11. "Airline Accused of Bias," *Boston Globe*, April 26, 2003, p. D1.

12. "Man in Terror Scare Says Woman Is Lying," CNN.com, September 13, 2002, http://wwwcnn.com.

13. Alice Mcquillan, "Cops Nab Brooklyn Thrill Killer," *New York Daily News*, March 30, 2003, http://www.nydailynews.com.

14. "Officer Suspended after Videotaped Beating," CNN.com, July 9, 2002, http://www.cnn.com.

15. "Man Shoots Three in New York City," *USA Today*, June 17, 2002, http://www.usatoday.com.

16. Jack Levin and Monte Paulsen, "Hate," *Encyclopedia of Human Emotions* (New York: Macmillan Reference, 1999), 1:324–31.

17. Valerie Jenness and Kendal Broad, *Hate Crimes: New Social Movements and the Politics of Violence* (New York: Aldine De Gruyter, 1997); James B. Jacobs and Kimberly A. Potter, *Hate Crimes: Criminal Law and Identity Politics* (New York: Oxford University Press, 1998); Jack Levin and Jack McDevitt, *Hate Crimes: The Rising Tide of Bigotry and Bloodshed* (New York: Plenum Press, 1993); Barbara Perry, *In the Name of Hate: Understanding Hate Crimes* (New York: Routledge, 2001); Frederick M. Lawrence, *Punishing Hate: Bias Crimes Under American Law* (Cambridge: Harvard University Press, 1999).

18. Jack Levin and William C. Levin, *The Functions of Discrimination and Prejudice* (New York: Harper and Row, 1982).

19. Thomas F. Pettigrew, "The Affective Component of Prejudice: Empirical Support for the New View," in *Racial Attitudes in the 1990s: Continuity and Change,* ed. Steven A. Tuch and Jack K. Martin (Westport, CT: Praeger, 1997), pp. 76–91.

CHAPTER 2: HATE AS VIOLENCE

1. See Neal Miller and Richard Bugelski, "Minor Studies of Aggression: The Influence of Frustrations Imposed by the In-Group on Attitudes Expressed Toward Out-Groups," *Journal of Psychology* 25 (1948): 437–42.

2. Roger Lane, *Murder in America: A History* (Columbus: Ohio State University Press, 1997).

3. Olivier Zunz, *The Changing Face of Inequality* (Chicago: Uni-

versity of Chicago Press, 1982); Gilbert Osofsky, *Harlem: The Making of a Ghetto* (New York: Harper & Row, 1968).

4. Thomas L. Philpott, *The Slum and the Ghetto: Immigrants, Blacks, and Reformers in Chicago, 1880–1930* (Belmont, CA: Wadsworth Publishing, 1991).

5. George Galster, "Racial Discrimination in Housing Markets during the 1980s: A Review of the Audit Evidence," *Journal of Planning Education and Research* 9, no. 3 (1990): 165–75.

6. Not a real name.

7. Scott S. Greenberger, "Landlord Agrees to Pay for Rejecting Black Family; Belmont Owner Agrees to $50,000 Settlement," *Boston Globe,* August 23, 2003, p. B1.

8. "Uppity Women," *Ms Magazine Online,* http://www.msmagazine.com, June 1999.

9. Kathleen Blee, *Inside Organized Racism* (Berkeley: University of California Press, 2002).

10. Associated Press, "Teen Charged with Assaulting Lesbian on July 4th Pleads Innocent," July 16, 2003, http://www.ap.org.

11. Steve Miller, "Special Day Probed in Girl's Beating," *Washington Times,* June 20, 2003, p. A12.

12. Not a real name.

13. Jim Adams, "Anoka Family Finds Racist Graffiti Spray-Painted on Garage," *Star Tribune,* June 13, 2003, p. 18.

14. This is a fictional name.

15. Bruce Lambert, "Advocates for Immigrants Say Suffolk Officials Foster Bias," *New York Times,* August 2, 2003, p. B5.

16. Paul Vitello, "Another Exercise in Hate," *Newsday,* August 3, 2003, p. 8.

17. "Four German Youths Sentenced for Anti-Foreigner Attacks," *Deutsche Presse-Agentur*, January 24, 2003, http://www.nexis.com.

18. "Ethnic and Religious Conflict in France Today," *Frontline/World,* May 2003, http://www.nexis.com.

19. David Cracknell and Dipesh Gadher, "Labour Is Warned of Asylum Backlash," *Sunday London Times,* January 26, 2003, p. 8.

20. Timo Virtanen, Preface, Finnish Youth Research Society, 2000, http://www.abo.fi/~tivirtan.

21. Chris Hedges, "What Every Person Should Know About War," *New York Times,* July 6, 2003, http://www.nytimes.com.

CHAPTER 3: HATE AS FEAR

1. Efrain Hernandez Jr. and Doreen E. Iudica, "Wellesley Chief Apologizes to Celtics Pick," *Boston Globe*, September 25, 1990, p. B1.

2. Andrew Jacobs, "Mistaken Arrest Makes Actor Miss 'Ragtime,'" *New York Times*, July 17, 1999, p. B3.

3. All names are changed to protect the victims.

4. David Wessel, "Racial Discrimination Is Still at Work," *Wall Street Journal,* September 4, 2003, p. A2.

5. Ibid.

6. Harry J. Holzer, *What Employers Want: Job Prospects for Less-Educated Workers* (New York: Russell Sage, 1996).

7. US Department of Education, National Center for Education Statatistics (NCES), Common Core of Data 1995. Cited in "Education and Race, A Journalist Handbook," by Rebecca Gordon, *Applied Research Center*, September 20, 2003, http://www.arc.org/downloads/RaceandEducation.pdf.

8. Meghan Tench, "Questions Follow Lapse on Wellesley Metco Bus," *Boston Globe Online*, September 6, 2003.

9. Dean Johnson, "WEEI Benches Duo; Hosts Suspended for Two Weeks over Remarks," *Boston Herald*, October 7, 2003, p. 5.

10. US Department of Education, National Center for Education Statistics, *National Education Longitudinal Study of 1988, Second Follow-up Survey* (Washington, DC: Government Printing Office, 1992).

11. *Metropolitan Estate Journal* (1987): 14, cited in Hillel Levine and Lawrence Harmon, *The Death of an American Jewish Community: A Tragedy of Good Intentions* (New York: Free Press, 1992), p. 195.

12. Ibid., pp. 195–96.

13. Ann E. Donlan, "Judge Slams Door on Slaying Suspect," *Boston Herald,* December 23, 1995, p. 1.

14. "Hispanics Say They're Increasingly Being Blamed for Crimes," Associated Press, February 5, 2003, http://www.ap.org.

15. Federal Bureau of Investigation, *Crime in the United States* (Washington, DC: US Government Printing Office, 2000), p. 291.

16. Curt Anderson, "Prison Populations, Costs Climbing," *Boston Globe,* July 28, 2003, p. A2.

17. "Prisoners in 2002," Bureau of Justice Statistics, September 15, 2003, http://www.ojp.usdoj.gov/bjs/pub/pdf/p02.pdf; "Justice Expenditure and Employment in the United States, 1999," *Bureau of Justice Statistics Bulletin,* February 2002, NCJ 191746, http://www.ojp.usdoj.gov/bjs/pub/pdf/jeeus99.pdf.

18. Timothy J. Flanagan and Kathleen Maguire 1994, cited in Ann Dryden Witte, *Urban Crime: Issues and Policies: Housing Policy Debate* 7, no. 4 (Fannie Mae Foundation, 1996), pp. 731–48.

19. "Prisoners in 2002."

20. Ibid.

21. "Crime Control and Common Sense Assumptions: Underlying the Expansion of the Prison Population," by William Sabol, Urban Institute, http://www.urban.org/crime/module/butts/youth-crime-drop.html).

22. Not a real name.

CHAPTER 4: HATE AS REVENGE

1. Jack McDevitt, Jack Levin, and Susan Bennett, "Hate Crime Offenders: An Expanded Typology," *Journal of Social Issues* 58 (Summer 2002): 303–18.

2. Eric Convey, Laurel Sweet, and Franci Richardson, "Strangled to Death: Pedophile Priest Geoghan Killed by Neo-Nazi Prison Inmate," *Boston Herald,* August 24, 2003, http://www.bostonherald.com.

3. Jack Levin and Jack McDevitt, *Hate Crimes Revisited* (Boulder, CO: Westview Press, 1993); Jack Levin and Gordana Rabrenovic, "Hate

Crimes and Ethnic Conflict: An Introduction," *American Behavioral Scientist* 45, no. 4 (December 2001): 574–87.

4. Ravi Nessman, "Helicopter Attacks Spotlight Israel's Policy of Targeted Killings," *Associated Press*, June 12, 2003, http://www.ap.org.

5. Ian James, "Israel Will Respond with Force," Associated Press, August 20, 2003, http://www.ap.org; Jacques Pinto, "Israeli Retaliation Crosses Another Red Line with Tulkarem Invasion," Agence France-Presse, January 22, 2002, http://www.nexis.com.

6. Anna Badkhen, "Kashmir Crisis Reflects Religious Hate in India," *San Francisco Chronicle*, June 20, 2002, p. A10.

7. Ibid.

8. "After the Slaughter, What Hope," *Economist*, March 7, 2002, http://www.economist.com.

9. Celia W. Duggar, "Fire Started on Train Carrying Hindu Activists Kills 58," *New York Times*, February 28, 2002, p. A3.

CHAPTER 5: HATE AND HUMAN NATURE

1. Harold Fishbein, *Peer Prejudice and Discrimination* (Boulder, CO: Westview Press, 1996).

2. Ibid.

3. Roger Brown, *Social Psychology,* 2d ed. (New York: Free Press, 1986); Fishbein, *Peer Prejudice and Discrimination.*

4. Henri Tajfel, Michael Billig, R. P. Bundy, and C. Flament, "Social Categorization and Intergroup Behavior," *European Journal of Social Psychology* 1 (1971): 149–78.

5. Michael Billig and Henri Tajfel, "Social Categorization and Similarity in Intergroup Behavior," *European Journal of Social Psychology* 3 (1973): 27–52; Anne Locksley, Vilma Ortiz, and Christine Hepburn, "Social Categorization and Discriminatory Behavior: Extinguishing the Minimal Intergroup Discrimination Effect, *Journal of Personality and Social Psychology* 39, no. 7 (1980): 73–83.

6. Aaron Beck, *Prisoners of Hate: The Cognitive Basis of Anger, Hostility, and Violence* (New York: HarperCollins, 1999).

7. M. Rothbard, M. Evans, and Solomon Fulero, "Recall for Confirming Events: Memory Processes and the Maintenance of Social Stereotyping, *Journal of Experimental Social Psychology* 15 (1979): 343–55.

8. C. D. Batson, "Sociobiology and the Role of Religion in Promoting Pro-Social Behavior," *Journal of Personality and Social Psychology* 45 (1983): 1380–85.

9. Paul Connolly, Alan Smith, and Berni Kelly, "Too Young to Notice? The Cultural and Political Awareness of 3–6 Year Olds in Northern Ireland," Report by Northern Ireland Community Relations Council (Belfast, Northern Ireland, June 2002).

10. Rosie Cowan, "Thousands Join Ulster Anti-Violence Protest," *Guardian* (London), January 19, 2002, p. 8.

11. Theodore Adorno, W. E. Frankel-Brunswick, Daniel J. Levinson, and N. H. Sanford, *The Authoritarian Personality* (New York: Harper and Row, 1950); J. Sidanius, F. Prado, and L. Bobo, "Social Dominance Orientation and the Political Psychology of Gender: A Case of Invariance," *Journal of Personality and Social Psychology* 67 (1994): 998–1011.

12. Carl Goldberg, "Fanatic Hatred and Violence in Contemporary America," *Journal of Applied Psychoanalytic Studies* 5, no. 1 (January 2003): 9–19.

13. Konrad Lorenz, *On Aggression* (New York: Harcourt, Brace, 1966).

14. Eric Fromm, *The Anatomy of Human Destructiveness* (New York: Holt, 1973).

15. See James A. Fox and Jack Levin, *The Will to Kill: Making Sense of Senseless Murder* (Boston: Allyn and Bacon, 2001).

16. Personal conversation with Kevin Borgeson, September 2, 2003.

17. Not a real name.

18. Kathleen Blee, *Inside Organized Racism: Women in the Hate Movement* (Berkeley: University of California Press, 2003).

CHAPTER 6: THE POLITICAL USES OF HATE

1. Richard Gambino, *Vendetta* (Garden City, NY: Doubleday Books, 1977).

2. Ibid.

3. Ibid.

4. Ibid.

5. Ibid.

6. Rahul Bedi, "Islamic Gunmen Kill 29 in Attack on Hindu Temple," *Daily Telegraph* (London), September 25, 2002, p. 17.

7. Luke Harding, "Fears for Secular India after BJP Win: Religious Hatred Nets Hard-line Hindus a Landslide in Gujarat," *Guardian* (London), December 16, 2002, p. 13.

8. Ibid.

9. Amy Waldman, "Hopes and Fears in India Stirred by Hindu Nationalist," *New York Times,* December 15, 2002, p. A22.

10. Mannika Chopra, "In a Corner of India, Vote Widens Rift; Muslims Are Wary of New Strife after a Hindu Triumph," *Boston Globe*, December 22, 2002, p. A15.

11. Edward Luce, "The Ram Battering at India's Coalition: Hindu Militants Fighting for Temples on Holy Sites Are Stepping Up the Pressure with Nationwide Agitation," *Financial Times* (London), March 16, 2002, p. 9.

12. "One Step Forward, One Step Back," *Economist Online*, April 7, 2001, http://www.economist.com/displaystory.cfm?story_id=561431 (August 4, 2003).

13. Eric D. Gordy, *The Culture of Power in Serbia: Nationalism and the Destruction of Alternatives* (University Park: Pennsylvania State University Press, 1999).

14. Helsinki Committee for Human Right in Serbia, *Report on Human Rights and Minorities* (Belgrade, Yugoslavia, 1996).

15. Noah J. Efron, *Real Jews: Secular Versus Ultra-Orthodox and the Struggle for Jewish Identity in Israel* (New York: Basic Books, 2003).

16. Tedd Robert Gurr, "Ethnic Warfare on the Wane," *Foreign Affairs* 79, no. 3 (May/June 2000): 55.

17. Margaret Brearley, "The Persecution of Gypsies in Europe," *American Behavioral Scientist* 45, no. 4 (December 2001).

18. Guenter Lewy, "The Travail of the Gypsies," *National Interest* (Fall 1999).

19. Chris Hedges, "Another Victim, 14, in Serbia's War Against Gypsies," *New York Times*, October 22, 1997, p. A8.

20. Carlotta Gall, "Gypsies and Others Said to Draw Kosovar Fury," *New York Times*, November 5, 1999, p. A18.

21. Riccardo Orizio, *Talk of the Devil: Encounters with Seven Dictators* (New York: Walker & Company, 2003).

22. Simon Schama, *The History of Britain* (New York: Miramax Books & Hyperion, 2003).

23. "Tragedy of a Death Foretold," *Economist*, March 20, 1999, p. 59.

24. "Northern Ireland: Roadblock," *Economist*, November 7, 1998, p. 60.

25. Suzanne Breen "Continuity IRA Threatens to Target Security Force Members; The Organisation Says It Has No Intention of Calling a Ceasefire and Claims the Omagh Bomb Has Not Ended Dissident Republicanism," *Irish Times,* November 7, 1998, p. 6.

26. Kevin Cullen, in "Ulster, Grief, Guilt as Victims Are Counted," *Boston Globe,* August 17, 1998, p. A1.

27. Ibid.

28. Jim Cusack, "The Killing of Rosemary Nelson," *Irish Times,* March 16, 1999, p. 7.

29. Ibid.

30. Marie-Therese Fay, Mike Morrisey, and Marie Smyth, *Mapping Troubles-Related Deaths in Northern Ireland 1969–1994*, Center for the Study of Conflict, INCORE, Belfast, Northern Ireland, 1998.

31. Fionnuala McKenna, "Security and Defense," Background Information on Northern Ireland Society, CAIN, July 12, 2003, http://www. cain.ulst .ac.uk/ni/security.htm.

32. Paul Tanney, "Violent Summer Turns to Autumn of Discontent," *Irish Times,* August 30, 2001, p. 9.

33. Ibid.

34. "Belfast Crisis Talks Aim to Ward off Bloodletting," *Financial Times* (London), September 6, 2001, p. 2.

35. Paul Tanney, "Dispute Could Spread to Other Schools," *Irish Times*, September 5, 2001, p. 9.

36. John Murray Brown, "Belfast's Patchwork of Communities Rips Apart at the Seams: This Week's Violence May Be Symptomatic of a Wider Malaise among Northern Ireland's Protestants," *Financial Times* (London), January 11, 2002, p. 2.

CHAPTER 7: HATE AND CULTURE WARS

1. Andrew Baruh Wachtel, *Making a Nation, Breaking a Nation: Literature and Cultural Politics in Yugoslavia* (Stanford, CA: Stanford University Press, 1998).

2. Ibid.

3. *Statisticki Bilten SFRJ,* no. 1295 (Belgrade: Governement Prinint Office, 1982) and *Statisticki Godisnjak SFRJ* (Belgrade: Governement Prinint Office, 1981).

4. Ibid.

5. Wachtel, *Making a Nation, Breaking a Nation.*

6. Kemal Kurspahic, *Prime Time Crime: Balkan Media in War and Peace* (Washington, DC: United States Institute of Peace Press, 2003).

7. Ibid.

8. Ibid.

9. Kathryn L. Lindholm and Zierlein Aclan, "Bilingual Proficiency as a Bridge to Academic Achievement: Results from Bilingual/Immersion Programs," *Journal of Education* 173, no. 2 (1991): 99–113.

10. Derrick Z. Jackson, "Black Slang White Jive," *Boston Globe*, January 3, 1997, p. A27.

11. Rebecca Gordon, "Education and Race," report by Applied Research Center, Oakland, CA, 1998, p. 31, http://www.arc.org.

12. US Department of Education, Institute of Education Sciences, "Status and Trends in the Education of Blacks," *National Center for Education Statistics* (September 2003), p. xi.

CHAPTER 8: HATE IN POPULAR CULTURE

1. G. Gordon Liddy show, August 26, 1994.
2. David Wild, "Who Is Howard Stern?" *Rolling Stone,* June 11, 1990, p. 87.
3. David Bauder, "MSNBC Fires Savage on Anti-Gay Remarks," Associated Press, July 7, 2003, http://www.ap.org.
4. S. S. Brehm and J. W. Brehm, *Psychological Reactance: A Theory of Freedom and Control* (New York: Academic Press, 1981).
5. George Gerbner, *Television and Its Viewers: What Social Science Sees* (Santa Monica, CA: Rand Corporation, 1976); George Gerbner, "Fairness and Diversity in Television," *Screen Actors Guild Report* (Philadelphia: Temple University, 1998).
6. Gerbner, *Television and Its Viewers.*
7. Ibid.
8. Janine Jackson, "Anything but Racism," *Extra,* January / February 2000, http://www.fair.org/extra.
9. Jean Griffin, "Racism and Humiliation in the African-American Community," *Journal of Primary Prevention*, 12, no. 2 (1991): 149–67.
10. Jack Levin and Jack McDevitt, *Hate Crimes: The Rising Tide of Bigotry and Bloodshed* (New York: Plenum Press, 1993); Michael Moynihan and Didrik Soderlind, *Lords of Chaos* (Venice, CA: Feral House, 1998).
11. "Lethal Garbage: Anti-White Rap Lyrics," *American Renaissance,* March 4, 2004, http://www.amren.com.
12. Jerry Adler, "The Rap Attitude," *Newsweek,* March 19, 1990, pp. 56–59.
13. Richard Reese, "From the Fringe: The Hip Hop Culture and Ethnic Relations," Paper presented at the Far West Popular Culture Conference, Las Vegas, NV, February 1998.
14. Ibid.
15. Derrick Z. Jackson, "Unlikely Embrace," *Boston Globe*, February 14, 2001, p. 10.
16. Mary Ballard and Steven Coates, "The Immediate Effects of Homi-

cidal, Suicidal, and Nonviolent Heavy Metal and Rap Songs on the Moods of College Students," *Youth and Society* (December 27, 1995): 148–68.

17. Fred Bruning, "The Devilish Soul of Rock and Roll," *Maclean's,* October 21, 1985, p. 13.

18. Adler, "The Rap Attitude," p. 56.

19. Ballard and Coates, "The Immediate Effects of Homicidal, Suicidal, and Nonviolent Heavy Metal and Rap Songs on the Mood of College Students."

20. Moynihan and Soderlind, *Lords of Chaos.*

21. Anti-Defamation League, "Bigots Who Rock: An ADL List of Hate Music Groups," ADL Web site, May 2001, http://www.adl.org.

22. Mark Potok, "The Year in Hate [2003]," Southern Poverty Law Center, January 2003, http://www.splcenter.org.

23. Anti-Defamation League, "Bigots Who Rock."

24. Anti-Defamation League, "Deafening Hate: The Revival of Resistance Records," ADL Web site, May 2000, http://www.adl.org.

25. Anti-Defamation League, "Growing Proliferation of Racist Video Games Target Youth on the Internet," ADL Web site, February 19, 2002, http://www.adl.org.

26. Jeffrey M. Jones, "What Do Islamic World Residents Like About the West?" Gallup Organization, May 28, 2002, http://www.gallup.com.

27. Gallup Organization, "Poll of the Islamic World: Perceptions of Western Culture," March 12, 2002, http://www.gallup.com.

28. Gallup Organization, "Does Modernity Challenge Islamic Values?" March 12, 2002, http://www.gallup.com.

29. Jones, "What Do Islamic World Residents Like About the West?"

30. Gallup Organization, "Poll of the Islamic World: Perceptions of Western Culture."

31. Gallup Organization, "Does Modernity Challenge Islamic Values?"

32. Jeffrey M. Jones, "Does Western Contact Affect Islamic Opinions?" May 7, 2002, http://www.gallup.com.

33. Anti-Defamation League, "September 11 and Arab Media: The Anti-Jewish and Anti-American Blame Game," November 26, 2001, http://www.adl.com.

34. Samuel Walker, *Hate Speech* (Lincoln: University of Nebraska Press, 1994).

35. Ziauddin Sardar and Merryl Wyn Davies, *Why Do People Hate America?* (New York: Disinformation Company, 2002).

CHAPTER 9: WHEN THE ECONOMY GOES SOUTH, HATE TRAVELS NORTH

1. Muzafer Sherif and Carolyn Sherif, *The Robbers Cave Experiment: Intergroup Conflicts and Cooperation* (Norman: University of Oklahoma Press, 1961).

2. Richard Burkholder, "Despite Improved Ties, Pakistanis Cool to U.S.," Gallup Web site, September 10, 2002, http://www.gallup.com.

3. Ziauddin Sardar and Merryl Wyn Davies, *Why Do People Hate America?* (New York: Disinformation Company, 2002).

4. Ibid.

5. Oscar Handlin, *The Newcomers* (Garden City, NY: Anchor Press, 1962); Max Lerner, *America as a Civilization*, (New York: Simon and Schuster, 1972).

6. Steven Camarota, "Immigrants in the United States—2002," Center for Immigration Studies, November 2002, http://www.cis.org/topics/ currentnumbers.html.

7. Salvatore LaGumina, *Wop!* (San Francisco: Straight Arrow Press, 1973).

8. Betty Lee Sung, *Mountain of Gold* (New York: Macmillan, 1961).

9. LaGumina, *Wop!*

10. Jack Levin and Jack McDevitt, *Hate Crimes: The Rising Tide of Bigotry and Bloodshed* (New York: Plenum Press, 1993).

11. "Violence against Immigrants," Brookhaven Citizens for Peaceful Solutions, April 24, 2001, http://www.geocities.com/bcpsolutions.

12. Levin and McDevitt, *Hate Crimes*.

13. "Four German Youths Sentenced for Anti-Foreigner Attacks," *Deutsche Presse-Agentur,* January 24, 2003, http://www.nexis.com.

14. Jack Levin and Jack McDevitt, *The Violence of Hate* (Boston: Allyn and Bacon, 2002).

15. David Cracknell and Dipesh Gadher, "Labour Is Warned of Asylum Backlash," *Sunday Times,* January 26, 2003, p. 8.

16. Timo Virtanen, "Youth, Racist Violence and Anti-Racist Responses in the Nordic Countries," Preface, Finnish Youth Research Society, December 2000, http://www.abo.fi/~tivirtan.

17. Kenneth Stampp, *The Peculiar Institution* (New York: Vintage, 1956).

18. Edna Bonacich, "A Theory of Ethnic Antagonism: The Split Labor Market," *American Sociological Review* (October 1972): 547–59; Marvin Harris, *Patterns of Race in America* (New York: Walker, 1964)

19. Bonacich, "A Theory of Ethnic Antagonism."

20. Susan Olzak, *The Dynamics of Ethnic Competition and Conflict* (Stanford, CA: Stanford University Press, 1992).

21. John Hope Franklin and Isadore Starr, *The Negro in Twentieth Century America* (New York: Vintage Press, 1967), p. 25.

CHAPTER 10: MANUFACTURING HATE

1. FOX News Channel, Special Report, August 9, 2000.

2. Anti-Defamation League, "Deafening Hate: The Revival of Resistance Records," ADL Web site, May 2000, http://www.adl.org.

3. Ibid.

4. National Journal Group, Inc. "Lieberman: Dallas NAACP Chapter Pres. Gone After 'Jew' Comment," August 10, 2000, http://www.nationaljournal.com.

5. Melissa Radler, "ADL: Anti-Semitism up 49% in NYC," *Jerusalem Post*, March 22, 2001, p. 5.

6. Paul Iganski and Barry Kosman, *A New Antisemitism?* (London, England: Profile Books, 2003).

7. Kevin Alan Brook, *The Jews of Khazaria* (Northvale, NJ: Jason Aronson, 1997).

8. The Nizkor Project, "The Protocols of the Elders of Zion," February 10, 1993, http://www.nizkor.org.

9. Anti-Defamation League, "September 11 and Arab Media," November 26, 2001, http://www.adl.org.

10. Editorial, "Inexcusable," *Newsday,* October 18, 2003, p. A16.

11. Arnaud de Borchgrave, "Loony Lucubrations," *Newsday,* October 10, 2003, p. 12.

12. Jeffrey M. Jones, "Fear of Terrorism Increases Amidst Latest Warning," Gallup Organization, February 12, 2003, http://www.gallup.com.

13. Warren P. Strobel, "Iraq Victory Has Failed to Reduce Perils," *Deseret News,* May 25, 2003, p. A1.

14. Paul Krugman, "Pattern of Corruption," *New York Times*, July 15, 2003, p. A21.

15. Strobel, "Iraq Victory Has Failed to Reduce Perils."

16. Steve LeBlanc, "Kennedy Says the Case for War against Iraq Was a 'Fraud,'" Associated Press, September 18, 2003, http://www.nexis.com.

17. Dana Milbank and Claudia Deane, "Hussein Link to 9/11 Lingers in Many Minds," *Washington Post,* September 6, 2003, p. A1.

18. George W. Bush, weekly radio address, December 28, 2002.

19. George W. Bush, State of the Union Address, January 29, 2003.

20. Remarks by George W. Bush from the USS *Abraham Lincoln,* "Strengthening Intelligence to Better Protect America," May 2, 2003.

21. Robert Parry, "Bush's' Crusade," September 25, 2001, http://www.consortiumNews.com.

22. Swapan Dasgupta, "An Alternative to the Jihadis," http://www.rediff.com/news, October 13, 2003.

23. Richard Burkholder, "Jihad—'Holy War,' or Internal Spiritual Struggle?" Gallup Organization, December 3, 2002, http://www.gallup.com.

24. Daniel Nassim, "Pearl Harbor: The Prequel," Spiked Culture Web site, May 30, 2001, http://www.spiked-online.com/Articles.

25. Christopher R. Browning, *Ordinary Men* (New York: Harper-Perennial, 1992).

26. Raul Hilberg, *Perpetrators, Victims, Bystanders: The Jewish Catastrophe 1933–1945* (New York: HarperCollins, 1992).

27. Tasha Robertson, "Staking Claim to a Hidden Past," *Boston Globe,* June 25, 2003, p. A1.

28. Patricia A. Turner, *I Heard It Through the Grapevine* (Berkeley: University of California Press, 1999).

CHAPTER 11: ORDINARY PEOPLE; EXTRAORDINARY COURAGE

1. Raul Hilberg, *Perpetrators, Victims, Bystanders: The Jewish Catastrophe 1933–1945* (New York: HarperCollins, 1992).
2. I. M. Piliavin, J. A. Piliavin, and J. Rodin, "Costs, Diffusion, and the Stigmatized Victim," *Journal of Personality and Social Psychology* 32 (1975): 429–38.
3. Ibid.
4. John M. Darley and Bibb Latane, "When Will People Help in a Crisis?" *Psychology Today* 2, 1968, pp. 70–71.
5. Samuel P. Oliner, *Do Unto Others: Extraordinary Acts of Ordinary People* (Boulder, CO: Westview Press, 2003).
6. Paul London, "The Rescuers: Motivational Hypotheses about Christians Who Saved Jews from the Nazis," in *Altruism and Helping Behavior*, ed. J. Macaulay and L. Berkowitz (New York: Academic Press, 1970).
7. D. L. Rosenhan, "On Being Sane in Insane Places," *Science* 179 (1973): 250–58.
8. M. A. Barnett, J. A. Howard, L. M. King, and G. A. Dino, "Antecedents of Empathy: Retrospective Accounts of Early Socialization," *Personality and Social Psychology Bulletin* 6 (1980): 361–65.
9. The Holocaust Martyrs' and Heroes' Remembrance Authority, http://www.yad-vashem.org.il/about_yad/index_about_yad.html.
10. Yukiko Sugihira, *Visas for Life* (1993; English translation, San Francisco: Edu-Comm. Plus, 1995).
11. Ibid.
12. Varian Fry Foundation Project, International Rescue Committee, New York.
13. Michael Smith, *Foley: The Spy Who Saved 10,000 Jews* (Abingdon, Great Britain: Hodder & Stoughton General Division, 1999).
14. The Garden of the Righteous Worldwide, http://www.gariwo.net/eng/index.html.
15. The Garden of the Righteous in Sarajevo, http://www.gariwo.net/ethnic_c/garden.htm.
16. http://www.gariwo.net/eng/ethnic_c/ethnic_c_5_5.htm.

17. Ibid.

18. Hartmut Keil, *Race and Ethnicity: Slavery and the German Radical Tradition*, talk given in Madison, WI, February 3, 1999, http://www.csumc.wisc.edu/mki/Resources/Online_Papers/keil.html.

19. "German Attitude Toward the Civil War," *The Handbook of Texas Online*, http://www.tsha.utexas.edu/handbook/online/articles/print/GG/png1.htm.

20. Samuel P. Oliner, *Do Unto Others: Extraordinary Acts of Ordinary People* (Boulder, CO: Westview Press, 2003).

21. John Rabe, *The Good Man of Nanking: The Diaries of John Rabe,* ed. Erwin Wickert (Vintage, 2000).

22. "Monument to Le Chambon-Sur-Lignon," September 20, 2003, http://www.yad-vashem.org.il/visiting/sies/chambon.html.

23. Otpor Web page, http://www.otpor.com.

24. "Bringing Down the Dictator," York Zimmerman, Inc. and WETA Video Production, http://www.pbs.org/weta/dictator/otpor/.

25. Matthew Collin, "Inside Serbia's Rock'n'Roll Revolution," *Independent* (London), April 3, 2001, p. 1.

26. Lindsay Clydesdale, "The Dictator Domino Effect," *Scottish Daily Record*, April 10, 2003, p. 8.

CHAPTER 12: COOPERATION AND COMMUNITY ACTION

1. Emily Rutherford, "Foreign Parts," *Brookline Tab,* August 14, 2003, p. 1.

2. Gordon Allport, *The Nature of Prejudice* (Reading, MA: Addison-Wesley, 1954).

3. Ibid.

4. Jenny Berrien and Christopher Winship, "An Umbrella of Legitimacy: Boston's Police Department—Ten Point Coalition Collaboration," in *Securing Our Children's Future: New Approaches to Juvenile Justice and Youth Violence,* ed. Gary S. Katzmann (Washington, DC: Brookings Institution Press, 2002).

5. Bettye H. Pruitt, "The Boston Strategy: A Story of Unlikely Alliances," Robert Wood Johnson Foundation, 2001, http://www.Boston-Strategy.com (September 10, 2003).

6. John E. Eck and Dennis Rosenbaum, "The New Police Order: Effectiveness, Equity, and Efficiency in Community Policing," in *The Challenge of Community Policing,* ed. Dennis P. Rosenbaum (Thousand Oaks, CA: Sage, 1994), p. 11.

7. Jenny Berrien, Omar McRoberts, and Christopher Winship, "Religion and the Boston Miracle: The Effect of Black Ministry on Youth Violence," in *Who Will Provide? The Changing Role of Religion in American Social Welfare,* ed. Mary Jo Bane, Brent Coffin, and Ronald Thiemann (Boulder, CO: Westview Press, 2000).

8. Urban Institute, analysis of data from Federal Bureau of Investigation, *Crime in the United States,* annual (Washington, DC: FBI, US Department of Justice).

9. Boston Police Department, Public Safety Citizen Survey, 2001, http://www.tbf.org/indicators/public-safety/indicators.asp?id=1272# (August 15, 2003).

10. Jack Levin, "An Effective Response to Teenage Crime Is Possible and Cites Are Showing the Way," *Chronicle of Higher Education,* no. 35 (May 7, 1999): B10.

11. "Prisoners in 2002," Bureau of Justice Statistics http://www.ojp.usdoj.gov/bjs/pub/pdf/p02.pdf (September 10, 2003).

12. Boston Police Department, Public Safety Citizen Survey, 2001.

13. Christian Swezey, "Courting Unity; Group Uses Basketball to Try to Bring People Together," *Washington Post,* June 25, 2003, p. D1.

14. John O'Farrell, "Crossing the Divide," *Irish Times,* April 13, 2002, p. 50.

15. Darcy Ribeiro, *The Brazilian People: The Formation and Meaning of Brazil* (Gainesville: University Press of Florida, 2000).

16. Gertrude J. Selznick and Stephen Steinberg, *The Tenacity of Prejudice* (New York: Harper Torchbooks, 1969).

17. E. Elliott Aronson, N. Blaney, J. Sikes, C. Stephan, and M. Snapp, "Busing and Racial Tension: The Jigsaw Route to Learning and Liking," *Psychology Today* 8 (August 1974): 43–59.

18. B. Shlachter, "Jasper Breathes a Sigh of Relief," *Fort Worth Star-Telegram*, February 27, 1999, p. 4.

19. Dina Temple-Raston, *A Death in Texas* (New York: Henry Holt, 2002).

20. J. Labalme, "Discussion Focuses on Hate Crimes," *Indianapolis Star*, November 17, 1999, p. B1.

21. Shlachter, "Jasper Breathes a Sigh of Relief."

22. Jack Levin and Gordana Rabrenovic, "Hate Crimes and Ethnic Conflict: An Introduction," *American Behavioral Scientist* 45, no. 4 (December 2001): 574–87.

23. John Darby, *Intimidation and the Control of Conflict in Northern Ireland* (Syracuse, NY: Syracuse University Press, 1986).

24. Fictional name but real town.

25. Darby, *Intimidation and the Control of Conflict in Northern Ireland.*

26. Chris McGeal, "Kibbutz Unshaken in Pursuit of Utopia," *Guardian* (London), November 16, 2002, p. 16.

27. Ibid.

28. Ibid.

29. Mazin Qumsiyeh, "Shame, Revulsion, and Sadness," *Jerusalem Post*, November 17, 2002, p. 6.

CHAPTER 13: WOMEN AS PEACEMAKERS

1. Nathan Stoltzfus, *Resistance of the Heart: Intermarriage and the Rosenstrasse Protest in Nazi Germany* (New Brunswick, NJ: Rutgers University Press, 2001).

2. Cynthia Cockburn, *The Space Between Us: Negotiating Gender and National Identities in Conflict* (London and New York: Zed Books, 1998).

3. Rada Boric, "Against the War: Women Organizing Across the National Divide in the Countries of the Former Yugoslavia," in *Gender and Catastrophe*, ed. Ronit Lentin (London and New York: Zed Books, 1997), pp. 36–49.

4. Marilyn Gittel, Isolda Ortega-Bustamante, and Tracy Steffy, eds., *Women Creating Social Capital and Social Change: A Study of Women-Led Community Development Organizations* (New York: Howard Samuels State Management and Policy Center, Graduate School and the University Center of the City University of New York, 1999).

5. Gordana Rabrenovic and Laura Roskos, "Civil Society, Feminism, and the Gendered Politics of War and Peace: Introduction," *National Women's Studies Association Journal* 13, no. 2 (Summer 2001): 40–54.

6. Cockburn, *The Space Between Us.*

7. Ibid.

8. Ibid., p. 80.

9. Radha Kumar, "Women's Peacekeeping During Ethnic Conflicts and Post-Conflict Reconstruction," *National Women's Studies Association Journal* 13, no. 2 (Summer 2001): 68–73.

10. Sheila Arnopoulos, "Women's Front Line for Peace in India," *Gazette* (Montreal, Quebec), March 20, 2002, p. B5.

11. Robert Putnam, *Bowling Alone: The Collapse and Revival of American Community* (New York: Simon and Schuster, 2001).

12. Jennifer Turpin, "Many Faces: Women Confronting War," *The Women and War Reader*, ed. Lois Ann Lorentzen and Jennifer Turpin (New York: New York University Press, 1998), p. 4.

CHAPTER 14: SOCIETIES THAT RESIST HATE AND VIOLENCE

1. Jack Levin and William C. Levin, *The Functions of Discrimination and Prejudice* (New York: Harper and Row, 1982).

2. Daniel Jonah Goldhagen, *Hitler's Willing Executioners: Ordinary Germans and the Holocaust* (New York: Basic Books, 1996).

3. Michael Bar-Zohar, *Beyond Hitler's Grasp: The Heroic Rescue of Bulgaria's Jews* (Avon, MA: Adams Media Corporation, 1998).

4. Tzvetan Todorov, *The Fragility of Goodness: Why Bulgaria's Jews Survived the Holocaust* (Princeton, NJ: Princeton University Press, 1999).

5. Ibid.

6. Jacky Comforty and Lisa Comforty, *The Optimists: The Story of the Rescue of the Bulgarian Jews from the Holocaust* (Film by Comforty Media Concepts, Evanston, IL, 2001).

7. Ashutosh Varshney, *Ethnic Conflict and Civic Life: Hindus and Muslims in India* (New Haven, CT: Yale University Press, 2002).

8. Ibid.

9. Ibid., p. 127.

10. Ibid., p. 124.

CHAPTER 15: ENDING HATE AND VIOLENCE

1. Tzvetan Todorov, *The Fragility of Goodness: Why Bulgaria's Jews Survived the Holocaust* (Princeton, NJ: Princeton University Press, 1999).

2. Yuri Kochiyama, "Then Came the War," in *The Social Construction of Race and Ethnicity in the United States*, 2d ed., ed. J. Ferrante and P. Browne Jr. (Upper Saddle River, NJ: Prentice Hall, 2001).

3. Ronald Takaki, *Strangers from a Different Shore: A History of Asian Americans* (Boston: Little, Brown and Company, 1989), p. 380.

4. Ibid., p. 384.

5. Ibid.

6. Ibid., p. 381.

7. Ibid., p. 382.

8. Ibid., p. 379.

9. Mitchell Maki, *Achieving the Impossible Dream: How Japanese-Americans Obtained Redress* (Urbana: University of Illinois Press, 1999).

10. Truth Commission Report, Special Report: 1998, "Truth and Reconciliation," October 1998, http://news.bbc.co.uk/2/hi/special _report/1998/10/98/truth_and_reconciliation.

11. Ibid.

12. Ibid.

EPILOGUE: THE MODERN MADNESS OF HATE

1. Dan McGinn, "Governments Urged to Press Loyalists to Disarm," Press Association Limited, http://www.nexis.com (October 17, 2003).
2. Roger Mac Ginty, "Ethno-National Conflict and Hate Crime," *American Behavioral Scientist* 45, no. 4 (2001): 639–53.
3. Ibid.
4. Richard Ryan, "Michigan, Arabs See Peace, Profit in Partnership," *Detroit News*, September 21, 2003, p. 1.
5. Tim Shipman and Julia Hartley-Brewer, "Focus," *Sunday Express*, October 28, 2001, p. 11.
6. Richard Pendlebury, "Beneath the Mask," *Mercury*, October 18, 2003, p. 45.
7. Mari Fitzduff, "The Northern Ireland Troubles," INCORE background paper, http://www.cain.ulst.ac.uk/othelem/incorepaper.htm.
8. Tedd Robert Gurr, "Ethnic Warfare on the Wane," *Foreign Affairs* 79, no. 3 (May/June 2000): 55.

APPENDIX: FLAG-WAVING AND ATTITUDES TOWARD ARAB AMERICANS

1. Jennifer Mergy, "Totems and Flags: Collective Symbolism in Durkheimian Thought," *Durkheimian Studies* 2 (1996): 99, B121.
2. Robert N. Bellah, "Civil Religion in America," *Daedalus* (Winter 1967): 1–21.
3. *Smithsonian* 28, no. 3, June 1997, p. 70; *Time,* February 25, 1991, p. 55; *Economist* 354, no. 8154, January 22, 2000, p. 36; *Newsweek,* October 1, 2001, p. 63.
4. Robert Putnam, "Bowling Together: The United States of America," *American Prospect* 13, no. 3 (February 11, 2002): 20–23, http://www.web5.infotrac.galegroup.com, pp. 1–7 (March 14, 2002).
5. Dean E. Murphy and David M. Halbfinger, "9/11 Bridged the Racial Divide, New Yorkers Say, Gingerly," *New York Times,* June 16, 2002, p. A25.

6. Robert Reich, "The Nationalism We Need," *American Prospect* 11, no. 2, December 6, 1999, p. 64.

7. Ibid.

8. Murphy and Halbfinger, "9/11 Bridged the Racial Divide."

9. Eric Sorensen, "The Newfound Desire to Fly Old Glory," *Seattle Times*, September 25, 2001, p. A1.

10. Erving Goffman, *The Presentation of Self in Everyday Life* (New York: Anchor Books, 1959).

11. Adam Piore, "Red, White and What a Deal!" *Newsweek International*, November 26, 2001, p. 59.

INDEX